INTOLERANCE

Divided Societies on trial

BRIAN HARRIS

Copyright © 2008 by Brian Harris

Intolerance: Divided Societies on Trial

British Library Cataloguing-in-Publication Data:

A catalogue record for this book is available from The British Library

ISBN 9780854900251

First published in 2008 by

Wildy, Simmonds & Hill Publishing Ltd.
58 Carey Street, London WC2A 2JB
England

CONTENTS

For

Hannah, Adam, Sarah and Mollie,

the new generation

LIST OF ILLUSTRATIONS

ACKNOWLEDGEMENTS

I am indebted to Paul Fitzsimons, Jack Maurice, Dr. Tom McMorrow, John Spencer and Andrew Tabachnik for reading and commenting on various parts of the text. I also owe a debt of gratitude to my son Neil for removing many of the bees in my literary bonnet and to Andrew Riddoch for his intelligent and perceptive sub-editing of the text. Needless to say, the remaining errors and infelicities (and there are bound to be some, though as yet I know them not) are all mine.

I continue to be grateful to the staff of Olney library for their cheerful support in tracing and speedily acquiring the most recondite works from all over the country.

INTRODUCTION

Father, Mother, and Me,
Sister and Auntie say
All the people like us are We,
And every one else is They.
And They live over the sea,
While We live over the way,
But - would you believe it? - They look upon We
As only a sort of They!

A Friend of the Family, Rudyard Kipling[1]

Richard Langhorne was a successful barrister of the Inner Temple who lived in a rural lane to the north of Holborn and had chambers nearby. Generous almost to a fault, he would sometimes ask his friends to pay his professional fees 'in love and affection'.[2]

The fifty-five year old Richard was a Roman Catholic, two of his four children were Catholic priests and among his clients was the order of Jesuits in England. But to be a Catholic in seventeenth century England was to be the object of constant suspicion. Richard was not surprised therefore when after the Great Fire of London he was arrested and brought before a Parliamentary Committee on suspicion of having been involved in a plot to burn down the capital. Nothing came of this unsettling experience, but he was arrested again some eleven years later and thrown once more into prison. This time it was serious.

After two and a half months in solitary confinement Richard was brought before the Earl of Shaftsbury and two other lords who said that he could only save himself from a charge of

1   Rudyard Kipling, *Debits and Credits* (London, Macmillan, 1926).
2   James Long and Ben Long, *The Plot Against Pepys* (London, Faber and Faber, 2007), p.101.

treason by making a full confession; as an innocent man, it was an offer he could not accept. Three months later he was offered a free pardon, but he still could not bring himself to admit to something he had not done. When he was eventually able to read transcripts of other 'treason' trials his lawyer's brain quickly realized that the evidence of the prosecution witnesses was often inconsistent and did not hold up. Despite the fact that others had already been sentenced to death on such evidence, Richard was confident that, as a lawyer, he could demonstrate that they were lying; he was wrong.

When Richard was finally brought to trial at the Old Bailey, it was before the notorious Chief Justice Scroggs who refused to hear his objections. He was quickly convicted and sentenced to be hung, drawn and quartered. He met his death bravely at Tyburn on 14 July 1679, declaring King Charles II to be his 'true and lawful sovereign' and denying that the Pope had power to depose him.

At a time when Catholicism and the Catholic powers were feared and hated it took only a few self-serving politicians and a couple of lying witnesses to generate a frenzy of fear; even level-headed people became convinced that there was a plot abroad to overthrow the King, destroy the liberties of Englishmen and massacre all Protestants. Some even took to carrying a loaded cosh to defend themselves. Though the King had his doubts, these improbable stories were accepted by the Privy Council and the courts of law and dozens of innocent people, both high and low, were thrown into gaol, some twenty of them being sent to a horrifying death. In fact, the plot existed only in the heads of the villainous Titus Oates and his partner in crime, William Bedloe, aided and abetted by a credulous Protestant fanatic, Israel Tonge.[3] The best that can be said of the first two is that their motives were pure, pure greed. They concocted the story of a Popish plot simply in order to claim the reward money.

---

3   Even when his lies were exposed, the worst that happened to Oates was that he was imprisoned, pilloried and whipped. Later he was pardoned and died peacefully in his bed, a pensioner of the government.

There was nothing unique about the persecutions which Richard Langhorne and his fellow Catholics suffered in the seventeenth century. Something even worse had happened to the Jews of twelfth-century York. It was to happen again in twentieth-century America when artists were sacked or even imprisoned in apprehension of a largely non-existent communist threat. The feature common to all these events was intolerance, intolerance of the stranger in the midst, of the deviant, the nonconformist. When this sentiment is strong enough, a small threat can be blown up, by accident or design, into a mass panic in which reason seems somehow to desert otherwise rational people, leading all too often to persecution or suppression.

Most of us are intolerant of something, whether it is our neighbour's dog, his politics or the colour of his skin, but we may not always recognize our lack of tolerance. While I rejoice in my opinions, others groan under their prejudices. Sensible people keep their bigotries to themselves, but sometimes they break out and cause offence, or worse. This book is not an academic treatise on this most difficult subject, but merely a look at some of the famous and less famous examples of intolerance which ended up in the courts and, as a result, are fairly well documented.

The cases that I have chosen range from the seventeenth to the twentieth century, from the old world to the new. In some instances the intolerance is that of the defendant, in others that of society. In too many of them we find the court supporting instead of standing up to intolerance. Occasionally, there has been a ringing victory for the little man; in too many instances society seems to have learnt nothing from the experience.

Any attempt to classify intolerances is probably doomed to failure, but for practical purposes I have arranged the cases in this book into five categories, religious bigotry - which, I fear, contains the lion's share - the intolerance of dissent, censorship (or literary intolerance), the intolerance of sexual deviancy, and, perhaps most interesting of all, the intolerance of those who do bad things with good intent.

RELIGIOUS BIGOTRY

As soon as primitive man began to live in groups he sought to understand the world around him; where did it come from, who controlled it and how could 'He' be influenced? It was to be the genesis of a host of religions; some simple, some sophisticated, some cruel, some compassionate. Nothing in what follows should be taken as a criticism of religion as such, but it is a terrible indictment of how the faithful have sometimes acted.

Compassion features strongly in most of the world's great religions, but seems to be in short supply among some of their followers when it comes to dealing with dissenters or, worse, apostates. Heresy, or the promotion of unorthodox religious opinions, was for centuries an ecclesiastical offence for which people could be burned at the stake; blasphemy was its equivalent at common law. With Christianity now competing with a number of other religions, and orthodox faith itself on the wane, the crime was rarely invoked and is prospectively abolished. Nevertheless, dissenters are still reviled by many religions on the authority of their sacred texts.

Muslims, for example, are called upon to shun the company of infidels (Koran 2:118, 3:118, 4:89), even to strike off their heads and fingertips (Koran 8:012), at least until they become taxpayers in a state of subjection (Koran 9:029). This is perhaps understandable because Allah has cursed unbelievers (Koran 2:89), who will accordingly be subject to 'an awful doom' (Koran 2:7). Some Islamic scholars believe that Muslims are under a duty to kill anyone who converts to another religion, but the Koranic authority for this is disputed.

By the same token, Christians are told by the Bible that cities which refuse to admit them will suffer a fate worse than that of Sodom and Gomorrah (Mark 6:11). People sacrificing to any God but Jehovah must be 'utterly destroyed' (Exodus 22:20), or stoned to death (Deuteronomy 17:2-5). A similar fate awaits those who try to persuade a believer to convert (Deuteronomy 13:6-10). Even those who simply fail to seek the Lord must be slaughtered, 'whether small or great, man or woman' (2 Chronicles 13). As for the Jews, gentle Jesus (who, it will be remembered, 'came not to send peace but a sword: Matthew 10:34) taught that they should be 'thrown outside, into the darkness, where there will be weeping and gnashing of teeth' (Matthew 8:12).

Liberal religious opinion today rejects a literal interpretation of these passages, preferring instead to understand them in their historical context. Nevertheless, there are many individuals who see their respective holy books as the inerrant word of God which must be strictly observed. Such literalism has led to homophobia, holocaust and 'holy' war. As Swift wrote in *Thoughts on Various Subjects* (1711), 'We have just enough religion to make us hate, but not enough to make us love one another'. One of the more notorious examples of religious persecution was the pogrom of witches which swept Europe and the New World from the fifteenth century to the dawn of the enlightenment.

A microcosm of the great witch fever occurred in a tiny New England village in the year 1692. Although resulting in the deaths of only twenty people, the events so impressed themselves on the national conscience that they were to be immortalized two and a half centuries later in Arthur Miller's play, *The Crucible*.[4] Despite the liberties which the author took with the facts (he was using them as a metaphor for the McCarthy 'witch-hunt' of communists during the Cold War) the resulting work convincingly recreates the claustrophobia and superstitious fear of the time. 'The Triumph of Credulity' attempts to unravel the origins, tragic history and lessons of the historical event, and goes on to compare Salem with present day 'witch-hunts' and their equally horrifying consequences.

The New England witch-hunt was a relatively localized and contained instance of religious persecution. Far more serious events occurred in old England a century later when religious conflict caused hundreds of deaths and nearly led to the destruction of the capital. While most people may have heard of the Gordon riots, not many are aware of the vast extent of those disorders or the events which led up to them. Ultimately, they went back to a king's burning desire to sire a male heir.

The Church of England was born almost as a side wind out of Henry VIII's dynastic ambitions, but it was soon followed by religious strife in which hundreds were condemned to the block or the stake. An unsuccessful Catholic rising in the North failed and its lead-

---

4 Even today, the police cars of Salem bear on their doors a logo featuring a witch on a broomstick.

ers were dealt with according to the harsh usages of the day. Rome reacted by excommunicating Henry's daughter, Queen Elizabeth, and depriving her of 'her pretended title to the aforesaid crown and of all lordship, dignity and privilege whatsoever'. It was an act of war and the persecution of Catholics now began in earnest.

It took nearly a century after the death of Elizabeth before England's Prime Minister, William Pitt, thought that it safe to venture the first tentative steps towards the emancipation of Roman Catholics; unfortunately, he misjudged the public mood and the results were disastrous. 'London Burning' tells the now largely forgotten story of the worst disorders that London has ever seen. It is a warning of how long folk memories can persist and of the hostility which people can feel towards what they perceive to be an alien religion in their midst. It also has much to teach us on how easy it is for an orderly demonstration to be transformed into something far more sinister.

One of the problems with religious faith is how intolerant it can be towards ideas which are seen to contradict its beliefs, even when those ideas are backed up by solid scientific evidence. And we do not have to go back to Galileo to demonstrate that.[5]

The trial of a young schoolteacher in a sleepy Tennessee town in the 1920s was seen at the time as a great battle between fundamentalist religion and science; and so it was, but the real story is far more complex. The religious folk of America's Bible Belt were scornful of the theory of evolution which they saw in simplistic terms as a claim that man was descended from the apes. Laws were passed to prevent this subversive notion being taught in their schools. When civil libertarians challenged them some of the townsfolk saw this as an opportunity to put their little borough on the map and a 'friendly' prosecution was swiftly arranged. The involvement of prominent lawyers on both sides ensured that the event received national, even international, coverage. Thirty years later a stage play and then a film were made out of the trial which left the world with an entirely misleading version of events – though, goodness knows, actuality was sensational enough.

5 Those who are interested in that case can consult Brian Harris, *Injustice* (Stroud, Sutton Publishing, 2006).

'The Monkey Trial' relates the true story of evolution resistance and its surprising resurgence in the present day.

Religion no longer wields the temporal influence it once did, but history has shown that the secular authorities can be no less intolerant of dissent than the religious.

THE INTOLERANCE OF DISSENT

Every government is convinced that it would be a disaster for the country if it were to be removed from power. When a threat to the administration is accompanied by armed force the reaction is likely to be correspondingly violent; and nobody did violence better than our Elizabethan forebears. A contemporary has left us a description of how, 'The greatest and most grievous punishment used in England for such as offend against the State is drawing from the prison to the place of execution upon an hurdle or sled, where they are hanged till they be half dead, and then taken down, and quartered alive; after that, their members and bowels are cut from their bodies, and thrown into a fire, provided near hand and within their own sight, even for the same purpose.'[6] Samuel Pepys gleefully described such an event in his diary: 'To my Lord's in the morning, where I met with Captain Cuttance, but my Lord not being up I went out to Charing Cross, to see Major-General Harrison hanged, drawn, and quartered; which was done there, he looking as cheerful as any man could do in that condition. He was presently cut down, and his head and heart shown to the people, at which there was great shouts of joy.'[7]

Women convicted of treason were spared this brutality; instead, their punishment was to be burned at the stake. Only a few years before Harrison died, this was the fate which faced a seventy year old lady charged with harbouring one of the soldiers of a defeated rebel army. Her trial, supervised by 'Bloody Judge Jeffreys', has long been

6 *Holinshed's Chronicles* (1587).
7 Diary entry for 13 October 1660. Major-General Thomas Harrison was one of the regicides who signed the death warrant of King Charles I. Imprisoned four times during the Protectorate for opposing Cromwell's elevation to Lord Protector, he refused to flee the country on the Restoration. At his execution, steps are said to have been taken to keep him alive until the last possible moment.

regarded as the epitome of injustice, (though recent scholarship suggests that this may be an exaggeration). Her pathetic story, as told in 'The Bloody Assizes', should give us pause to reflect whether, or indeed how, had we been the government of the day, we would have dealt with affairs differently. It is also a lesson on how difficult it can sometimes be to reconcile the law with the demands of friendship.

It is one thing for government to attempt to control dissent, quite another to control what people read.

CENSORSHIP AND THE INTOLERANCE OF FREE EXPRESSION

John Milton was the first and is still perhaps the most eloquent opponent of censorship:

> If we think to regulate printing, thereby to rectify manners, we must regulate all recreation and pastimes, all that is delightful to man. ... It will ask more than the work of twenty licensers to examine all the lutes, the violins, and the guitars in every house; they must not be suffered to prattle as they do, but must be licensed what they may say. And who shall silence all the airs and madrigals that whisper softness in chambers? The windows also, and the balconies must be thought on; there are shrewd books, with dangerous frontispieces, set to sale; who shall prohibit them, shall twenty licensers?[8]

It took half a century before censorship of books was abolished in England.[9] All that was left was post-publication accountability. The vital difference between them was explained by the eighteenth-century jurist Sir William Blackstone in his *Commentaries on the Laws of England*: 'Every freeman has an undoubted right to lay what sentiments he pleases before the public: to forbid this, is to destroy the freedom of the press: but if he publishes what is improper, mischievous, or illegal, he must take the consequence of his own temerity.' Even today, the State is still concerned that books should not be the medium whereby impure thoughts can enter into the heads of its citizens.

8 John Milton, *Areopagitica: A Speech for the Liberty of Unlicensed Printing,* (1644).
9 In 1694 Parliament declined to renew the Licensing Order under which governments claimed the right to license books.

Most people are content to see limits placed on what can be published; the problem is that few will agree what those limits should be. There would probably be a consensus against promoting crime through books. Paedophilia is a case in point. The real difficulty lies with books which simply offend. Should they be prohibited and, if so, what should be the test of offensiveness? In England books were long held to be obscene if they had 'a tendency to deprave or corrupt those whose minds are open to such immoral influences, and into whose hands a publication of this sort may fall'. As a yardstick this was pretty useless, since it simply threw the question of what should be prohibited back upon the tastes and prejudices of the particular magistrate or juror. Not only will one person disagree with another as to what will 'deprave and corrupt', but public tastes notoriously change with time. As Cole Porter wrote, 'In olden days a glimpse of stocking/Was looked on as something shocking/ Now, heaven knows, anything goes.'

With such a vague test of obscenity it is not surprising that under public pressure the prosecuting authorities sometimes go over the top. As Macaulay wrote nearly two centuries ago, 'We know no spectacle so ridiculous as the British public in one of its periodical fits of morality'. He could have been describing England's most notorious obscenity trial of the twentieth century.

The prosecution of the publishers of D.H. Lawrence's novel, *Lady Chatterley's Lover*, described in 'The Chatterley Affair' below, is a prime example of how problematic law enforcement can be in this area. The prosecution failed, leaving the Director of Public Prosecutions with egg on his face and prosecuting counsel lumbered for the rest of his professional life with what is probably the most notorious remark ever made to an English jury. Goodness and light triumphed but, in their zeal to secure an acquittal, defence witnesses of impeccable character and authority found themselves making improbably grandiose claims for what is one of Lawrence's most toe curling novels. But this was not the end of the matter.

At about the same time as the Old Bailey trial took place the book and a film based on it were hauled before the courts in America. The attorney who acted for the defence in these cases has argued convincingly that the American approach to the issue of obscenity is more principled than the British. Is it, perhaps, time for us to grow up and permit adults to read anything they like so long as it does not promote crime?

THE INTOLERANCE OF SEXUAL DEVIANCY

A little-noticed feature of the *Lady Chatterley* case was the apparent failure of the prosecution to spot Lawrence's lightly disguised references to what was then called the 'abominable crime'; which was curious, since in 1960 buggery was still an offence on the statute book carrying the possibility of life imprisonment.[10]

All societies seem to ostracize or even punish what they consider to be deviant sexual practices which changes over time. Boy love was regarded as normal, even desirable, in ancient Greece, but Christianity took a harder line. According to the Old Testament, Jehovah instructed Moses that, 'If a man also lie with a man as he lies with a woman, both of them have committed an abomination; they shall surely be put to death; their blood shall be upon them.'[11] Even after Christ's death Saint Paul warned, 'Be not deceived: neither fornicators, nor idolaters, nor adulterers, nor effeminate, nor abusers of themselves with mankind, Nor thieves, nor covetous, nor drunkards, nor revilers, nor extortioners, shall inherit the kingdom of God'.[12] Paul's heaven must be a thinly populated region.

There is no reason to think that male homosexuality was any less prevalent in the 'repressive' nineteenth century than it is in our more liberal age, but it was social death to own up to it. Sexual relations between men were known to take place without anyone being much bothered, provided only that those involved were discreet. Once, when an actress was offended by the attentions an actor was paying to a younger man, the great Mrs. Patrick Campbell is said to have remarked, 'Does it really matter what these affectionate people do – so long as they don't do it in the streets and frighten the horses.' It was

10   In Chapter Nine, for example, Mrs. Bolton discovers that even the paraplegic Sir Clifford could be aroused by anal stimulation. And Chapter Sixteen contains a thinly disguised description of Mellors buggering Connie.
11   Leviticus 20:13.
12   1 Corinthians 6:9-10.

a belief that he could ignore this rule that ruined the life of Ireland's most gifted wit, Oscar Wilde.

The public persona which Wilde adopted for himself was that of an extrovert 'queen'. Though he was married with children, there was hardly anyone in London's literary or social circles who did not guess his true sexual inclination; and he was content to encourage them in this, stopping short only of what is now called 'coming out'. But for all his wit and humanity there was a dark side to Wilde; his sexual proclivities were directed at young men, in particular at the sordid world of rent boys. It was Wilde's particular misfortune that his lover happened to be the son of a choleric and powerful person who believed that another of his sons had already been corrupted by an older man. At first, Wilde sought to avoid conflict, but he let himself be persuaded that he could win any forensic battle with the monster who was hounding him, and foolishly threw down the gauntlet. Wilde's story, told in 'Feasting with Panthers' below, is a tragic example of society's intolerance of sexual deviancy, but it was also an instance of what the Greeks called *hubris*, the actions of someone who thought that his extraordinary talents were enough to protect him from whatever dangers his risk-taking life style exposed him to. He was wrong in this assumption and he paid the price for it in full.

It would be good to think that society learned lessons from Oscar Wilde's tragic fate, but the official persecution of homosexuals in England did not end until nearly three quarters of a century later.

It is easy to see the mote in the homophobe's eye, but more difficult to notice the beam in our own when we condone what would normally be considered wrongful acts simply because they are being committed for 'good' reasons. Saint Paul, for example, condemned those who urge us to 'do evil, that good may come',[13] and in practice we seem to accept that the greater the good intended, the greater the evil to which we are entitled to resort. (Consider the British sinking of the French fleet in Toulon in 1940, or the 'collateral damage' to civilians in modern-day Iraq.) The question arises with special force when it comes to overthrowing a repressive form of government or doing away with a wicked institution.

13   Romans 3:8.

THE INTOLERANCE OF THE VIRTUOUS

Eighteenth-century France was stuck in the Middle Ages, with most of its population deprived, not only of the right to vote, but even of the necessities of life. In its time the French Revolution of 1789 was seen as a victory of democratic ideals over tyranny. Wordsworth spoke for many when he wrote in his poem, *The Prelude*: 'Bliss was it in that dawn to be alive,/But to be young was very heaven!' But Wordsworth was not living in Robespierre's France.

The French establishment proved ridiculously easy for the revolutionaries to overthrow. Few except those concerned mourned the passing of the religious orders and the nobility; even the King capitulated without any real struggle. The problem came from France's enemies. To stand up to all the foreign powers which France had provoked into war, it was necessary to have a secure base at home. For this reason the revolutionary government saw any manifestation of dissent as counter-revolutionary. But for every revisionist they imprisoned or executed another ten seemed to spring up in their place. What began as a fight for liberty, equality and fraternity spiralled into a brutal culling, not only of the *ci-devant* nobility and dissenters, but also of former friends and comrades. Even the efficient guillotine was not enough to satisfy the blood lust and ever more imaginative methods had to be found to dispose of the Republic's supposed enemies. Madame Roland – the former revolutionary aristocrat who had once demanded the head of the queen – famously exclaimed on the way to the scaffold, 'Oh Liberty, what crimes are committed in thy name.' Compared with the Terror, the reign of Louis XVI must have seemed almost benign.

It was only when self-immolation reached the very top with the death of Robespierre that the Terror ceased and the counter-terror began. The final irony was when the last vestiges of democracy meekly submitted to one of Europe's greatest autocrats, Napoleon Bonaparte. 'The End of a Revolutionary' tells the dramatic story of one of the revolutionary leaders, Georges-Jacques Danton, who fell victim to the horror which he himself had helped bring about, and compares the revolution in France with events then occurring in America.

It was ironic that, seventy years after the founding of the first nation dedicated to the freedom of the individual, almost one in eight of its population was a slave (one in three in the South) and few seemed to be concerned about it. The great Abraham Lincoln abhorred the 'peculiar institution' of slavery, but before hostilities broke out could not bring himself to believe that it justified war between the states. Others had no such doubts, among them an unsuccessful businessman called John Brown. His violent death was immortalized in a catchy tune which described him as 'a soldier in the Army of the Lord' who 'died that the slaves might be free'. He was indeed a martyr to the abolitionist cause, but he also had no qualms in massacring men and boys whom he believed to be in his way. Some even think that his most famous act, the seizure of a Federal armoury, instead of advancing abolition, simply helped bring about America's bloody civil war. Brown's story, with all its awful contradictions, is told in 'Revolt at Harpers Ferry'.

INTOLERANCE NOW AND IN THE FUTURE

Despite the vast sums ploughed into the human rights industry, intolerance today seems to be flourishing as strongly as ever. Witches are still feared, though dressed in the guise of paedophiles. Catholics are debarred from ascending the throne of England. The obscurantist 'creationism' of the 1920s, now evolved into 'intelligent design', is making great strides towards its aim of challenging a major scientific theory. And in the 1990s a group of men were found guilty of having masochistic sex together in private which hurt absolutely no one but themselves.[14] As for state-organized repression, the choice of examples is embarrassing, and all committed in the name of humanity.

Civilized society is a fragile plant; it depends in large measure upon its members' continued willingness to cooperate and live in reasonable harmony with each other. Irrational intolerance, whether on

---

14   *R v Brown and other appeals* [1993] 2 All ER 75. In a strong dissenting opinion Lord Mustill asserted that 'these are questions of private morality; that the standards by which they fall to be judged are not those of the criminal law; and that if these standards are to be upheld the individual must enforce them upon himself according to his own moral standards, or have them enforced against him by moral pressures exerted by whatever religious or other community to whose ethical ideals he responds.'

the part of terrorists, governments or individuals, is the greatest threat to this harmony. I hope that this book will serve to remind its readers of what has happened so many times in the past when minorities or individuals have borne the brunt of inflated fears simply for being different.

Brian Harris

THE TRIUMPH OF CREDULITY
THE TRIAL OF THE SALEM WITCHES, 1692

In the latter end of the year 1691 [1692 in the new style calendar] *Mr. Samuel Paris, Pastor of the Church in Salem-Village, had a Daughter of Nine, and a Neice of about Eleven years of Age, sadly Afflicted of they knew not what Distempers; and he made his application to Physitians, yet still they grew worse: And at length one Physitian gave his opinion, that they were under an Evil Hand. This the Neighbours quickly took up, and concluded they were bewitched... These Children were bitten and pinched by invisible agents; their arms, necks, and backs turned this way and that way, and returned back again, so as it was impossible for them to do of themselves, and beyond the power of any Epileptick Fits, or natural Disease to effect. Sometimes they were taken dumb, their mouths stopped, their throats choaked, their limbs wracked and tormented so as might move an heart of stone, to sympathize with them, with bowels of compassion for them.*

John Hale, *A Modest Inquiry Into The Nature Of Witchcraft* (1702).

So began the most infamous series of witch trials in modern times in which twenty people were judicially put to death and others suffered horribly and died in a vain attempt to put an end to a phenomenon which had no real existence outside the heads of the good people of New England.

The early church had been scornful of the idea of witches. The *Canon Episcopi* of 906 AD, for example, writing of women said to cavort through the air at night, asked, 'Who is so stupid and foolish as to think that all these things that are done in the spirit are done in the body?' For some reason the church changed its attitude in the fifteenth century and began hunting witches with a truly religious fury. And what began in Europe followed the European settlers to the New World.

England, where most of the New England settlers had come from, had been relatively free of witch hysteria until the superstitious King

A witchcraft trial in Salem. (Topfoto)

James I extended the mandatory death penalty to a wide range of witchcraft offences. The new law was swiftly put to use in Lancashire, where ten 'witches' were discovered in the small town of Pendle and hanged. Paranoia and persecution found their most extreme form, however, in the activities of a clergyman's son, Matthew Hopkins, who in 1645 arrogated to himself the title of Witchfinder General and for nearly two years caused havoc among the 'witches' of East Anglia. Some two hundred people are thought to have been hanged as a result of his exertions in the name of God.

It is not surprising that a similar outlook prevailed among the devoutly Puritan settlers of New England. Their Bible took a stern line on witches. Exodus 22:18 states, "Thou shalt not suffer a witch to live." And in Leviticus 20:27 it is written, "A man also or woman that hath a familiar spirit, or that is a wizard, shall surely be put to death: they shall stone them with stones: their blood shall be upon them."[1]

---

1   Doubt has since been expressed as to the meaning of the word in the Hebrew text which was translated in the King James Version of the Bible as 'witch'.

These texts had been given the force of law by the *Book of the Laws and Liberties of Massachusetts* (1648) which provided that, 'If any man or woman be a witch (that is, hath or consulted with a familiar spirit) they shall be put to death'. This belief in the supernatural seemed almost to be reinforced by the colony's harsh climate and its hostile Indian population. 'The forests which surrounded our ancestors were the abode of a mysterious race of men of strange demeanour and unascertained origin,' wrote the nineteenth-century historian Charles Upham in his book, *Salem Witchcraft*. 'It was the common belief, sanctioned ... not by the clergy alone, but by the most learned scholars of that and the preceding ages that the American Indians were the subjects and worshippers of the Devil, and their powwows, wizards.'[2] As a result, the Puritan settlers saw themselves, in the words of Cotton Mather, a New England divine, as 'a people of God settled in those, which were once the Devil's territories'.

It was against this background that the curious behaviour of the Salem children was to have such devastating effects.

A VILLAGE DIVIDED

Salem was a fishing settlement only a few miles to the north of what was already the great town of Boston. Known to the Indians as Naumkeag, it was given the Biblical name, Salem (from 'shalom' or peace) by the English settlers. Gradually, the town expanded to the north and west, creating what came to be known as Salem farms, later, Salem village.[3] Some have traced the witch frenzy to tensions between the poorer village folk and the more prosperous folk on the edge of town,[4] but later analysis has cast doubt on this. Nevertheless, Salem was not a happy place. Though it had a meeting house and minister of its own, Salem village had been refused a separate congregation

2   By 'powwow' Upham was referring, not to a meeting of Red Indians, but to a German system of magic brought to America by the Dutch.
3   Salem village was renamed Danvers in 1752, by which name it is still known.
4   Paul Boyer and Stephen Nissenbaum claimed in *Salem Possessed: The Social Origins of Witchcraft* (Cambridge, Mass., Harvard University Press, 1974) that almost all the accusers came from the former, whereas almost all the 'afflicted' came from the latter.

with the power to baptize and give communion. The move had been led by the Putnam family, one of the largest farmers in the village. The agricultural Putnams had long been in dispute with the mercantile Porter family over the flooding of their farms which led, eventually, to a complete breakdown of relations. At the centre of the storm was the church, whose ministers, James Bayley, George Burroughs and Deodat Lawson, had all left in unhappy circumstances. (The Putnams had even quarrelled among themselves over Burroughs.) In 1688 John Putnam invited a new man to become visiting preacher. He was the London-born Samuel Parris and his role in the ensuing events was to be pivotal.

THE NEW MINISTER

Parris' temporary appointment appears to have been a success because in 1689, after protracted negotiations over his salary and emoluments, he was appointed pastor and moved to the village. But the old pattern soon repeated itself and by the following year Parris acknowledged that 'a great hatred ariseth even from nearest relations.' When the elders of the church asked the village committee to impose the tithe which provided the minister's salary their request was ignored. Instead, an inquiry was set up into the legality of his title to the parsonage. Parris preached against those who opposed him and the church took the village to court. 'By 1692', commented the historian Bryan Le Beau, 'Salem Village had reached the point of institutional, demographic and economic polarization.' The first manifestation of the troubles to come occurred in the minister's own home.

When Parris came to the village he had brought with him his wife Elizabeth, his daughter, also called Elizabeth (or Betty) and his niece, Abigail Williams, as well as his slave, the twenty-five year old Tituba and her 'consort', Indian John. It was Betty and Abigail (now nine and eleven years old) who first began behaving oddly. A doctor was called but could find nothing wrong with them; their symptoms, he concluded, could only be the results of witchcraft. Within weeks two more village girls began to act in the same manner. They were seventeen year old Betty Hubbard and twelve year old Ann Putnam. Betty was the indentured maidservant of the physician who had first suggested witchcraft. Ann was the daughter of Thomas Putnam, the Parish clerk, and his wife, also called Ann, both strong supporters of Rev. Parris. A firm believer in witchcraft, Ann Sr. was, like other members of her family, an excitable, somewhat unbalanced person who seems to have greatly influenced her daughter's behaviour. Along with the Parris girls, the Putnams, mother and daughter, were to play prominent roles in the events which followed.

In an attempt to alleviate their symptoms, the Rev. Parris organized prayer meetings and days of fasting, but the girls covered their ears and would not listen. A neighbour resorted to a more unconventional method of getting at the truth; she asked Tituba and Indian John to make what was known as a 'witch cake'. This was a mixture of rye and barley meal. Old English superstition held that, when cooked together with Betty's urine and fed to a dog (a known familiar of the Devil), this mixture would cause the animal to reveal the identity of the girl's oppressor. When Parris learnt of this development he was horrified; the 'witch cake', he said, was 'the devil's own means to reveal the devil's presence'.

THE FIRST ACCUSATIONS

Under pressure from her father and other grown-ups Betty and Ann Jr. eventually named Tituba and two other women, Sarah Good and Sarah Osborne, as the source of their troubles. Born in Barbados, Tituba has been variously described as of West African or South American origin: we shall probably never know. The important point is that her contemporaries thought of her as an Indian, and thus an agent of the Devil. Because of her exotic origins Tituba was believed by some to have influenced the children's behaviour, but there is no real evidence for this.[5] Nevertheless, the possibility that a woman of Tituba's background could have spent the long New England winters filling the children's ears with stories of the supernatural cannot be entirely dismissed. The thirty-eight year old Sarah Good, already under suspicion for witchcraft, was a natural scapegoat.[6] After falling on hard times,

5   See, for example, Bernard Rosenthal, *Salem Story: Reading the Witch Trials of 1692* (New York, Cambridge University Press, 1995).
6   She has traditionally been described as much older. See Rosenthal, *Salem Story*, pp. 37-38.

she and her children wandered from door to door begging for charity; refusal was met by mutterings which the simple village folk took to be curses. Sixty year old Sarah Osborne (née Warren) was not a regular churchgoer and before her marriage had lived 'irregularly' with her Irish indentured servant. She had long been involved in litigation with her children over her first husband's estate, and the Putnam family were on the children's side.

Warrants were issued for the arrest of the three women and they were duly brought before the examining magistrates, John Hathorne and John Corwin on 1 March.[7] The magistrates' first question of Sarah Good shows exactly how little doubt they had of her guilt. Asked, 'What evil spirit have you familiarity with?' She denied having any. Asked what she had muttered when leaving the Parris household, Sarah said she was saying the commandments, changing her story later to saying a psalm. What happened next was to set a pattern for future examinations. Hathorne asked the children 'to look upon her, and see if this were the person that had hurt them.' They did so, and 'presently they were all tormented', going into paroxysms as if in pain. No doubt in desperation, Sarah Good named her fellow accused as the one who had tormented the children, and Sarah Osborne was duly ushered before the magistrates.

Sarah Osborne's appearance had the same effect on the children as Sarah Good's. Faced with a deposition from Betty Hubbard alleging that she had visited her in spectral form, Sarah answered 'I doe not know [but] that the devil goes about in my likeness to doe any hurt.' It was a good point; how should she know what the Devil got up to? But Sarah was as superstitious as anyone in Salem. She told the court that 'shee was more like to be bewitched, than that shee was a witch.' Asked what made her say so, 'shee answered that shee was frighted one time in her sleep and *either saw or dreamed* that shee saw a thing like an indian all black which did prick her in her neck and pulled her by the back part of her head to the dore of the house.' (Emphasis added.)

7   Hathorne was the great-great-grandfather of Nathaniel Hawthorne, but the story that the latter changed his surname in disgust at his ancestor's conduct is probably untrue.

6

Finally, the court turned to Tituba. At first, the slave denied having had any contact with the Devil, but under pressure from examiners determined to find evidence of witchcraft, dramatically 'confessed she was a Witch, and that she with the two other accused did torment and bewitch the complainers, and that these with two others whose names she knew not, had their Witch-meeting together.' She had seen 'a thing like a man, that tould me Searve him & I tould him noe I would nott doe Such thing.' Her imagination now took flight: the visitant was 'Sometimes like a hogge. Sometimes like a great black dogge.' She had also seen a yellow bird and '2 Catts, one Red, another black as bigge as a little dogge'. Asked what she rode upon to go to hurt the children, Tituba replied, 'I Rid upon a stick or poale & Good & Osburne behind me we Ride taking hold of one another don't know how we goe for I Saw noe trees nor path, but was presently there when wee were up.'

After three days' questioning all three accused were remanded to Boston Prison in chains to await their trial. Sarah Osborne cheated death by dying in prison on the day set down for the hearing. Sarah Good lasted only a few days longer before she was tried, condemned and hanged. Tituba was more fortunate. By confessing, she was saved from the gallows so that she could give evidence against other 'witches'. It cost her thirteen months in gaol.

But the Putnams had not finished with the Good family. Sarah's four year old daughter Dorothy (known as Dorcas) was the first child to be accused of witchcraft. Arrested and taken to Salem gaol, she was examined by three magistrates. It must have been a fearful experience for one so young and impressionable, for she was soon persuaded to display the finger upon which her familiar was supposed to suck. Dorothy's cooperation with the court was rewarded by committal to prison, where she remained for eight months with her legs in eight-pound irons like the grown-ups. (This practice was thought to prevent witches from sending their spectres abroad to torment good Christian folk.) Dorothy was eventually released when the witch hunt ended, but only after her now deranged mother had been hanged and her baby sister had died. She herself had been 'so hardly used and terrifyed that she hath ever since been very changeable haveing little or no reason to govern herself'.[8]

But even before the accusers had finished with little Dorothy they had trained their eyes on another target.

'IN THE HANDS OF AUTHORITY'

Seventy-two year old Martha Corey (Goodwife Corey) was a deeply religious person, though believed to have had an illegitimate child by a Red Indian, which smacked of witchcraft in the eyes of many. An independent-minded woman, she was known to be scornful of stories of witches. When Ann Putnam Jr. put it around that she had been visited by Martha's spirit, two local busybodies, Edward Putnam and Ezekiel Cheever, resolved to investigate. They decided to test her story by asking her how the spirit was dressed. According to Charles Upham, 'The girl told them that Goody Corey, knowing that they contemplated making this visit, had just appeared in spirit to her, but had blinded her so that she could not tell what clothes she wore.' Apparently accepting this ridiculous story at face value, the two then went to Martha's house. 'I know what you are come for.' She said. 'You are come to talk with me about being a witch, but I am none. I cannot help people's talking of me.' Martha, who denied that there were such things as witches, had earlier boasted that the magistrates' 'eyes were blinded and that she could open them.' In this she was sadly mistaken.

At Martha's first examination on 21 March, Magistrate Hathorne began as he intended to go on, 'You are now in the hands of Authority; tell me now why you hurt these persons'. When she denied having afflicted anyone Hathorne asked, 'Who did, then?' She replied, 'I do not know; how should I know?' A number of villagers then 'vehemently accuse[d] her in the assembly of afflicting them, by biting, pinching, strangling, etc.; and that they did in their fit see her likeness coming to them, and bringing a book to them.' Martha denied knowledge of any book. Charged with having a yellow bird that used to suck betwixt her fingers, she said she had no familiarity with any such thing, adding

8   Letter dated 13 September 1710 from her father requesting compensation.

indignantly that 'she was a gospel woman'. Of her accusers, Martha could only say, 'We must not believe all that these distracted children say.' But it was what they did that counted. The Rev. Deodat Lawson recorded that:

> It was observed several times that if [Martha] did but bite her underlip in time of examination, the persons afflicted were bitten on their arms and wrists and produced the marks before the magistrates, ministers, and others. And being watched for that, if she did but pinch her fingers, or grasp one hand hard in another, they were pinched, and produced the marks before the magistrates and spectators.

Some of the 'afflicted' even claimed to be able to see a black man whispering in Martha's ear. The last recorded exchange went:

Hathorne: 'What do you say to all these things that are apparent?'

Martha: 'If you will all go hang me how can I help it.'

Hathorne: 'Were you to serve the Devil ten years tell how many?'

'She laught.'[9]

There was nothing for it but to remand the obviously guilty Martha to prison. With one member of the church in prison on suspicion of witchcraft the accusers decided to aim for yet another, this time, in Upham's words, a person 'of acknowledged worth'.

THE ATTACK ON THE TOWNE FAMILY

For over half a century the Putnam family of Salem had been locked in a boundary dispute with the Towne family of Topsfield, a village some four miles to the north. Seventy year old Rebecca Nurse, née Towne, was known to be of the anti-Parris faction and Ann Putnam Sr. seems to have judged that this was the time to strike. The villagers were stunned when this pious, almost saint-like character was arrested and brought before the magistrates on 24 March. Abigail Williams, Ann Putnam and others told their usual rigmarole of having been tormented by Rebecca's apparition *that very day*. Even Rebecca's daughter, Sarah, was persuaded to testify against her. At one point in

9   Essex Institute, Mass., Historical Collections.

the proceedings Ann Putnam interrupted the questioning by shouting out, 'Did you not bring the Black Man with you, did you not bid me tempt God and dye?' Rebecca raised her hands to heaven and exclaimed, 'Oh Lord help me'; at which the children immediately went into fits. Later, the 'afflicted' were seen to mimic the poor woman's movements.

Rebecca denied the accusation of witchcraft 'before my eternal Father', but all the magistrate was concerned about was that the evidence of the afflicted had not reduced her to tears: 'It is very awful,' he said, 'to all to see these agonies … & yet to see you stand with dry eyes …' (As a contemporary, Thomas Brattle was later to observe, 'Some there are who never shed tears; others there are that ordinarily shed tears upon light occasions, and yet for their lives cannot shed a tear when the deepest sorrow is upon their hearts; and who is there that knows not these things?' The magistrates, apparently.) Rebecca was now, in Upham's words, 'infirm, half deaf, cross-questioned, circumvented, surrounded with folly, uproar, and outrage.' She exclaimed bitterly, 'You do not know my heart.'

Rebecca had two sisters, Sarah Cloyce (or Cloyse), and the fifty-seven year old Mary Easty. They were shortly to be the subject of similar accusations. At a church service on 20 March Ann Putnam Sr. had shouted, 'Look where Goodwife Cloyce sits on the beam [the roof beam of the church] suckling her yellow bird between her fingers.' A week later Rev. Parris took as the text of his sermon, 'Have I not chosen you twelve and one of you is a Devil?'[10] Sarah had had enough; taking this to be a condemnation of her sister, Rebecca, she 'rose up, and went out, the Wind shutting the door forcibly, gave occasion to some to suppose she went out in Anger, as might occasion a suspicion of her.' It did, and a warrant was promptly issued for Sarah's arrest. She was to languish in gaol until the following January when the charges against her were dismissed by a grand jury.

But when it came to the turn of Rebecca's other sister, Mary Easty, the evidence seems not to have been as convincing as usual. So much so, that the magistrate asked Ann Putnam, 'Are you certain that this is the woman?' For reasons unknown, most of the accusers seem to

10   John 6: 70.

10

have had second thoughts and Mary was discharged. This was too much for one of the 'afflicted', the nineteen year old Mercy Lewis, who went into paroxysms of unprecedented severity which lasted the whole day.[11] It was enough for the magistrate to order the unfortunate Mary to be rearrested. From prison she appealed to the Governor and judges:

> I Petition your Honors not for my own life, for I know I must die, and my appointed time is set, but the Lord he knows it is; if it be possible, that no more Innocent blood be shed, which undoubtedly cannot be avoided in the way and course you go in. I question not, but your Honors do the utmost of your powers, in the discovery and detection of Witchcraft and Witches, and would not be guilty of Innocent blood for the world; but in my own Innocency I know you are in the wrong way.

This moving plea made not a bit of difference and Mary was duly convicted and taken to the gallows, along with others, on 22 September. Before being turned off the ladder she prayed for an end to the witch-hunt.

THE PROCTORS

Also arrested at the same time as Sarah were John Proctor and his third wife, Elizabeth. Elizabeth managed her husband's tavern in Salem town, an occupation which was regarded by many as unsuitable for a woman. Her Quaker faith also gave cause for suspicion in the deeply Puritan town. So important was her examination thought to be that the regular magistrates were joined in the meeting house on 11 April by four colleagues from the Court of Assistants, and the court was presided over by the Deputy Governor of the Province.

The first witness was John Indian, who told the magistrates how Goody Proctor and Goody Cloyce had come to him at night and choked him 'a good many time'. Hearing this, Sarah could not contain herself and exclaimed, 'Oh. You are a grievous liar.' Two of the prosecution witnesses refused to speak, though for what reason it is impossible to

---

11 Mercy Lewis had been a servant in the family of former minister, George Burroughs (in Maine) and more recently of Thomas Putnam (in Salem).

say. When Abigail Williams gave evidence that Sarah had asked her to write in the Devil's book, the accused gently reminded the witness, 'Dear child. It is not so. There is another judgment, dear child'; it was enough to send Abigail and Ann into paroxysms in which they called out, "Look you! there is Goody Proctor upon the beam', indicating the rafters of the meeting house. (For some reason the villagers seem to have fastened on the idea that the Devil's servants had nothing better to do than hang around on roof beams.)

When order had been restored, the court decided to apply the acid test for witchcraft. Elizabeth was required to recite the Lord's Prayer, an accomplishment which everyone knew that witches could not perform inerrantly. Sure enough, the terrified woman pronounced the phrase, 'Hallowed be thy name' as 'Hollowed be they name'. It did not bode well for her.

Elizabeth's husband, the tall, sixty year old John Proctor, stood beside her during the examination. When one of the girls called out that the spectre of John would raise up a woman's feet; sure enough, the feet of Bathsheba Pope were seen to arise. Another woman, Goody Bibber suffered a similar indignity.[12] John was a farmer accustomed to speaking his mind and his mind scorned the whole idea of witches. He had once said, 'They should rather be had to the whipping post... If they are let alone we should all be devils and witches'. Before the magistrates two of the accusers 'cried out of'[13] John himself, saying that he was a wizard. Immediately, 'many if not all of the bewitched had grievous fits.' Deputy Governor Danforth asked John why they were suffering so. 'I know not,' he replied, 'I am innocent.' It did him no good and the following day he and his wife were committed to prison along with other suspected witches.

John Proctor ended on the gallows, a fate which his wife Elizabeth escaped only by reason of her pregnancy. In January of the following year, while still in prison, she gave birth to another child, but mother and daughter were not released until the general amnesty four months later. Three other children of the Proctors' had been arrested along

12   The diary of one of the judges, Samuel Sewall, reveals how impressed even a sane and compassionate observer could be by this trick.
13   That is to say, accused.

12

with their parents, but their fate is unknown. For the accusers, it had been an almost clean sweep.

THE ACCUSER WHO TURNED

There was now an extraordinary development. Two of the foremost accusers, Mercy Lewis and Ann Putnam, turned on a third, Mary Warren and declared that it was she who had forced Elizabeth Proctor to sign the devil's book. Cast into prison, Mary replied in kind, saying that her former accomplices were not to be believed any more than a simpleton. When she was examined on 19 April, Magistrate Corwin asked her, quite reasonably, 'You were a little while ago an afflicted person, now you are an afflicter: how comes this to pass?' Her enigmatic reply was that she took it to be 'a great Mercy of God'. The 'afflicted' children immediately went into fits, which were capped only by Mary doing the same, but repeatedly and at greater length.

When Mary had calmed down sufficiently to be examined further, she was reminded of her accusation that 'the afflicted persons did but dissemble'. This caused her to collapse again. On coming to, she said, 'Oh! I am sorry for it, I am sorry for it, & wringed her hands, & fell a little while into a fit again & then came to speak, but immediately her Teeth were set, & then she fell into a violent fit, & cryed out, Oh Lord help me, Oh good Lord save me!'

Later in prison Mary seems to have had yet another change of heart for she now declared that the Proctors, husband and wife, were both witches and that at their bidding she had signed the Devil's book and had tormented the children. Perhaps she had decided that it was best to give the inquisitor what he wanted, or perhaps she had been, as the historian Chadwick Hansen has suggested, 'literally driven insane'.[14] Whether from confusion or design, however, Mary's status as a confessed witch was to keep her off the gallows long enough to ensure her survival.

14   Chadwick Hansen, *Witchcraft at Salem* (London, Arrow Books, 1971), p. 87.

THE ONE WHO GOT AWAY

One who managed – narrowly – to avoid the fate of so many others was Elizabeth Cary (or Carey) of Charleston, across the river from Boston. Hearing that she had been accused of witchcraft, the doughty Elizabeth and her husband, Captain Nathaniel Carey determined to go to Salem to see what it was all about. When they arrived on 24 May, they met John Indian in a tavern in order to hear his story. Abigail Williams had promised to be there, but 'instead of one Accuser, they all came in, who began to tumble down like Swine, and then three Women were called in to attend them. We in the Room were all at a stand, to see who they would cry out of; but in a short time they cried out, "Cary"'. Elizabeth was immediately hauled before Hathorne and Corwin, where she was forced to stand with her arms apart in order to prevent her from tormenting the children. Later, her husband pathetically reported that, 'I did request that I might hold one of her hands, but it was denied me; then she desired me to wipe the tears from her eyes, and the sweat from her face, which I did; then she desired she might lean herself on me, saying she should faint.' With all his characteristic lack of impartiality and compassion Magistrate Hathorne remarked that if she had strength enough to torment those persons, she should have strength enough to stand.

The hearing ended with Elizabeth being committed to prison in leg irons. Nathaniel tried unsuccessfully to have her trial removed out of Salem; in desperation he arranged her escape from prison. The couple fled to New York, where they remained until the witch fever died down. Thomas Brattle thought that various 'high officials' had been complicit in her escape, which suggests that by this date a degree of cynicism with the witch-hunt had begun to set in at a high level.

THE BRAVE CAPTAIN

The accusers also met their match in the case of the redoubtable Captain Alden.

According to Calef, John Alden was an 'Indian fighter, naval commander, now at seventy a man of wealth, [and] one of the leading figures of New England'. Alden himself later recorded how, when he was examined on 31 May, 'Those Wenches being present, ... plaid their jugling tricks, falling down, crying out, and staring in Peoples Faces.' Alden turned to the magistrate and pertinently asked, 'What's the reason you don't fall when I look at you?' Hathorne had no answer. Alden was nevertheless committed to prison. He escaped three months later, along with another prisoner and was not seen again until his case was discharged by proclamation the following year.

But nothing could stop the accusations. In the month of May alone thirty-six warrants were issued for the arrest of suspect witches and by the end of that month about one hundred people were in prison. The ancient court system was groaning under the strain and something had to be done about it.

Massachusetts had been without a charter since 1684 following disagreements with the home country. A delegation had been sent to England under one of Massachusetts' most prominent divines, the Rev. Increase Mather. Their efforts bore fruit and on 14 May 1692 Mather returned to the colony with a new charter and a new Governor, the successful soldier and merchant Sir William Phips.[15] On 27 May Phips, acting on his own authority, set up a special Court of Oyer and Terminer to 'hear and determine' the witchcraft cases.[16] As chief justice, he appointed his Lieutenant Governor, William Stoughton. It was a disastrous choice.

THE FIRST TRIAL

The person with the dubious privilege of being the first to be tried by the new court was sixty year old Bridget Bishop. Despite the fact that she was a member in full fellowship of the church in the nearby village of Beverly, Bridget was suspect for various reasons; she owned a tavern where drinking and games of shovel board took place even on the Sabbath; she seldom had a good word to say about her neighbours and she was slow at paying her bills. Worse still, only six years before, Bridget had been accused of murder by witchcraft, but had been acquitted.

15　Phips had been knighted for his success in discovering Spanish treasure.
16　Technically, the appointment of a court was a question for the legislature. But the backlog of cases was so great that the determined Governor was not prepared to wait for its election.

Prof. Richard Frances has painted the scene in court on 2 June:

> On the one hand: the row of grave justices ... in long scarlet gowns with matching hoods, along with attending ministers like Samuel Parris from Salem village and Nicholas Noye from Salem town, in their black robes, white cravats around their necks conveying the dignity of spiritual office. On the other the accused, mainly girls, some of them small ones, shrieking, falling over going into paroxysms, staring at Bridget Bishop like children do in playgrounds, seeing who will be the first to blink, though here a life depended on it. Then there were the onlookers, fascinated by the spectacle but fearful a finger might suddenly, arbitrarily be pointed at them. Many were weather-beaten country people from Salem village and outlying parts, men in smocks or doublets and knee breeches with worsted stockings, the women with shawls – long handkerchiefs as they called them – their home-made dresses dirty at the bottom where they swirled over miry paths and fields ... Some better off townspeople were sprinkled among them, a glint of brass buckles and buttons on their shoes and surcoats, the women in gowns with virago sleeves, made of patterned quality material, sarcenet or velvet...[17]

On the morning of the trial Bridget was examined for witch marks. It was believed at the time that the Devil confirmed his pact with a witch by giving him or her some bodily confirmation, such as supernumerary nipples in the armpits or other concealed place. The result was a series of humiliating bodily examinations of suspects. If a witch mark was found it was proof of guilt; if absent, it was not proof of innocence. The jury of nine matrons which examined Bridget found a 'preternathurall Excresence of flesh between the pudendum and Anus much like to Tetts & not usuall in women'. It was a clear sign of witchcraft, but, frustratingly, 'upon a second search, within Three or four hours, there was no such thing to be seen...' The task of the witchfinder was truly difficult.

The prosecution began their case by calling witnesses who told how they had been visited at night by Bridget's spectre. A man spoke of having been kissed by her on the lips. (Could it be that he harboured sexual fantasies about this attractive woman who was notori-

---

17   Richard Francis, *Judge Sewall's Apology* (London, Fourth Estate, 2005), p. 119.

ous for wearing a scarlet bodice?) As had now become customary, 'the Bewitched were extreamly Tortured. If [the accused] did but cast her Eyes on them, they were presently struck down; and this in such a manner as there could be no Collusion in the Business. But upon the Touch of her Hand upon them, when they lay in their Swoons, they would immediately Revive; and not upon the Touch of any ones else…' Fifty year old Deliverance Hobbs, who had confessed to being a witch and was now probably out of her mind, claimed that Bridget had administered the sacrament to her at a witches' Sabbath. To crown it all, labourers employed to tear down a wall of Bridget's house gave incriminating evidence of 'poppets', or ritual dolls, concealed within it for which she could give no good explanation.

'There was,' wrote Cotton Mather, 'one very strange thing more with which the court was newly entertained. As this woman was under a guard passing by the great and spacious meeting house of Salem she gave a look towards the house and immediately a demon, invisibly entering the meeting house, tore down a part of it; so that there was no person to be seen there, yet the people, at the noise, running in, found a board, which was strongly fastened with nails, transported into another quarter of the house.' (Is it only in our more cynical days that we question how, if the devil was invisible, he could be seen entering the building?) Eight days after the inevitable verdict of 'Guilty', Bridget was taken to Gallows Hill and hanged, the first fatality of the Salem witch-hunt.

Gallows Hill was a promontory overlooking the North River. (The exact site is disputed.) It had been chosen, so the superstitious villagers believed, in order that Satan and his imps could survey the destruction of their kingdom in the New World. Drawn through the village on a cart and placed on a ladder before being launched into eternity, the condemned had to listen to the minister's sermon and confess their sins. Their end would not have been an easy one. Death by hanging was not the speedy dispatch perfected two centuries later. Instead of the immediate loss of consciousness which results from a broken neck, the condemned slowly strangled to death over a number of minutes. Afterwards, their bodies were thrown into a shallow grave, to be rescued secretly at night by any relatives brave enough to do so.

SPECTRAL EVIDENCE UNDER FIRE

The case against Bridget Bishop rested in large measure on what was known as spectral evidence, that is to say, evidence of the witness being visited by the spectre or apparition of the accused. A typical example of this was given by Bernard Peache in the trial of Rebecca Nurse: 'That being in Bed on a Lords-day Night, he heard a scrabbling at the Window, whereat he then saw Susanna Martin come in, and jump down upon the Floor. She took hold of this Deponents Feet, and drawing his Body up into an Heap, she lay upon him near Two Hours; in all which time he could neither speak nor stirr.'[18] Spectral evidence was thought to be particularly convincing because of the belief that the Devil could take the shape only of one of his followers, but not of a godly person. One of the first defendants to challenge this assumption was eighty year old George Jacobs:

> Jacobs: 'You tax me for a wizard. You may as well tax me for a buzzard. I have done no harm.'
>
> Court: 'Is it not harm to afflict these?'
>
> Jacobs: 'I never did it.'
>
> Court: 'But how comes it to be in your appearance?'
>
> Jacobs: 'The devil can take any license.'
>
> Court: 'Not without their consent.'

One of the judges, John Richards, had been worried about spectral evidence and, even before the Court of Oyer and Terminer had sat for the first time, he sought advice from one of New England's most respected ministers.

The Rev. Cotton Mather was the brilliant son of the famous Increase Mather. After graduating from Harvard College Cotton was ordained in 1684. At the age of twenty-two he was appointed teacher at the Old North Church, Boston, where his father was minister. Despite a lively interest in what we would now call science,[19] Mather

---

18 Symptoms which would nowadays be described as hallucinatory sleep paralysis.
19 He published a treatise on inoculation and in 1713 was made a Fellow of the Royal Society, England's foremost scientific body.

was, like most of his contemporaries, a firm believer in the existence of witches. In 1684 he published the influential '*Remarkable Providences*'. It was a 'defense of the existence of apparitions, witches, diabolical possessions and other remarkable judgements upon noted sinners.' He followed this up five years later with a book in which he adjured the reader to, 'Go tell Mankind, that there are Devils and Witches'. In one sermon he announced, 'let us go where we will, we shall still find a devil nigh unto us.' In August 1692, when the Salem witch-hunt was at its height, Mather proclaimed his belief that events in that village were proof of an 'Horrible Plot against the Country by Witchcraft' aiming to 'Blow up, and pull down all the churches in the Country.' The well-educated Mather in other words was a firm believer in witches and an enthusiastic supporter of the witch-hunt. On spectral evidence, however, he took a more pragmatic view than most, and he so advised Judge Richards. 'The Devil,' he wrote on 31 May, '*can* appear in the shape of an innocent person. For that reason, admitting spectral evidence only opens the door to false and malicious witness.'[20]

Another judge, Nathaniel Saltonstall, had been so 'very much dissatisfied' with the use of spectral evidence in Bridget Bishop's trial that he refused to sign any more warrants and resigned from the bench.[21] If the spectral evidence had been disregarded, he said, Bridget had been hanged for 'little more than wearing scarlet, countenancing shovel board, and getting herself talked about; all offenses, but hardly capital offenses.'[22] Almost immediately after speaking out, the judge's spectre was spotted by a number of girls, but he seems to have been too respected, or at any rate too important, a person to be attacked in this way.

Faced with such criticism, Governor Phips decided, after the manner of the time, to seek the advice of the clergy generally. The outcome of their deliberations was that, 'The evidence in this crime [of

20   Massachusetts Historical Society Collections, 4th series, VIII, pp. 391-397.
21   Saltonstall was replaced on the bench by Magistrate Corwin.
22   Marion L. Starkey, *The Devil in Massachusetts. A Modern Enquiry into the Salem Witch Trials* (New York, Alfred Knopf, 1949), p. 153.

witchcraft] ought to be as clear as in any other crimes of a capital nature.'[23] The ministers concluded:

> ... in the prosecution of these and all such witchcrafts, there is need of a very critical and exquisite caution. . . Presumptions, whereupon persons may be committed, and much more convictions, whereupon persons may be condemned as guilty of witchcrafts, ought certainly to be more considerable, than barely the accused person's being represented by spectre to the afflicted: inasmuch as it is an undoubted and a notorious thing, that a daemon may, by God's permission, appear even to ill purposes in the shape of an innocent, yea, and a virtuous man: nor can we esteem alterations made in the sufferers, by a look or touch of the accused, to be an infallible evidence of guilt: but frequently liable to be abused by the devil's legerdemains.

For reasons which are not fully understood, the ministers' warning fell on deaf ears, and spectral evidence continued to be admitted in court. However, as Increase Mather reported in *Cases of Conscience*, and recent research confirms,[24] no one was actually convicted on spectral evidence alone. Some argue that the ministers' advice actually did harm because it went on to recommend, 'the speedy and vigorous prosecutions of such as have rendered themselves obnoxious, according to the directions given in the laws of God and the wholesome statutes of the English nation for the detection of witchcrafts'. In fact, it is doubtful whether at that stage the ministers, or indeed anyone else, could have halted the good people of Salem in their headlong hunt for witches; and so the persecution went on.

REBECCA'S END

Rebecca Nurse, Sarah Good and three others were the next to be convicted of witchcraft on 30 June, though in the case of Rebecca in the most dubious circumstances.

---

23 *The Return of Several Ministers Consulted*, dated 15 June, was written by the ministers' amanuensis, Cotton Mather, and later published by Increase Mather (by then president of Harvard) in his 1693 book, *Cases of Conscience*.
24 Wendal D. Craker, 'Spectral Evidence, Non-spectral Acts of Witchcraft, and Confession at Salem in 1692' *The Historical Journal* vol. 40, 2 (1997), 331-359.

What happened was that when the jury returned with the unusual verdict of 'Not Guilty' the 'afflicted' screamed and jerked their bodies wildly. Judge Stoughton shared their dismay at the verdict and turned to the jury to direct their attention to a statement that Rebecca had made to the court. After Deliverance Hobbs had been brought in to give evidence Rebecca had said, 'What, do you bring her? She is one of us', or words to that effect. The implication which the judge invited the jury to draw was that the witness was a member of Rebecca's coven. This did the trick and the judge finally got the verdict of 'Guilty' that he sought. While he was, according to the laws of Massachusetts, entitled to invite the jury to reconsider their verdict, the judge should have first given the sick and deaf prisoner an opportunity to refute the implication of his remarks. The poor woman's first opportunity to do so was only after being sentenced to death when she wrote to the court desperately trying to correct the judge's remarks:

> I being informed, that the Jury brought me in guilty, upon my saying that Goodwife Hobbs and her daughter were of our Company; but I intended no otherwise, then as they were Prisoners with us, and therefore did then, and yet do judge them not legal evidence against their fellow prisoners. And I being something hard of hearing, and full of grief, none informing me how the Court took up my words, and therefore had not opportunity to declare what I intended, when they said they were of our Company.

The plea fell on deaf ears and Rebecca was hanged on 19 July, along with five other women, but only after she had been carried by chair from prison to her church to be excommunicated and condemned to eternal damnation. Alongside her was the plucky Sarah Good. Asked by the Rev. Noyes to repent, she said, 'You're a liar. I am no more a witch than you are a wizard! If you take my life away, God will give you blood to drink.' Local tradition has it that some years later Noyes died of a haemorrhage in the throat.

THE 'WHEEL WITHIN A WHEEL'

Isolated acts of witchcraft were bad enough, but events of an even more sinister nature had been hinted at when Abigail Williams gave evidence at the examination of the Proctors. She described to the magistrates a ceremony in the grounds of Samuel Parris's house at which about forty people had drunk the blood of those whom they had been tormenting. A picture was now beginning to emerge of an organized Satanic coven in the village.

In court Abigail had refrained from naming the person in charge of the coven, but a week or so after giving evidence she claimed to have seen at their meetings 'a little black minister that lived at Casco Bay'. This left little room for doubt since Casco Bay in Maine was where Salem's former minister, the dark-complexioned George Burroughs, had moved when he left Salem. This was confirmed the same day when the young Ann Putnam made a deposition claiming to have seen the apparition of a minister who choked her in an attempt to get her to write in his book. He said that his name was Burroughs and that he was 'above a witch, for he was a conjurer'. The very next day, Ann's father, the manipulative Thomas Putnam, wrote to the magistrates informing them 'of what we conceive you may not have heard, which are high and dreadful: of wheel within a wheel, at which our ears do tingle.' He gave no details, but his daughter's vision was confirmed by Abigail's stepmother, Deliverance Hobbs, and a warrant was issued for the arrest of Burroughs.

George Burroughs had been appointed to the church at Salem in 1680. His experience was similar to that of other preachers in that post before and after. When the village committee refused to levy the tithe by which his salary was paid, he had declined to preach. Despite legal proceedings designed to keep him in the village, Burroughs eventually left for Maine in 1683, still owed his unpaid tithes and funeral bills. The vengeful Thomas Putnam pursued him even there and had him thrown into prison for debt. The task of detaining 'the chief wizard' of Salem was put in the hands of the reluctant Marshal; the prospect scared him so much that two others had to be sent along with him. On the way back from Maine with their supernatural prisoner the officers of the law had to ride through deep woods in the middle of a thunderstorm. They were so terrified by the experience that their route has been known ever since as Witchtrott Hill and Witchtrott Road.

The unfortunate clergyman was produced before Magistrates Hathorne, Corwin, Sewall and Stoughton on 9 May. (The atmosphere must have been strained since Burroughs had known Sewall at Harvard.) The first examination was held in private, possibly because it dealt with his views on matters of doctrine. Under questioning, Burroughs had to admit that only the eldest of his children had been baptized and that he could not remember the last time he had received Holy Communion. The examination then moved to open court where Abigail Hobbs and others told of having been present 'at the great meeting in Mr. Parris's pasture' at which the prisoner had administered the sacrament. Among his accusers was Mercy Lewis, whom Burroughs had taken in after she had lost her parents in an Indian raid. The afflicted were so disordered at the presence of their 'tormenter' that they had to be removed for their own safety. Later, they told the magistrates of having seen the ghosts of Burroughs' former wives with napkins round their heads pointing to their death-wounds and saying that 'their blood did cry for vengeance'. (There is some evidence that he had treated his wives badly, but absolutely none whatever for the suggestion that he had killed them.)

Burroughs' case came up for trial on 2 August along with five others. There were thirty depositions to his guilt, (though it appears that some of them may have been inserted in the files after the trial). Mercy Lewis swore that 'a little black haired man' whom she identified as the minister, 'carried me up to an exceeding high mountain and shewed me all the kingdoms of the earth and tould me that he would give them all to me if I would writ in his book.'[25] The girl became so agitated that she had to be ordered out of court. Abigail Hobbs then testified that Burroughs had given her magical dolls and Ann Putnam swore that he had bewitched soldiers during a failed military campaign against the Indians three years before. When the children claimed to have been bitten by Burroughs the court solemnly examined his teeth and decided that they matched the bite marks on the children's bodies.

Perhaps the oddest evidence, however, was of Burroughs' party tricks, which in their unworldliness the witnesses translated into feats of supernatural strength. He was accused, for example, of having been able to lift a barrel of molasses with his finger and of having put 'the forefinger of his right hand into the muzzle of a gun and 'held it out att arms end only wth thatt finger'. Burroughs, a short, sleight man,

25   Probably an unconscious echo of Matthew 4:8.

explained to the court how he had done this old soldier's trick with the gun and claimed that an Indian who had been present could do the same. His accusers countered by saying that the Indian was the Devil in disguise.

When it was his turn to give evidence, the by now terrified Burroughs is said to have given 'Faltring, Faulty, unconstant, and contrary Answers'. Certainly, he made a number of damaging admissions, such as that he had a toad problem in his home in Maine. (Toads were closely associated with witchcraft.) When his accusers writhed in agony, Magistrate Stoughton asked the prisoner, '"How comes the Devil is so loath to have any testimony borne against you?" Which cast [Burroughs] into very great confusion.' No doubt fearful of being unable to respond as he would wish, Burroughs handed the court a written statement in which he expressed his doubts that witches actually possessed the powers ascribed to them, and expounded his doctrinal view that 'signing a compact with the Devil did not enable a Devil to torment other people at a distance.' These theological niceties did not go down well with the court.

Despite a petition signed by thirty-two villagers, Burroughs was convicted and went to the gallows on 19 August, along with others. His end is described in *The History of Salem, Massachusetts*:

> ... when he was upon the ladder, he made a speech for the clearing of his Innocency, with such Solemn and Serious expressions, as were to the Admiration of all present; his prayer (which he concluded by reading the Lords' prayer) was so well worded, and uttered with such composedness, and such (at least seeming) fervency of Spirit, as was very affecting, and drew tears from many (so that it seemed to some, that the Spectators would hinder the Execution).[26]

This display of public concern so disturbed Cotton Mather that he felt compelled to declare to the assembled throng that, 'Mr. Burroughs was not an ordained minister and that [the] Devil was often transformed into an angel of light. This somewhat appeased the people.'

---

26 I have omitted some gory details which Calef supplied in *More Wonders of the Invisible World*, but which have for good reasons been doubted. See William Frederick Poole, 'Cotton Mather and Salem Witchcraft' *North American Review*, vol. 108, issue 223, (April 1869).

Not everyone in Salem surrendered to the sleep of reason.

THE CONSTABLE WHO REFUSED TO ARREST

One of those who met his end along with Burroughs was John Willard. Willard was a respected citizen and land speculator who had his doubts about the witch craze. He was also a deputy constable. When in March, Willard had been ordered to bring in several of the accused, he complained that their accusers were attention seekers who used their sightings to get even with their enemies. Fortunately, the Rev. Parris was on hand to ensure that no witch went unpunished. When a relative of Willard's was confined to bed with a pain in his side the sick man blamed it on the constable. When the sick man's son fell ill the girls confirmed that they could see Willard's spectre crushing his chest. The boy died and a coroner's jury found that he had been killed by Willard's spectre. Nathaniel Putnam was the foreman of the jury.

As soon as he heard that a warrant had been issued for his arrest Willard fled the county but was soon apprehended. Ann Putnam told the magistrates that his spectre had threatened to kill her. Another witness actually saw 'the black man' speaking in Willard's ear while he was being examined. When Willard failed to recite the Lord's prayer correctly in court, he is said to have joked, 'I think I am bewitched as well as they.' John Willard was put on trial and hanged, maintaining his innocence to the last.

THE 'DREADFUL WIZZARD'

Undoubtedly the most frightful fate of anyone involved in the Salem witch trials was that of Martha Corey's farmer husband, Giles. Giles was said to be eighty, but was probably nearer seventy. He was a violent man; some eighteen years before, he had beaten a servant to death but had managed to avoid conviction when the servant died before he could give evidence. More to the point, he had fallen out with Thomas Putnam during George Bayley's stewardship of the church, and time had not lessened the two men's dislike for each other. Giles was at first inclined to give credence to the witch stories, but when the accusations began to be directed against his Martha he poured scorn on them; scorn which turned to rage when he found himself the subject of accusations too.

Hauled before the magistrate on 19 April he had to listen to Ann Putnam give evidence that she had seen:

> ... the Apperishtion of Gilles Cory com and afflect me urging me to writ in his book and so he continewed hurting me ... dureing the time of his examination Giles Cory did tortor me a grat many times ... severall times sence Giles Cory or his Apperance has most greviously afflected me by beating pinching and almost Choaking me to death urging me to writ in his book... I veryly beleveue that Giles Cory [is] a dreadfull wizard.

Other witnesses accused him of murdering his first wife and of only refraining from murdering the second because she too was a witch. Giles' presence had the now predictable effects on his accusers. When he held his head on one side, the girls did likewise. When he drew in his cheeks, so did the girls. Magistrate Hathorne exclaimed, 'What? Is it not enough to act witchcraft at other times, but must you do it now in face of authority?', and ordered the prisoner's hands to be tied so that he could not torment his accusers.

Remanded to prison, Giles addressed a desperate plea for help to Cotton Mather and four other ministers on behalf of himself and other prisoners. He blamed their fate on 'the Enmity of our Accusers and our Judges, and Jury, whom nothing but our Innocent blood will serve their turn'. The only evidence against them, he wrote, had been from confessed witches, three of whom, including his son, having refused to cooperate 'till they tyed them Neck and Heels till the Blood was ready to come out of their Noses.'[27] Against this background the prisoners were unlikely to get justice and he asked either for the judges to be changed or the case transferred to Boston. Corey's plea was ignored. Nevertheless, he never got to stand trial. Judge Sewall's diary records briefly that 'About noon, at Salem, Giles Corey was press'd to death for standing mute.' He certainly was pressed to death – probably on 19 September – but how this came about and why are still matters of conjecture.

---

27   This was a regular punishment at the time, but not authorised as an interrogation technique. Since this account is the only one of its kind it must be viewed with caution.

The commonest explanation, enshrined in books, plays and films, is that Giles refused to plead 'Not Guilty' because he knew that he stood no hope of being acquitted and because he believed that by doing so he would preserve his inheritance for his children. As Charles Upham tells it: 'When called into court to answer to the indictment found by the Grand Jury, he did not plead "Guilty," or "Not guilty," but stood mute. How often he was called forth we are not informed; but nothing could shake him. No power on earth could unseal his lips.'[28]

It is true that at common law if a prisoner charged with a felony refused to plead the trial could not go ahead. As a means of securing a plea the court was allowed to order the *peine forte et dure* [hard and severe punishment]. This archaic procedure required that the prisoner:

> ... be laid upon the bare Ground without any Litter, Straw or other Covering, and without any Garment about him, saving something to cover his Privy Members and that he shall lie upon his Back, and his Head shall be covered, and his Feet bare, and that one of his Arms shall be drawn with a Cord to one side of the House, and the other Arm to the other side, and that his Legs shall be used in the same manner, and that upon his Body shall be laid so much Iron and Stone as he can bear, and more, and that the first Day after he shall have three Morsels of Barley Bread, without any Drink, and the second Day he shall drink so much as he can three times of the Water which is next the Prison Door, saving running Water, without any Bread: and this shall be his Diet until he die....[29]

Strangely enough, there were people willing to undergo this appalling ordeal. The advantage to them was that, if they died under it, their property would not be forfeit to the Crown, as would normally be the case for a convicted felon. However, the idea that this was what motivated Giles seems unlikely since forfeiture of a prisoner's

---

28   An interpretation which led to Longfellow's lines, 'I will not plead / If I deny, I am condemned already, / In courts where ghosts appear as witnesses / And swear men's lives away. If I confess, / Then I confess a lie, to buy a life, / Which is not life, but only death in life.' (*Giles Corey of Salem Farms*).
29   *The Proceedings at the Sessions of the Peace, and the Oyer and Terminer, for the City of London and the County of Middlesex 13–15 January 1720/1.*

property had been abolished as long ago as 1641. And Corey had little inheritance to protect since before the trial he had conveyed his land by deed to his two sons-in-law. The 'refusal to plead' scenario is flatly contradicted by another account. A century and a half closer to the events than Upham, Robert Calef wrote, 'Giles Cory *pleaded not guilty* to his indictment, but would not put himself on Tryal by the Jury (they having cleared none upon tryal) and knowing there would be the same witnesses against him, rather chose to undergo what death they would put him to.'[30] (Emphasis added.) Chadwick Hansen supports this version of events.[31] But there is a problem here; in such a case the court was obliged, in the words of Blackstone's *Commentaries on the Laws of England*, perhaps the most revered authority on the common law, 'to impanel a jury, to enquire whether he ftands obftinately mute, or whether he be dumb *ex vifitatione Dei* [by visitation of God].' While we cannot be sure that such a procedure did not take place, there is no record of it. (It might be added that if Hansen's account was correct, the *peine forte et dure* was pronounced illegally and Giles' death was judicial murder.)

In the absence of proper court records, the only fact that we can be sure of is that Giles died after two days of agony administered by Sheriff Corwen under the supervision of Judge Stoughton. Robert Calef (not always the most scrupulous witness) provides a gruesome detail: Giles's 'tongue being prest out of his mouth, the Sheriff with his cane forced it in again, when he was dying. The prisoner's last words are said to have been: 'More weight'. Before their deaths both Giles and Martha Corey were excommunicated by their loving brethren.

In what was to prove to be a last sputter of superstitious prejudice Abigail Hobbs, Samuel Wardwell and seven others were tried on 17 September and condemned.[32] Wardwell, who had confessed to witch-

30   This peculiar order was abolished in England in 1772.
31   Hansen, *Witchcraft at Salem*, p. 185. The court asked, 'How will you be tried? The prisoner was expected to reply, 'By God and my country', which was the passport to trial by jury.
32   Three of the women prisoners who temporarily escaped death by reason of pregnancy, were later condemned by Judge Stoughton and reprieved only by a general amnesty.

craft at his examination, bravely retracted it at his trial, saying that 'he knew he should dye for it; whether he owned it or no.' The witch cart clattered up Gallows Hill for the last time on 22 September with a cargo of eight 'witches'. All that the Rev. Nicholas Noyes of Salem could say was, 'What a sad thing it is to see eight firebrands of hell hanging there.'

'OUR ERROUR IS GREAT'

Shortly after this, Salem's blood lust seems to have finally run its course, at least for the more thoughtful members of society, although some of them seem to have been spurred to protest only when the finger of suspicion was pointed in their direction.

After his wife had been accused of witchcraft, Increase Mather used the occasion of his October sermon publicly to disapprove of spectral evidence. 'It were better that Ten Suspected Witches should escape,' he declared, 'than that the Innocent Person should be Condemned ... It is an awful thing, which the Lord has done to convince some amongst us of their Error: I declare and testifies [sic] that to take away the life of any one, merely because a spectre or Devil, in a bewitched or possessed person does accuse them, will bring the guilt of innocent blood on the land...'[33]

A few days after Mather's sermon the first comprehensive criticism of the trials appeared in the form of a letter written 'to whom we know not' by Thomas Brattle, a wealthy merchant and treasurer of Harvard college and a Fellow of the recently founded Royal Society of London (now the Royal Society). In his letter he dismissed as fanciful such matters as the Devil's book, the witches' meeting, the Devil's Baptism and the mock sacraments. More importantly, he dissected the cavalier attitude of the courts towards the evidence of persons who 'do say, and often have declared it, that they can see Spectres when their eyes are shutt ... I am sure they lye, at least speak falsely, if they say so; for the thing, in nature, is an utter impossibility... if our officers and Courts have apprehended, imprisoned, condemned, and executed our guiltlesse neighbours, certainly our errour is great, and we shall rue it

---

33   The sermon was later published in *Cases of Conscience.*

in the conclusion...' Brattle's views were all the more telling because he was no unthinking critic of the judges and magistrates involved.

No doubt emboldened by this change in informed opinion, the Rev. Francis Dane, minister of the church in Andover, wrote to the Governor, along with twenty-three others, seeking mercy for those still in custody on the basis of unfounded accusations. Dane had an additional reason to feel strongly on this point. His own daughter Abigail had been convicted and sentenced to death only the month before, but given a temporary stay of execution because she was pregnant.

Returning from business in the eastern part of the country, Governor Phips declared that he was concerned at what he called a 'strange ferment of dissatisfaction' and ordered 'a stop to the printing of any discourses one way or other' about witchcraft. His edict was ignored almost as soon as it was issued by the publication of a pamphlet pleading for greater rigour in assessing evidence in cases of witchcraft.[34] 'God hath appointed that there shall be good and clear proof against the Criminal: else he is not Providentially delivered into the hands of Justice, to be taken off from the earth. Nor hath God exempted this Case of Witchcraft from the General Rule. Besides, reason tells us, that the more horrid the Crime is, the more Cautious we ought to be in making any guilty of it.'[35] The pamphlet's author was Boston minister, the Rev. Samuel Willard (no connection with John). Willard had personal experience of the problem since he too had been accused of witchcraft by Abigail Williams – until a magistrate told her that she must be mistaken.

A SUPERIOR COURT?

Phips also discovered that his deputy, Stoughton, had been ignoring the fact that 'many considerable persons of unblamable life and conversation [had been] cried out upon as witches and wizards', and resolved to put things right. (His resolve must have been strengthened by the fact that even his own wife had not escaped suspicion.) He im-

34 It was entitled, *Some Miscellany Observations A Dialogue between 'S' and 'B'.*
35 A model statement of English law on the standard of proof.

mediately released on bail those against whom the only evidence was of a spectral nature and put a stop to any further arrests for witchcraft pending the King's pleasure. His Majesty duly responded, urging 'the greatest moderation and all due circumspection' in the future prosecution of witches. Shortly after, the Court of Oyer and Terminer was dissolved and replaced by a Superior Court of Judicature in which spectral evidence was to be of presumptive value only. Unfortunately, Judge Stoughton was elected chief justice of the new court and immediately declared his intention to order the execution of all the 'witches' who had been saved from death by reason of their pregnancy. Phips, acting on the advice of the Attorney General, put a stop to this by reprieving everyone concerned. Stoughton, 'filled with passionate anger', stormed off the bench. He returned at a later date, but by then the wind had veered round so far that a woman was actually prosecuted for making a false accusation of witchcraft.

Witchcraft trials did not immediately cease after these reforms; they merely became less frequent. The witch-hunt was only brought to an end on 3 April 1695 when Increase and Cotton Mather met the Massachusetts Bay elders who jointly issued a strong warning against the making of further complaints. One by one those involved began to acknowledge their faults. Some, like Tituba and the sixteen year old Margaret Jacobs, had admitted lying shortly after doing so; others took longer to reflect on their errors. Among the first was Rev. Parris.

THE FIRST APOLOGY

In his sermon on Sunday, 18 November 1694, Samuel Parris 'humbly owned':

> yt [that] God has been righteously spitting in my face... I am very desirous (upon farther light) to own any errors I have therein fallen into, and can come to a discerning of ... I do most heartily, fervently, and humbly beseech pardon of the merciful God, through the blood of Christ, of all my mistakes and trespasses in so weighty a matter; and also all your forgiveness of every offence in this and other affairs, wherein you see or conceive I have erred and offended; professing, in the presence of the Almighty God, that what I have done has been, as for substance, as I apprehended was duty — however through weakness, ignorance, &c., I may have been mistaken.'

This half-hearted apology seems to have been forced out of the minister by demands for his removal from office. However, it satisfied the village committee who resolved the following year:

> That albeit in ye Late and ye Dark Time of ye confusions, wherein Satan had obtained a more than ordinary liberty to be sifting of this Plantation, there were sundry unwarrantable and uncomfortable steps taken by Mr. Samuel Parris …, then under ye hurrying Distractions of amazing Afflictions, yet the said Mr. Parris, by ye Good Hand of God brought unto a better sense of things, hath so fully expressed it, that a Christian charitie may and should receive satisfaction therew it.

The loving spirit did not last and, as Upham records, 'Samuel Parris, after a ministry of seven years, crowded from the very beginning with contention and animosity, and closed in desolation, ruin, and woes unutterable, havoc scattered among his people and the whole country round, was driven from the parish, the blood of the innocent charged upon his head, and, for the rest of his days, consigned to obscurity and penury.'

The Salem flock had to wait until 1696 for the appointment of a new minister; he proved to be exactly what they needed. Young Joseph Green cajoled members of the warring families to sit in the same pews and finally effected a true reconciliation in the troubled community. In 1703 he even persuaded his congregation somewhat tardily to revoke the excommunication of their former sister, Martha Corey.

The next to see the light was the Rev. John Hale. His change of heart, fortuitously occurred only after his wife, Sarah had been accused of witchcraft, but it was not until 1697 that he publicly admitted in his *Modest Enquiry Into the Nature of Witchcraft* that there had been 'a going too far in this affair,' because 'It cannot be imagined that in a place of so much knowledge, so many in so small compass of land should abominably leap into the Devil's lap at once.' The sheer number of accused, he wrote, 'gave just ground to suspect some mistake.' It was small comfort to those whom he had helped to a dusty grave.

Samuel Sewall was the only judge to admit his mistakes; and he did so handsomely. On a day in January 1697 appointed for fast, penance and reparation Judge Sewall attended a service at the Old South Church in Boston, where he handed the Rev. Willard a paper to read out on his behalf. The judge remained standing while it was read out, and at the close bowed his head:

> Samuel Sewall, sensible of the reiterated strokes of God upon himself and family, and being sensible that as to the guilt contracted upon the opening of the late Commission of Oyer and Terminer at Salem ..., he is, upon many accounts, more concerned than any that he knows of, desires to take the blame and shame of it, asking pardon of men, and especially desiring prayers that God, who has unlimited authority, would pardon that sin and all his other sins, personal and relative. And according to His infinite benignity and sovereignty, not visit the sin of him or of any other, upon himself or any of his, nor upon the land. But that he would powerfully defend him against all the temptations to sin for the future, and vouchsafe him the efficacious, saving conduct of His Word and Spirit.

It is possible that the death of Sewall's baby daughter Sarah, on Christmas Day 1696, may have prompted this confession, but of its fulsome sincerity there can be no doubt. Unfortunately, no other judge followed his example and it took the jurors to put them to shame. Writing on the same day as Sewall's apology, Thomas Fiske and his fellow jurors confessed that:

> ... we ourselves were not capable to understand, nor able to withstand, the mysterious delusions of the powers of darkness and Prince of the air, but were, for want of knowledge in ourselves and better information from others, prevailed with to take with such evidence against the accused, as, on further consideration and better information, we justly fear was insufficient for the touching the lives of any.

They expressed to God and to the survivors of the affair their 'deep sense of, and sorrow for, our errors in acting on such evidence to the condemning of any person; and do hereby declare, that we justly fear that we were sadly deluded and mistaken – for which we are much disquieted and distressed in our minds ...'

They 'would none of us do such things again, on such grounds, for the whole world...'

Finally, on 25 August 1706, at the urging of Pastor Green, the now twenty-seven year old Ann Putnam Jr. made her confession at a meeting before the Salem village church. She said that she desired:

... to be humbled before God for that sad and humbling providence that befell my father's family in the year about '92; that I, then being in my childhood, should, by such a providence of God, be made an instrument for the accusing of several persons of a grievous crime, whereby their lives were taken away from them, whom now I have just grounds and good reason to believe they were innocent persons; and that it was a great delusion of Satan that deceived me in that sad time...

She had been 'instrumental, with others, though ignorantly and unwittingly, to bring upon myself and this land the guilt of innocent blood; ..., being deluded by Satan.'

She added that for having been 'a chief instrument of accusing of Goodwife Nurse and her two sisters, I desire to lie in the dust, and to be humbled for it, in that I was a cause, with others, of so sad a calamity to them and their families...'

We will probably never know whether this expression of 'ignorance' and 'unwittingness' was genuine or feigned.

Many of the accused and their dependants had lost out financially when their property was seized by Sheriff Corwin. (The legality of his actions is still disputed). After his death Phillip English had the last word when he put a lien on the corpse. The body was deposited on his front lawn until his executors paid £60. 3s., almost all that was left of the estate. Others looked to the General Court for compensation and on October 1711 it was finally ordered, but only to a mere twenty-two petitioners. (The largest sum was £150 to John Proctor and his wife.) Descendants of the wrongly condemned continued to seek pardons until 2001 when legislation was passed proclaiming the innocence of all the accused.

WHY DID IT HAPPEN?

By the time the witch-hunt had come to its end over one hundred and fifty people had been accused and imprisoned, nineteen had been hanged, five had died in prison and one had been deliberately crushed to death. How did this calamity come about?

Various medical causes have been advanced for the behaviour of the girl accusers, including epilepsy, ergot poisoning,[36] *encephalitis lethargica* (inflammation of the brain),[37] asthma and even child abuse,[38] but none of these is now thought to provide a satisfactory explanation of their 'symptoms'.

In the 1970s the historian Chadwick Hansen put forward a new explanation for the behaviour of the 'afflicted':

> We must bear in mind that in a society which believes in witchcraft, it works. If you believe in witchcraft and you discover that someone has been melting your wax image over a slow fire or muttering charms over your nail parings, the probability is that you will get extremely sick. To be sure, your symptoms will be psychosomatic rather than organic. But the fact that they are obviously not organic will make them only more terrible, since they will seem the result of malefic and demonic power.[39]

The idea that some of the 'afflicted' could actually have suffered in the manner they so graphically described to the court is a fascinating possibility, but one which is unlikely to be verifiable, one way or the other. Hansen may have been on stronger grounds when he suggested that the phenomenon 'was not fraudulent, as some have claimed, but pathological; these people were hysterics in the clinical rather than the popular sense of the term.'[40] It is not surprising that young children, particularly girls, brought up in a stiflingly religious atmosphere with little in the way of opportunities for self-expression, should display hysterical group behaviour, but why did the hysteria last so long? When the time came at which the girls could have been expected to resume control over their emotions their parents and others in author-

36   *Science* vol. 192 (1976) by Linda Caporael. But see Spanos, N. P., J. Gottlieb. 'Ergots and Salem village witchcraft: A critical appraisal'. *Science* vol. 194. (1976), 1390-1394.
37   See Laurie Winn Carlson, *A Fever in Salem: A New Interpretation of the New England Witch Trials* (Chicago, Ivan R. Dee, 1999).
38   See Richard A. Gardner MD, *Sex Abuse Hysteria – Salem Witch Trials Revisited* (New Jersey, Creative Therapeutics, 1991).
39   Hansen, *Witchcraft at Salem*, p. 31.
40   *The Encyclopedia of Medicine* states: 'hysteria is a feature of hysterical disorders in which a patient experiences physical symptoms that have a psychological, rather than an organic, cause...'

ity stepped in to tell the girls that they had been bewitched. Many of their parents had probably read Cotton Mather's best seller, *Memorable Providences,* which described remarkably similar behaviour on the part of girls in nearby Boston only a few years before. The Rev. Deodat Lawson's sermon of 19 March put down the girls' afflictions to 'the effects of Diabolical malice.' It must have been difficult for the children to resist living up to the adults' expectations. It is notable that, under pressure to reveal their 'persecutors', the girls had been careful to name two elderly women on the fringe of society who could not be expected to stand up for themselves. And when challenged, they cast aspersions upon anyone who doubted them. What had started as hysteria may have turned into wish fulfilment and then into a vicious conspiracy. It is a tempting theory.

A few of the adult accusers were to some extent victims of their environment. The influences at work on Ann Putnam Sr., for example, were described graphically by Charles Upham:

> For two months, her house had been the constant scene of the extraordinary actings of the circle of girls of which her daughter and maid-servant were the leading spirits. Her mind had been absorbed in the mysteries of spiritualism. The marvels of necromancy and magic had been kept perpetually before it. She had been living in the invisible world, with a constant sense of supernaturalism surrounding her. Unconsciously, perhaps, the passions, prejudices, irritations, and animosities, to which she had been subject, became mixed with the vagaries of an excited imagination; and, laid open to the inroads of delusion as her mind had long been by perpetual tamperings with spiritual ideas and phantoms, she may have lost the balance of reason and sanity. This, added to a morbid sensibility, probably gave a deep intensity to her voice, action, and countenance.

There is no question that some of the accusers did lie consciously. As Charles Upham wrote, 'There is too much evidence of guile and conspiracy to attribute all their actions and declarations to delusion.' On 28 March Mercy Lewis, went into a 'fit' and cried out, 'Goody Proctor. Old Witch. I'll have her hang.' Accused of lying, she swiftly came out of her trance and said, 'It was for sport. I must have some sport.' Even more suggestive of conscious falsehood is the consistency of the girls' accusations, some of which sound as though they had been worked out together. The carefully orchestrated attack on

George Burroughs is a case in point. And the 'afflicted' were cunning enough to know how to deal with difficult questions. When the young Ann Putnam was brought before the magistrates and asked what her spectre was wearing she replied, suspecting a trap: 'I am blind now; I cannot see.' Some of the accusers were actually caught in the act of lying, such as the girl who produced a knife blade which, she swore, had been used on her by the accused. (Its true provenance was only revealed by chance when a young man who happened to be in court came forward to claim the knife as his own; it made no difference to the trial.)

But why should they lie?

Some, like Tituba, probably lied out of pressure. According to Calef, 'The account she since gives of it is, that her Master did beat her and otherways abuse her, to make her confess and accuss (such as he call'd) her Sister-Witches, and that whatsoever she said by way of confessing or accusing others, was the effect of such usage.' Tituba actually visited Burroughs in his cell the day before his execution to beg pardon for her lies. Others, like Margaret Jacobs, had been co-erced into falsehood by the oppressive questioning, threats and prom-ises of the examining magistrates. In a letter to her father written from the dungeon at Salem Prison on 20 August, Margaret confessed to '... having, through the Magistrates Threatnings, and my own Vile and Wretched Heart, confessed several things contrary to my Conscience and Knowledge, though to the Wounding of my own Soul, the Lord pardon me for it.' Later, she wrote to the judges explaining:

> ... they told me, if I would not confess, I should be put down into the dungeon and would be hanged, but if I would confess I should have my life; the which did so affright me, with my own vile wicked heart, to save my life; made me make the like confession I did, which confession, may it please the honoured court, is altogether false and untrue.

But was there something more sinister at work? One cannot help noticing how many of the accused were enemies of the vengeful and manipulative Putnam family. The two Anns, Sr. and Jr., were at the heart of the accusations. The simple-minded Mercy Lewis had worked in the Putnams' household and had experienced their tirades against the accused. Grudge seems to have played a part in the case of other prosecution witnesses also. Benjamin Abbot is an example of such a case when he claimed that Martha Carrier had threatened him *after quarrelling with him over land* and that thereafter he 'was taken with a swelling in his Foot, and then with a pain in his side, and exceedingly Tormented.' Another witness told how, *after an argument with the accused*, he had 'lost a Cow in a strange Preternatural unusual manner.' (The court did not bother to check that the death was indeed 'preternatural'.)

COULD THE WITCHES HAVE BEEN REAL?

Hansen makes another interesting suggestion, namely that despite their denials some of the accused may actually have believed themselves to have been witches. As examples, he points to Bridget Bishop with her hidden 'poppets' and to George Burroughs with his reputation for occult powers and his faltering defence. (Interestingly, Cotton Mather claimed in a letter to a friend that after Burroughs' death five Andover witches had confessed that he was their leader.) It would not be surprising if some of the accused had persuaded themselves that they really did possess occult powers (and were thus, incidentally, guilty according to the law of the day), but this was by no means true of the majority of the accused. Most of those who confessed to witchcraft probably did so because they saw it as the only way to avoid the rope. And this was a realistic expectation; no one who admitted being a witch was actually hanged (though, as we have seen, some of them came perilously close before being finally pardoned).

But it took more than a few hysterical children and a twisted and embittered family to cause so much pain and misery in this little community. Why was it allowed to happen?

WHO WAS AT FAULT?

It is easy to blame the examining magistrates. As Charles Upham wrote: 'They acted throughout in the character and spirit of prosecuting officers, put leading and ensnaring questions to the prisoners, adopted a browbeating deportment towards them, and pursued them with undisguised hostility. They assumed their guilt from the first, and endeavored to force them to confess; treating them as obstinate culprits because they would not. Every kind of irregularity was permitted.' All this was true, but Upham was writing in the mid nineteenth century and the practices he described were not considered improper at the time of the Salem trials, but were regarded merely as part of the investigative process. Did the judges do any better? [41]

Of the trials themselves, Upham comments that, 'every thing that the gossip of the credulous or the fertile imaginations of the malignant could produce; every thing, gleaned from the memory or the fancy, that could have an unfavorable bearing upon an accused person, however foreign or irrelevant it might be to the charge, was allowed to be brought in evidence before the magistrates, and received at the trials.' Comparison with English practice of the day suggests that, though the law of evidence was still in its infancy, lawyer judges might have adopted a more rigorous approach to spectral evidence. Unfortunately, none was available in seventeenth-century Salem and the senior judge saw nothing wrong with the practice.

A final judgement on Stoughton is still awaited. For all his faults, he had a reputation as a political moderate and even Thomas Brattle 'highly honoured and reverenced' his 'wisdom and integrity'. But it is difficult to justify his continuing willingness to admit spectral evidence long after its weaknesses had become publicly apparent. Nor is it easy to justify his bullying manner in court, his treatment of Giles Corey and his cruel resolve to have the 'confessed witches' executed after their convictions had been discredited. And he never learned; long after the trials were over and Judge Sewall had apologised, Stoughton steadfastly refused to admit any error on his part.

As for the church, there is no getting away from the fact that its ministers were in the forefront of the witch-hunt and were often present to gloat at the executions. Even the highly educated and relatively liberal Cotton Mather took this line and it was only his belated realisation of the dangers of spectral evidence that offers any mitigation to his reputation. Even then he was still urging enthusiastic continuance of the witch-hunt.

41   When the magistrates were sitting to hear the case, as opposed to sitting as examining magistrates, they were called 'judges'.

It would not be fair to place blame on any single group within Salem because at the root of the persecution was a weakness which was shared by almost every one of its inhabitants.

CREDULITY

For six terrible months in 1692 the one characteristic that the churchmen, magistrates and people of Salem had in common was a suspension of disbelief. Their willingness to accept, not merely the improbable, but also the manifestly impossible is difficult for the modern mind to grasp. Much of the explanation lies in the fact that Salem was a deeply religious community. The Puritans' fervent faith required its members to believe in the literal truth of witches,[42] exorcisms,[43] angels,[44] demons,[45] and the bodily resurrection[46] of a God whose body and blood they consumed weekly in the Eucharist. As William Frederick Poole wrote in 1869, 'Cotton Mather believed that devils were concerned in the proceedings at Salem. If this be superstition, he was very superstitious. But not a single person who held the faith of the Christian Church at that day can be named who had any other belief.' Predisposed to see the supernatural everywhere about them, there was, as Mather wrote of the judges, 'little occasion to prove the witchcraft, this being evident and notorious to all beholders'.

Mather also wrote of 'the Bewitched People' being 'grievously harassed with Preternatural Mischiefs, *which could not possibly be Dissembled.*' (Emphasis added). He described Burroughs' simple party tricks with the barrel and the gun as 'such Feats of Strength, *as could not be done without a Diabolical Assistance.*' The magistrates were no better. Nathaniel Carey told Calef how: 'The justices ordered that [the children] should be taken up and carried to the prisoner, that she might touch them; and as soon as they were touched by the accused, the justices would say, "they are well," before I could discern any alteration.' Calef records how, 'At Examination, and at other

42 Deut. 18:10-1.
43 Matthew 7:22.
44 Matthew 4:11.
45 Mark 15:9.
46 Matthew 28:1-20.

times, it was usual for the Accusers to tell of the black Man, or of a Spectre, as being then on the table, etc. The people about would strike with Swords, or sticks at those places. One Justice broke his cane at this exercise…' It apparently did not occur to them to consider why, given the likely consequences, a defendant who was denying a charge of witchcraft should choose to demonstrate to her judges powers of the sort she was claiming not to possess.

Common sense seemed just as absent during the trials. In one case the court accepted without question the evidence of a self confessed 'witch' who told them, 'That the Devil carry'd [Martha Carrier and her] on a Pole, to a Witch-Meeting; but the Pole broke, and she hanging about Carrier's Neck, they both fell down, and she then Received an Hurt by the Fall, whereof she was not at this very time Recovered.' Perhaps the most extraordinary example of indefensible credulity, however, was when Cotton Mather described how children 'would fly like Geese; and be carried with an incredible Swiftness thro the air, having but just their Toes now and then upon the ground, and their Arms waved like the Wings of a Bird.' As Upham observed, 'No one seems to have dreamed that their actings and sufferings could have been the result of cunning or imposture.'

The Rev. John Hale even managed to attribute a supernatural cause to the ending of the witch hunt: 'When this prosecution ceased, the Lord so chained up Satan, that the afflicted grew presently well. The accused are generally quiet, and for five years since, we have no such molestations by them.' He wrote too soon.

YET MORE WONDERS?

To this day the idea of Satanic abuse continues to exercise an unhealthy grip on the popular imagination, an obsession to which even education seems to offer little defence.

The modern fascination with witches is thought by some to have had its origins in the 1972 publication, *From Witchcraft to Christ*, a book which claimed to have been the autobiography of a former high priestess of Satan.[47] Equally important was *Michelle Remembers,* writ-

47   The work is described by the Christian Bookshop as 'The sensational true

ten in 1980 by Lawrence Pazder, a Canadian psychiatrist, who coined the term, 'ritual abuse', and his patient and later wife, Michelle. It purported to detail Michelle's 'recovered memories' of her own ritual abuse. Some critics have labelled the book a hoax, but of its influence on the new Satanism there can be little doubt.

The first case of Satanic ritual abuse in action concerned a series of charges brought before the courts in California in the 1980s when some 460 children were alleged to have suffered child molestation. Perhaps the most notorious case concerned members of the McMartin family. Seven teachers in an award winning day-care centre were accused of the abuse of some forty children in their care. The allegations, which originated in the mind of an alcoholic, were truly bizarre, involving the forced murder of children, children being flushed down toilets, flying through the air, satanic rituals and strange goings on in a non-existent cavern under the school; yet they were all taken seriously by the social workers, doctors and lawyers involved. After six years of legal proceedings, in which three of the defendants spent up to five years in gaol, all convictions were overturned and the remaining charges dropped.

The same chilling sequence of events spread to England, where social workers began touring the country lecturing on how to identify ritual abuse. The 1987 case of the Nottingham Broxtowe estate, involving allegations of incest within an extended family, resulted in seven children being taken into care. There were stories of strange goings-on in underground rooms, tunnels and passages, adults with dead babies hung round their necks, babies being buried and dug up, an adult putting on a cloak and flying, and children being turned into frogs. A joint police and social services report of 1989[48] 'found no evidence to substantiate the claims of the children and the corroborating adults. Tunnels and rooms that they had identified did not exist...' The report concluded:

> Our own research in Satanism and witchcraft left us with the view that there is very little if any empirical physical evidence to substantiate the claims that have been made. We doubt the existence of organised Satanic abuse as currently promulgated. Nevertheless it must be rec-

---

story of a woman rescued from Satan's grasp by the power of God.'
48   The Nottingham Police/Social Services Joint Enquiry Team report (JET).

ognised that rent boys and paedophile rings do exist...

The report found that:

> an unshakeable belief system in Satanic ritualistic abuse appears to have developed which could easily lead into a modern day "witch hunt" (as has happened in the USA). All the elements appear to us to be present; rigid preconceived ideas, dubious investigative techniques, the unwillingness to check basic facts, the readiness to believe anything, however bizarre, the interest in identifying prominent people, with widening of the net to implicate others and the unwillingness to accept any challenge to their views.

Scandalously, the Social Services department in question refused to allow the report to be published; as a result its conclusions were ignored until years later, during which time a growing witch-hunt continued to add to the sum of human misery.

In 1990, nineteen Rochdale children were taken from their homes and placed in care. Their families were not even permitted to send them Christmas cards for fear they might contain hidden Satanic messages. Three years later, members of four families in Bishop Auckland, County Durham, were arrested as a result of accusations from a teenager who had been convicted of molesting children. His fantasies were supported by an Evangelical Christian minister who was subsequently accused of having coached the children in Satanic ritual. All the accused adults were released without charge. And in 2003, on the Isle of Lewis, nine more adults were accused of sexually abusing children in Satanic rituals. The arrests had been prompted by allegations of animal sacrifice and orgies made by a Lewis resident who had been convicted of making false allegations of a similar nature elsewhere. The charges were later dropped for lack of evidence and the prime suspect was never brought to court.

In 1992 an American FBI report, *Satanic Ritual Abuse*,[49] concluded that, 'We now have hundreds of victims alleging that thousands of offenders are abusing and even murdering tens of thousands of people as part of organized satanic cults, and there is little or no corroborative evidence.' Two years later at the request of the British Health

---

49   By Kenneth V. Lanning.

Secretary, Professor Jean La Fontaine conducted an evaluation of all known British ritual abuse cases and found no evidence of Satanic ritual abuse. She attributed the reports of such to a climate of belief in the supernatural brought about by the upsurge in Evangelism.[50]

The fact that most Satanic abuse proceedings have eventually collapsed in one way or another – usually when sufficient people came to realize how ridiculous the allegations were – does not mean that organized child abuse does not take place; it does. It is not impossible that some child abusers dress or describe themselves as witches, either in order to intimidate and subdue the children they are abusing or because they actually believe that they possess supernatural powers. Where things have gone wrong is in the willingness of the authorities to believe, on the basis of wholly incredible evidence, that people have been abused as part of a large-scale Satanist conspiracy, a belief that has been enthusiastically supported by the Evangelical churches, into whose dogma such events neatly slot, and fortified by dubious 'medical' tests and procedures.[51] As a result, children have been seized in dawn raids, suffered degrading physical examinations and placed unnecessarily in what is euphemistically known as care; families have been broken up, often permanently, and innocent people have spent years in prison.

It seems strange that in a time when we are told that faith in God is on the wane people are increasingly willing to believe in Old Nick.

50   J. La Fontaine, *The Extent and Nature of Organised and Ritual Abuse* (London, HMSO, 1994).
51   Such as the now discredited anal dilation test, recovered memory techniques and the use by untrained workers of sex dolls.

LONDON BURNING

THE TRIAL OF LORD GEORGE GORDON, 1780

Israel bar Abraham was nearing his end, but the fire of reform still burned fiercely in his breast. He spent much of the day in his comfortable prison cell corresponding with radicals all round the world; in the evenings he received a motley crowd of visitors, ranging from Dukes to mechanics, from Members of Parliament to American merchants, from Polish peddlers to Cambridge grammarians. Anyone who shared his interests was welcome, save only those of his co-religionists who failed to keep their beards trimmed and their heads covered in the manner required by their faith. Once a fortnight the prisoner gave a formal dinner party with music and dancing, sometimes accompanied by a performance from the host on the bagpipes, once by the Duke of York's band. After 1792 it became the practice to end the evening with a singing of the French revolutionary song, the 'Marseillaise'. If there had been anyone unfamiliar with the prisoner's history (and that is unlikely) he might have had difficulty believing that this elderly orthodox Jew was the Godson of a King, the brother of a Duke, a former Member of Parliament and onetime leader of the largest Protestant movement in England. The irony is that he was not in prison for his part in the frightful disorders for which his name will forever be associated, but for blackening the names of the Queen of France and of His Majesty's judges.

George Gordon was born into the most privileged background on 26 December 1751. He was the third son of Cosmo George Gordon, third Duke of Gordon and his wife, Lady Catherine Gordon. His Godfather was King George II. Upon his father's death his mother married Colonel (later Major-General) Staats Long Morris. Young George was sent to Eton College at the age of eleven, where he was bullied and flogged after the manner of the time. Upon leaving school he was appointed ensign in his stepfather's regiment, but his army career was cut short when his mother, for reasons which are not known, decided to remove him into the navy as a midshipman. Despite the fact that he had not been consulted over this dramatic career change, the new way of life with its camaraderie and foreign

The burning of Newgate Prison during the Gordon Riots (Topfoto)

travel suited Gordon well and he began to display that combination of fierce humanitarianism, naïve enthusiasm and lack of judgement that was to dictate the course of his life. On one occasion while still a midshipman Gordon ordered his ship's biscuits to be thrown overboard because they were weevil ridden, an action at which delighted the sailors as much as it annoyed his superiors. On another occasion the Governor of Kingston was put out by being lectured by a midshipman on the plight of the slaves. Promoted lieutenant in 1772, Gordon was disappointed when the First Lord of the Admiralty declined to find a ship for him to command. After consulting his friend, the forty-two year old barrister and Member of Parliament, Edmund Burke, Gordon decided at the age of twenty-one to go into politics, where he thought he might be able to do something about the glaring inequalities that he had become so aware of in society.

The seat he chose to contest was that of Inverness, the home of the Lovat clan. Gordon threw himself vigorously into electioneering, learning Gaelic, playing the pipes and wearing the philabeg (or little kilt). He had a good eye for publicity and on one occasion hired a yacht to bring fifteen attractive young ladies of the Macleod clan from the island of Skye to a grand ball. So popular did the young contender become that Lord Lovat, the sitting Member and head of the clan, took fright. With the agreement of Gordon's stepfather, he arranged for his rival to be bought the pocket borough of Ludgershall in Wiltshire.[1] Gordon duly resigned his commission and entered Parliament in 1774.

The new MP's attendance at Westminster was meagre at first and when he did vote it was for the government. But it was not long before he fell under the influence of his friend Burke, who was already making a nuisance of himself with the establishment.[2] He claimed that Lord North, the Prime Minister, had tried by bribes, threats and promises, through an intermediary and directly, to secure his support, but without success.[3] The claim, though far from unlikely, was never proved. Gordon's first recorded speech, in 1778, was a bitter attack on

1 A pocket borough was a Parliamentary constituency 'owned' by one man.
2 Burke had entered Parliament at the relatively advanced age of forty-six.
3 Strictly speaking, Lord North was head of the Ministerial party; the term, 'prime minister' not coming into use until the time of Pitt.

the war against the American colonists, a war with which the reigning monarch, King George III was intimately associated. He did nothing to repair his standing at court when he asked whether the House of Commons would 'congratulate [the King] on his drawn battle at sea or his retreat at land…Would they thank him for the honours and emoluments he has heaped upon his favourites during the summer…? Will they thank him for saying he is ready to carry on the war with America?' The heat of Gordon's rhetoric was not confined to any party, but was felt as much by the Tories as the Whigs. So sharp were his strictures that a popular aphorism declared that 'there were three parties in parliament – the Ministry, the Opposition and Lord George Gordon.' It was not long before Gordon found a cause worthy of his great enthusiasms, resistance to what many saw as the dangerous resurgence of Roman Catholicism.

THE NATIONAL BOGEYMAN

Fear of Catholicism had been endemic in England since the time of Queen Mary when nearly four hundred Protestants were burned at the stake for heresy. The tensions were not merely religious: Rome had good cause to fear the English Reformation and Catholic France and Spain had long been jealous of English expansion. Catholicism in other words was perceived by many Englishmen to be both a spiritual and a political threat and the law was altered to protect them against it. On Mary's death it was the turn of Catholics to be persecuted by the Protestant Queen Elizabeth. Religious differences were reinforced by temporal fears after the failed invasion of England by Catholic Spain (1588) and by the Catholic-inspired 'Gunpowder Plot' (1605).[4] Even the 'Great Fire of London' (1666) was blamed on the Catholics, along with a wholly imaginary 'Popish Plot' (1678). Increasingly severe restrictions were placed on Catholic priests and worshippers. Romish priests were still liable to be burnt at the stake. Every office holder was required to take an oath denying the spiritual jurisdiction of the Pope. This effectively barred Catholics from all important public appointments. Recusancy, that is to say attending any but the established church, was made punishable by a fine (as Shakespeare's father could

---

4   A fear still ritually remembered on 5 November every year.

bear witness) and practising Catholics were made subject to all manner of disabilities.

By the late eighteenth century, zeal to enforce these draconian provisions had begun to slacken and in 1788 the government of William Pitt the Younger determined to make a further gesture towards toleration. A back bencher, Sir George Savile, was persuaded to introduce a Bill intended to ameliorate some of the more repressive features of the law. Catholics willing to take a revised oath of allegiance were to be allowed to own property unmolested and to join the army. The laws concerning the taking and prosecution of priests were repealed, along with the penalties for keeping a Catholic school. What the Catholic Relief Act did not do, however, was give Roman Catholics freedom of worship – although many assumed that it did. The Bill caused much greater resentment than had been anticipated, bolstered by the belief, not entirely without foundation, that it was no more than an attempt by the government to secure support and soldiers for continuance of the American Revolutionary War. The Anglican bishops did not opposed the measure, but the Evangelicals, Dissenters and Presbyterians did, and with passion. Nevertheless, the government were surprised at the strength of anti-Catholic sentiment; it can still be heard in the words of one of Wesley's hymns:

> Oh, how shall I presume,
> Jesus to call on Thee,
> Sunk in the lowest dregs of Rome,
> The worst idolatry!

In February 1779, after it had been announced that the Act would be extended to Scotland, violent anti-Catholic riots broke out in Edinburgh and Glasgow. The houses of Catholic priests were set on fire and Catholic women were forced to take refuge in Edinburgh Castle. It was Gordon's moment. Despite the fact that he had not spoken against or even voted on the Catholic Relief Bill when it had been debated in the Commons, he embarked on an anti-Catholic tour of Scotland. It was hugely successful. Protestant societies sprang up all over the country and Gordon was elected president of the Protestant committee of Edinburgh. The government reacted by giving an assurance that the Savile Act would not be extended to Scotland, but the concession came too late and Gordon was elected president of the English Association also.

One of the Association's first acts was to present a petition of thirty thousand names to the Prime Minister demanding repeal of the Act. Lord North declined to accept it, but what did Gordon expect when on 25 November he had been so indiscreet as to make an implied threat of violence in the House of Commons: 'The indulgences given to Papists have alarmed the whole country...I do not deliver my sentiments only; Government will find 120,000 men at my back who will avow and support them.' Frustrated by his lack of success with the Prime Minister, Gordon decided to exercise the right of access to the monarch, which was his as the son of a Duke. Horace Walpole's account of the meeting between the sovereign and his critic suggests that Gordon was less than diplomatic. He was nevertheless granted a second audience. Though accounts differ as to what was said, it is clear that George III considered Gordon to have pressed his point too intemperately. This was hardly surprising from a man who had only recently told Parliament that his petition extended 'from your [i.e. the Speaker's] chair to a window in Whitehall that Kings should often think of'.[5]

With no official support whatever Gordon resolved to appeal to the masses and called a meeting of his Association in Coachmakers' Hall on the evening of 29 May.

THE MARCH ON WESTMINSTER

At the meeting Gordon reported his lack of progress by conventional methods and declared that the Association's only recourse would be to hold a mass demonstration at the Houses of Parliament. He vowed that he would not attend unless twenty thousand followed him; he was not, he said, a man to do things by half. The proposal was given a rapturous welcome and next day an announcement appeared in the press inviting the public to support a demonstration to take place in St George's Fields, the traditional meeting point for the discontented not

5   This was, of course, a reference to the window out of which George's predecessor, Charles I, had stepped onto the scaffold.

far from what is now the site of Waterloo Station. Participants were instructed to wear blue cockades in their hats to distinguish them from the Papists. Magistrates, the notice went on, were invited to attend 'so that their presence may overawe and controul [*sic*] any riotous or evil-minded persons who may wish to disturb the legal and peaceable deportment of His Majesty's Protestant subjects.'

A vast throng, estimated variously as between 20,000 and 100,000, duly assembled at 10 a.m. on Friday, 2 June. It was an oppressively hot day and, following speeches from their President and others, the crowd marched around the field a few times to the singing of hymns. They then divided, as the press announcement had instructed, into three columns, one consisting of the Protestants of the City of London, one of the Protestants of the City of Westminster and one of Scottish expatriates. Preceded by a Highland piper and bearing banners emblazoned with the words 'NO POPERY', the demonstrators marched across the Thames six abreast to Westminster by four different routes; their discipline is said to have been impressive.

But the crowd which arrived at Palace Yard, Westminster at about 2.30 p.m. was not the same as that which had left St. George's Fields. A ragbag of hangers–on and mischief makers had been drawn to the procession who were to transform the nature of the protest. As the Members of Parliament arrived to begin the business of the day they found the entrances to both Houses blocked by demonstrators. Scuffles broke out in which dukes and bishops were abused and beaten. The Chief Justice of the King's Bench, Lord Mansfield was a particular object of opprobrium because of his supposed sympathy for Catholics, and the windows of his carriage were broken and his wig stolen.[6] The coach of Sir George Savile, promoter of the Catholic Relief Bill, was destroyed utterly. Some of the mob ran to Downing Street where they were faced by a party of Grenadier Guards. The Prime Minister, Lord North, went outside to warn them of the dangers they could face, and the crowd dispersed.

When the House of Lords eventually managed to convene, the only action which the noble lords could think of taking was to instruct Lord

6   He had summed up recently in favour of a Catholic priest charged before him with the crime of saying mass.

Mansfield and another judge to 'try to disperse the mob'. These worthies could get no further than the doors of their chamber, which was now besieged by a crowd of some fourteen thousand. In the House of Commons, Gordon, who had arrived separately from the demonstrators, produced his petition, which was said to bear 125,000 signatures, and asked for it to be debated immediately. He was said to be agitated, incoherent, almost hysterical, and his intemperate language was resented by many present. Cries of 'No Popery' nearly drowned out debate, but the House refused to depart from its normal practices. Members told Gordon exactly what they thought of him, some even threatening violence. His uncle, the Hon. William Gordon said, 'My Lord George, do you intend to bring your rascally adherents into the House of Commons? If you do – the first man of them that enters, I will plunge my sword not into his, but into your body'.[7] Gordon left the chamber a number of times during the debate in order to harangue his supporters from the gallery of the lobby. He went out of his way to identify by name those Members who were supporting or opposing discussion of their petition.

It was not until about 8.30 p.m. that the Peers finally managed to leave the Palace, but the demonstrators refused to disperse. The Horse Guards were called and eventually ordered to charge the mob; the result was bathos rather than tragedy. To everyone's amusement, the demonstrators fell about like ninepins when they were struck by the horses, and the charge failed to achieve its object. The crowd besieging the lower House was only persuaded to leave by a Justice of the Peace who offered to order the troops to leave first. A more ordered discussion was now able to take place in the Commons, which ended in the overwhelming defeat of Gordon's motion to debate the petition. Further discussion was adjourned to 6 June. An exhausted Lord George had to beg a lift from a fellow Member to make his way home. The more sensible demonstrators followed his example. Some were so disgusted at what had taken place that, before going home, they went to the offices of the Association to withdraw their names from the petition. Others had more sinister objectives.

7 *Annual Register* (1780), Appendix to the Chronicle, p. 258.

Hundreds of men were now wandering around London armed with spades and pickaxes, hammers and crowbars and carrying lighted torches. A little before midnight they separated into two groups, one going to the private chapel of the Sardinian ambassador in Lincoln's Inn Fields, the other to the chapel of the Bavarian ambassador in St James. (By reason of diplomatic privilege, the embassies were exempt from the laws against mass houses.) In each case the windows were forced, the building sacked and the furniture thrown into the street to be burned. Sampson Rainsforth, the King's tallow chandler, made a citizen's arrest of one looter, but the man was promptly rescued by the mob. Rainsforth ran off for help and brought back a hundred soldiers from the barracks at Somerset House. Though too late to prevent the chapel being gutted by fire, the troops were able to make thirteen arrests. They proved to be a collection of small fry, together with a few wholly innocent bystanders.

The following afternoon a large crowd gathered around the Bow Street police office[8] where the arrested men were being examined by the magistrate, Sir John Fielding.[9] It was broken up by Foot Guards who had been stationed there against that eventuality, but not before a great deal of damage had been done to property. In the House of Lords the Peers were puzzled at the ineffectiveness of the civil authorities the previous day. Lord Shelburne blamed the magistrates: the commission of the peace,[10] he said, was filled by 'man, base to the last degree, and capable of every mean act derogatory and opposite to the justice of the laws which their office obliged them to administer with truth, equity and wisdom'. The Duke of Northumberland offered a half-hearted defence of this 'exceeding troublesome office'. 'Justices get very little for their pains. It is for this reason impossible to persuade gentlemen of family and fortune to undertake it…' The rest of the day passed off peaceably enough until about 9 p.m. when crowds assembled in the Moorfields district of the City determined to wreak vengeance on another despised section of the population.

Moorfields was the home of the Irish labourers who, like unskilled immigrants in any era, were resented by the indigenous population

8   The City's first attempt at a police force set up in 1740.
9   Half-brother of Henry Fielding who had set up the Bow Street Runners.
10   That is, the office of justice.

for their willingness to work for low wages. In the rioters' eyes the newcomers bore the additional stigma of being Catholics, and they paid for it dearly. More mass houses were now destroyed, along with Catholic houses and schools. A City merchant appealed to the Lord Mayor of London, Brackley Kennett, but the former bawd and liquor merchant was reluctant to help. 'I must be cautious', he said, 'what I do lest I bring the mob to my house.' The soldiers arrived and sought his instructions, but Kennett still refused to act. All day Sunday the crowds continued to roam Moorfields shouting, 'No Popery' and 'Down with the Papists' and attacking every Irishman they came across. The Secretaries of State wrote to the Lord Mayor the following day reminding him of his duty, but to no effect.[11]

The disorders continued overnight and all day Monday. The mob, incensed by notices offering a reward of £500 for the apprehension of chapel burners, set off again, some of them bearing trophies looted from the now ruined buildings. Once more, they divided into two groups. One of them made for the homes of people mentioned in the press as having witnessed or criticized the riots, including that of Sir George Savile, and that of the magistrate who had ordered the arrest of the rioters at the Bavarian chapel two nights before. Their homes were reduced to burning embers. The house of Rainsforth, the King's tallow chandler, suffered a similar fate, the roadway outside it running with melted tallow and reeking with offensive fumes. By now, the fire and destruction had spread well beyond the Moorfields area. Once again, the magistrates, save for those attached to Bow Street, were either absent or ineffective. The soldiers, lacking any leadership, roamed the streets ineffectively. In the end it was the much maligned George III who took action. At midnight he wrote to the Secretary of War and to the Commander-in-Chief of the army conveying his desire for a 'large body of military force' to be made available to the City. His instructions were acted upon promptly, but the assembly of such a large force inevitably took time, and the mob had already got the scent of blood.

Gordon realized that matters had got out of hand and on Tuesday, 6 June, published a resolution in the *Morning Chronicle* and other

11   There were two Secretaries of State in those days, one for the North and one for the South.

papers. It condemned the chapel burning and the obstruction of Parliament and asked 'all true Protestants to show their attachments to their best interests by a legal and peaceable deportment.' The plea fell on deaf ears and the mob, many of them armed with axes, cutlasses and cudgels, once again surrounded the Palace of Westminster. Inside the Commons Lord George Gordon assured the House that the crowd would disperse if only they would appoint a day for a debate on the petition. It sounded like blackmail and one Member remarked that it was strange that Gordon should disclaim responsibility for the mob while attending Parliament wearing their cockade. In the end the House, including Gordon, unanimously resolved that the obstruction of Members by the mob was a 'high violation' of its privileges and demanded that the chapel burners should be prosecuted. The King was petitioned to inquire into the damages suffered in the riots and to order compensation. Nevertheless, when the Members attempted to leave at about 5 p.m., they were jostled and abused and some of their carriages wrecked.

The mob were finally dispersed by the actions of one brave magistrate, Justice Hyde, who read the Riot Act while riding on his white horse.[12] His reward was to be followed to his home in St Martin's Street, which was destroyed and its contents reduced to ashes. (So extensive were they that the rioters needed six bonfires to consume them.) When a party of soldiers tried to intervene they were ignored. The homes of Justice Cox and the elderly Sir John Fielding suffered the same fate. The mob seem to have been curiously discriminating at this stage. The writer Susan Burney describes how 'they order'd the

12   The Riot Act was an Act of 1715 under which it became a serious offence for a crowd of twelve or more people to refuse to disperse within an hour of being ordered to do so by a magistrate. The Act required that a magistrate 'or other person authorized by this act to make the said proclamation shall, among the said rioters, or as near to them as he can safely come, with a loud voice command, or cause to be commanded silence to be, while proclamation is making, and after that, shall openly and with loud voice make or cause to be made proclamation in these words, or like in effect: "Our sovereign Lord the King chargeth and commandeth all persons, being assembled, immediately to disperse themselves, and peaceably to depart to their habitations, or to their lawful business, upon the pains contained in the act made in the first year of King George, for preventing tumults and riotous assemblies. God save the King."' The Riot Act was abolished by an Act of 1986.

Engine to play on the neighbouring Houses, to prevent their catching fire'.[13] Gordon was the rioters' hero; when he left the House of Commons his carriage was unfastened from his horses and dragged with him inside to the City, stopping only at the Mansion House to give three cheers for the Lord Mayor, the supine Kennett. While all this was happening a furious attack was being mounted on the Downing Street residence of the Prime Minister. It was only narrowly frustrated by the soldiers.

At about 6 p.m. the mob resolved upon its boldest action yet, to secure the release of four of their number who had been arrested and remanded into custody. The men were confined in London's largest and oldest prison, the recently rebuilt Newgate.[14] Denied admittance by its keeper, the mob first threw his furniture into the street and burned it, then set fire to his house. Next to fall victim to the flames were the great doors of the prison itself, allowing the mob to rush in and liberate three hundred of the inmates. *Flambeaus* and other incendiary devices were thrown into the gaol, completing its destruction. A hundred constables who had been called to the scene proved insufficient to stop the destruction, and the freed prisoners, some of them awaiting sentence of death, hobbled away to find a blacksmith as fast as their chains would allow.

Later, at about 11.30 p.m., a large party of rioters made their way to the Bridewell Prison, broke down its doors and released its inmates.[15] They then turned to the nearby New Prison, whose custodians wisely elected to throw open its doors rather than have them forced. Now believing themselves to be untouchable, the rioters sent messages to all the other London prisons announcing when they would each in turn be liberated. This provoked a pert response from the prisoners in the Fleet Prison, who begged not to be disturbed so late in the evening. Their wish was granted!

Shortly after midnight on the Wednesday morning some of the rioters, inflamed by drink, determined to 'roast' Lord Mansfield. The seventy-six year old Chief Justice could not understand why he was

13 Letter of 8 June.
14 Now the site of the Central Criminal Court or Old Bailey.
15 The prison was named after St Bride's Well.

being singled out in this way and pathetically asked his friend and neighbour, the Archbishop of York, 'What have you and I to do with the Popery bill?'[16] Forty soldiers arrived to defend him at his residence in Bloomsbury Square. Mansfield refused to have them inside lest they should provoke the rioters further, but nothing could stop the mob and the judge and his wife were barely able to escape through the back before the rioters rushed in at the front. The contents of Mansfield's cellar were the first to go, followed by his furniture, which was burned in the street, along with his extensive library of valuable books and manuscripts. Mr. Burden, a magistrate possessed of more determination than most of his colleagues, arrived at about 4 a.m. accompanied by soldiers under command of a Colonel Woodford.[17] Burden 'read the Riot Act', but it had no effect, so he ordered the soldiers to disperse the mob. There followed a brisk but effective action which cost the lives of six or seven of the rioters and scared off the rest; it was the first time that the forces of order had opened fire. A quarter of an hour after the army left, however, the mob returned more determined than ever. Armed with turpentine and tar-soaked rope, they proceeded to complete their task of destroying Mansfield's house.[18] They then turned their attentions to the Archbishop of York's residence, where one of them was heard to say, 'Come my lads, that one house more and then to bed'. The prelate was lucky to escape by the back door with his life. The Lord Chancellor did not share Lord Mansfield's scruples against using the army and, as a result, managed to keep his home safe.

Early on Wednesday morning, an ironmonger's shop in Holborn was broken into by the mob and its stock of crowbars seized.[19] They were soon put to use. Dr. Johnson records that 'The Protestants were plundering the Sessions House at the Old Bailey. There were not, I believe, a hundred; but they did their work at leisure, in full security,

16   J. P. de Castro, *The Gordon Riots* (London, H. Milford, Oxford University Press, 1926), p. 97.
17   Ironically, Woodford was the brother-in-law of George Gordon.
18   Later that day it was only military intervention that prevented some five thousand rioters from burning down the judge's country house in Caen Wood, Hampstead.
19   The government instructed the gunsmiths to hide their weapons out of sight and send them, if possible, to the Tower of London for safety.

without sentinels, without trepidation, as men lawfully employed in full day'. Gordon, now seriously worried, went to the Queen's House (later renamed Buckingham Palace) with the intention of offering his assistance in quelling the riots. He was told that 'It is impossible for the King to see Lord George Gordon until he has given sufficient proof of his allegiance and loyalty by employing those means which, he says, he has in his power to quell the disturbances and restore peace to this capital.'[20] In other words, 'I will only see you after you have put an end to the riots.'

By now, the destruction had become widespread and indiscriminate, encompassing houses, commercial buildings and shops. Those premises that were not destroyed were closed and bolted by their owners, some prudently daubing 'No Popery' signs on the buildings. Grimaldi, the famous clown, ironically painted the words, 'No Religion' on his. The authorities put up notices warning people that they were mistaken in believing that they would be safer by wearing a blue cockade. '...it is an act of charity to inform them that for the future whoever appears with the ensign of rebellion will be consider'd as an enemy of Peace and Order and treated as such.'[21] And a royal proclamation was issued declaring that 'the utmost force' would be used on future rioters. None of it was of much comfort to those who had the mob outside their home. By an act of supreme idiocy, Kennett's Council passed a resolution calling on the government to comply with the mob's demands and repeal the Catholic Emancipation Act.[22] (At a later stage the timorous Lord Mayor took it upon himself to order the release of the arrested rioters; it took an order from Lord Amherst, Commander-in-Chief of the Home Forces, to stop it.) A second house belonging to Justice Hyde was now put to the flames, along with the home and police office of another justice in Bethnal Green.

One group of rioters now came across a prime target, the Catholic-owned gin distillery at the north-west corner of Fetter Lane in Holborn. After drinking the raw gin it contained, often with fatal results, they set the building on fire and used a pump to feed the flames with

20   Lord Stormont at the trial of Lord George Gordon.
21   de Castro, *The Gordon Riots*, p. 311.
22   In part, this was the work of the one-time rioter, the notorious John Wilkes, whose part in these events has still not fully come to light.

the remaining liquor, thus extending the blaze to twenty-one neighbouring houses. When the fire grew sufficiently intense the huge vats ignited, burning many to death. The mob were only dispersed by the Northumberland Militia who had arrived after a forced march of twenty-five miles. Next to burn were the Fleet Prison in Farringdon Road (near the now ruined distillery) and, across the river, the King's Bench and Surrey Prisons in Southwark and the Clink at London Bridge. To avoid further destruction the authorities ordered that the inmates of all other prisons should be released. As well as the original rioters there were estimated to be about sixteen hundred convicts at large in London, along with many of the disaffected poor and hundreds of habitual criminals, many of them drunk from stolen liquor. Despite scattered actions by the troops which resulted in perhaps a hundred deaths, it seemed now that nothing could stop the violence.

After putting parts of Barnard's Inn to the torch the mob turned to the tollbooths on Blackfriars Bridge with a view to seizing the money they contained. This time the army made a stand; a bayonet charge resulted in over a hundred rioters paying for their greed with their lives; it was the first serious check to mob violence. After this setback the rioters moved eastwards, but once again the army was prepared. Sailors had blocked the streets with hempen ropes which merely stretched when they were charged. When the mob did attack they were met with gunfire, leaving twenty of them dead in the street. Perhaps the most audacious assault that day was on the Bank of England. Beginning at about 11.30 p.m. it was the subject of three determined attacks led by a brewer's drayman on a cart brandishing a chain and fetter stolen from Newgate; his voice was said to have 'boomed like the crack of doom'. Some of the militia blocked the road, while others manned the interior of the Bank building, where its leaden inkstands were being cast into bullets. When at about 4 a.m. the rioters fired on the soldiers they were vigorously dispersed by the Horse Guards and the Light Infantry, and the street was filled with their dead and wounded. Lord George Gordon eventually appeared at the scene frantically attempting to defuse the violence to which his actions had given rise.

The City was now well ablaze and it was only the lack of a stiff enough breeze that prevented the conflagration from becoming all-consuming. A commentator wrote that London resembled, 'the picture of a city sacked and abandoned to a ferocious enemy [with] [t]he shouts of the populace, the cries of women, the crackling of the fires, the blaze reflected in the stream of the Thames, and the irregular firing which was kept up both in St George's Fields as well as towards the quarter of the Mansion House and the Bank …'[23] When the glare of the flames was reflected in the windows of Bethlehem (Bedlam) Hospital the patients were said to have danced with glee or shrieked with horror. The rioters finished their night's work with a celebratory bonfire. So ended 'Black Wednesday', as Walpole was to describe it, the worst day of the riots.

Next day, with the disorders continuing in Southwark and Bermondsey, the Privy Council convened early in secure accommodation behind St James Palace where the King had been removed to for his safety. The outcome was a proclamation summoning troops and militia to the capital in large numbers and authorizing the use of force without the need to wait for directions from the magistrates. (The King and the Attorney General had to push this order through against the opposition of a number of Councillors who deplored the use of troops.) The moat of the Tower of London was flooded and the drawbridge raised. Lord Amherst ordered the army to patrol the City in force and to seize the three bridges over the Thames. It did the trick. The last outbursts of disorder at Blackfriars, Holborn and the Strand were contained successfully with bayonet charges. By evening, calm had generally descended, except in Fleet Street where an isolated mob attacked the Horse Guards. It cost the rioters twenty dead and thirty-five injured and was the last, dying spasm of the riots; by nightfall all organized resistance had ceased. Three men were seen hanging from a lamp-post, but tales of widespread summary justice are without foundation. The following day the army strengthened its hold on the City and shops were able to re-open for business. By Saturday all was quiet.

When the dust settled, it was officially estimated that 200 people had died on the streets. Modern historians put the figure between 700 and 850; many more, of course, were injured. As well as the chapels, fifty-seven buildings had been destroyed, most of them belonging to

23 de Castro, *The Gordon Riots*, p. 136.

Irish Catholics, and many householders had been dispossessed. Over £28,000 was paid out in compensation by the City, and £5,200 by the Government. The distiller Langdale, who had incurred losses of about £100,000, wisely agreed to have his taxes waived for a year in lieu of compensation. Gradually City life got back to normal, but it was not until two centuries later that the government felt it safe to discontinue the picquet which the Guards had been providing to the Bank of England nightly since the riots. How had it been possible for the capital of this great nation to be brought to its knees in so short a time?

THE REASON WHY

While public disorder was far from unknown in England, riots on the scale of 1780 were unprecedented in recent times and the authorities were totally unprepared for them. Even when the enormity of the disorders was realised the state had no effective machinery to deal with them. No organised police force existed; indeed the idea of such an institution was regarded as unthinkably un-English.[24] The students of the Middle and Inner Temple formed a self-defence association, as did other groups, but their request to bear arms was denied because of the difficulty of discriminating between armed civilians and armed rioters, and their contribution was minimal. That left only the militia and the regular army. The former was ill-trained and the latter over-stretched by reason of the American Revolutionary War. In any event there was great resistance, even in the Privy Council, to the idea of using troops against the civil population. Edmund Burke, for example, described it as 'a mistaken idea to imagine the people of this country could be bullied by legions of armed men'. And the Opposition leader, Charles James Fox, declared that he would 'rather be governed by a mob than a standing army'.[25] Martial law was never imposed during the Gordon riots; instead, the defence of London was left, at first at least, in the hands of the magistrates and a few constables, and they were not up to the challenge.

24   England had to wait until the Metropolitan Police Act of 1829 for the formation of the first modern police force.
25   Christopher Hibbert, *King Mob* (Stroud, Sutton Publishing, 2004), p. 98.

The Secretary of War, Charles Jenkinson, complained on 6 June of magistrates who had failed to attend when the soldiers arrived and of magistrates who, when present, had refused to act.[26] And the King condemned 'the great supineness of the civil magistrates'.[27] But all could not be put down to incompetence. Some magistrates made no secret of their anti-Catholic leanings. Their constables were no different; one of them, for example, was heard to remark that his duty consisted in seeing that 'no honest Protestant got hurt by Popish conspirators.'[28] Some officials made themselves scarce for fear for their own safety; it is surprising that none of them was brought to book for neglect of duty.

Ultimately, it was the soldiers who put down the riots, though many of them were loathe to fire on civilians attacking what they perceived to be their country's enemies. And the soldiers' misgivings were compounded by confusion over their legal status. Some of them quoted as their reason for inaction the opinion of a former Attorney General that they could not intervene to prevent civil disorder otherwise than by order of a magistrate. Fortunately, the King had no such qualms and at the Privy Council meeting on Wednesday George III pressured his Attorney General into declaring his predecessor's opinion wrong.

WHO WERE THE RIOTERS?

The crowd that assembled in St George's Fields consisted mainly of hymn-singing evangelicals with a scattering of secular chauvinists fearful of foreign influences. The mob that laid waste to the City was of a very different character. No doubt some of them had remained from the original demonstration, but the vast majority consisted of London's disaffected underclass, bolstered by escaped convicts and debtors, petty thieves and the mentally disordered. The lawyer Thomas Erskine made the point that not one of those subsequently tried for riot was among those who had signed the Petition to Parliament. The black valet Ignatius Sancho, writing on the Tuesday of the riots, described 'at least a hundred thousand poor, miserable, ragged rabble

26   de Castro, *The Gordon Riots*, p. 72.
27   *Ibid.*, p. 82.
28   Hibbert, *King Mob*, p. 75.

from twelve to sixty years of age with blue cockades in their hats, besides half as many women and children'.[29] These people's resentment of authority may have accounted for the targeting of authority figures and nationally iconic buildings. Greed was the predominant motivation of many. Passers-by were assailed by demands for money 'for the mob' and houses were marked by signs indicating whether the householder had paid tribute or not. But none of this explains the swift devastation of the City of London.

How was it that a demonstration turned into a riot and a riot turned into what could easily be mistaken for an insurrection?

WHO WAS BEHIND THE RIOTS?

A mob is by its nature disorganized and fickle, but there are a number of aspects of the rioters' behaviour which suggest that they may in certain respects have acted under direction. The Attorney General was later to speak of the work of 'our inveterate enemies' and some pointed the finger of blame at France (which was seething with revolutionary discontent), or at the American colonists (who were in rebellion to the Crown). At one point the navy was ordered out to sea in order to safeguard the country against any opportunistic enemy. But these were no more than suspicions: there is little or no evidence to support the stories of foreign intervention.

Nevertheless, at critical stages of the riots there were signs of a guiding mind. It took someone with organizing ability to realize that it would confuse and divide the authorities to split the mob up into different cohorts. It took forethought to provide them on the first night of the riots with spades and pickaxes, hammers, crowbars and torches. It took discipline for the mob to fire some houses, while playing fire hoses on their neighbours'. It took someone literate and intelligent to identify the people named in the press as witnessing or suppressing the riots and single them out for special treatment, and it took someone with a knowledge of London society to identify from the

29   Ignatius Sancho, *Letters of the Late Ignatius Sancho, An African. In Two Volumes. To Which Are Prefixed, Memoirs of His Life.* (London, Printed by J. Nichols, 1782).

newspaper reports the homes of those mentioned. (Remember, this was in the days before the telephone book.)

Although Sir Samuel Romilly, the lawyer and social reformer, wrote of the riots being no more than 'the accidental effects of the ungovernable fury and licentiousness of a mob', some saw organization behind the disorders. Lord Mayor Kennet, for example, said, 'I can assure you that there are very great people at the bottom of this riot'. Lord Mansfield himself speaking in the Lords claimed that the riots were 'formed upon a systematic plan to usurp the government of the country'. And Fanny Burney was convinced that the mob was 'secretly directed by somebody above themselves'. A story circulated to the effect that Lord Effingham, the Opposition Peer, had been spotted leading the rioters on Blackfriars Bridge. His wounded body, disguised as a chimney sweep, was said to have been thrown into the river and only revived by the cold. (The noble Peer's subsequent appointment as Treasurer to the Royal Household gives the lie to this story.) The fact is that the houses of prominent members of the Opposition were destroyed equally with those of government figures. The historian George Rudé has noted the large proportion of those brought to trial who resided in the neighbourhood, if not in the actual parish, of the incidents for which they were said to be responsible.[30] In the absence of stronger evidence to the contrary the most likely scenario is one of a disorganized rabble, whose activities occasionally fell under the direction of their natural leaders.

Whether the disorders were organized or not, there is ample evidence of the involvement in them of 'men of quality'. The Archbishop of York, for example, noted that the body of a rioter dug from the ruins of a demolished house wore ruffles with a diamond pin at his shirt breast, while another was well dressed with a plan of London in his pocket. A Colonel Stuart in a letter to his father remarked that the mob attacking the Bank 'were led by a person in a Navy uniform with his sword drawn, that many decently dressed people encouraged them till they were near the Guard, but that they then retired and pretended to

---

30   George F.E., Rudé, *The Gordon Riots; a Study of the Rioters and their Victims* (Transactions of the Royal Historical Society, Fifth Series, Vol. 6, London, 1956), p. 102.

be spectators.'[31] As is so often the case, however, the authorities seem to have decided that it would be more prudent to ignore these stories and to fix responsibility where it naturally fell, namely on the discontented elements among the lower classes. But what was in the minds of the men and women who went beyond protest into insurrection?

George Rudé argues that 'behind the slogan of 'No Popery' and the other outward forms of religious fanaticism lay a deeper social purpose, a groping desire to settle accounts with the rich, if only for a day, and to achieve some rough kind of social justice'.[32] However, we should not ignore the tendency of all mobs to use the passions of the few as an excuse for the release of that mindless urge to violence and destruction which for most of the time lurks silently in so many of us awaiting only the excuse of the anonymity of a mob to be released.

THE RIOTERS' TRIALS

More than 450 people had been arrested during the disorders; 160 of them were to stand trial at the Old Bailey on 28 June, little more than a fortnight after the riots had ended.[33] Horace Walpole described the accused as 'a pack of boys and ruffians and a regiment of street walkers', including 'two gypsies, a West Indian slave, a cross-eyed beggar, three abscess-covered climbing boys and a negro prostitute'.[34] In the end, eighty-five were found not guilty and discharged. Sixty-two were convicted and sentenced to death, of which only twenty-five were actually hanged. Twelve were sentenced to imprisonment and one to be 'privately whipped'. Few of them were represented by lawyers, a notable exception being a Mr. Maskell (or Mascel), an apothecary and a well-known objector to the American war. Evidence was called of his having encouraged a boy to burn books stolen from Mansfield's library, but his counsel made such a good job of demolishing the witness that Maskell was acquitted. One wonders how many of the other

---

31   Hibbert, *King Mob*, p. 114.
32   Rudé, *The Gordon Riots,* p. 111.
33   Others were dealt with at Southwark Sessions.
34   Hibbert, *King Mob*, p.143. One of those saved from the gallows was the common hangman, Edward Dennis, known by the generic name of 'Jack Ketch'.

defendants would have been as fortunate with proper legal representation.

The former Lord Mayor, Brackley Kennet, was charged with criminal neglect of duty, his case being heard by Lord Mansfield in March of the following year. He was convicted, but cheated justice by dying, possibly by his own hand.

And what of the man widely blamed as the initiator of these events?

GORDON'S TREASON TRIAL

A warrant for the arrest of Lord George Gordon had been sworn out as soon as the riots subsided. On 9 June he was brought from his house in Welbeck Street to the Horse Guards in Whitehall, where he was questioned for four hours before being conveyed to the Tower of London under conditions of extraordinary security. (The guard consisted of a party of infantry, a whole regiment of dragoons, a colonel's guard of the Foot Guards and a party of militia; no one was taking any chances.) Two days later the Protestant Association published a disclaimer of any involvement with the 'lawless rioters' who 'under the pretence of opposing Popery and promoting the success of the Protestant petition [had] committed the most flagrant and dreadful depredations'. The Association declared its 'utmost abhorrence of such atrocious conduct'.

For reasons which are not clear, it was another six months before Gordon was arraigned before the Court of King's Bench. (It had taken an application for *habeas corpus* by the prisoner to bring on the commencement of his trial.[35]) The indictment (or charge) on which Gordon was eventually tried alleged that he:

> not having the fear of God before his eyes but being seduced by the instigation of the devil... unlawfully, maliciously and traitorously did compass and imagine and intend to raise and levy war against our Lord the King. And on the second day of June with a great multitude of persons, armed and arrayed in a warlike manner... with colours

35 An application of *habeas corpus* (literally, 'have the body') requires the person to whom it is addressed to produce a named person to the court.

66

flying and with clubs, bludgeons and staves …did ordain, prepare and
levy publick war against the King.

It was the gravest charge that could be brought, but at least as the
son of a Duke, Gordon knew himself to be exempt from the normal
punishment for such a crime, namely being hung, drawn and quartered.

Gordon was not a wealthy man and it took a contribution of over
£3,000 from his friends to obtain for him the services of two brilliant barristers, Lord Kenyon and Gordon's cousin, the young Thomas Erskine. (Kenyon was later to become Attorney General and then
Master of the Rolls; Erskine became Lord Chancellor. At that time
neither had much experience of criminal cases.) Gordon's trial began
on Monday, 5 February 1781 before Lord Mansfield, sitting with his
fellow judges, Justices Willes, Ashhurst and Buller. No one seems to
have thought it odd that Gordon should be tried by someone whose
house had been destroyed in the riot for which he was being tried; in
fact, Mansfield seems to have conducted the proceedings in a totally
disinterested manner. The case attracted great public interest and, in
addition to Gordon's two brothers, the Duke and Lord William, the
crowded courtroom contained the Duke of Richmond, Lord Derby,
Charles James Fox and the playwright Richard Brinsley Sheridan.

The trial started three quarters of an hour late because Gordon's
progress from the Tower had been treated by his supporters almost as
a triumphal procession.[36] After 'George Gordon Esq. commonly called
Lord Gordon'[37] had pleaded 'Not Guilty', the case for the prosecution was opened by the Attorney General, the much respected James
Wallace. He explained that there were two types of treason, levying
war against the King in person, and levying war against the King's
Majesty. The latter, called 'constructive treason', included insurrec-
tions designed to alter the law of the land or to redress grievances,
real or imaginary. The recent riots, he said, were such an insurrection
and the prisoner was 'the author of all these violent and disgraceful
proceedings'. While not in so many words calling for his supporters
to barricade the Palace of Westminster, Gordon had by his language

36 The following account of the trial is based on Howell's *State Trials* (1814).
37 The prefix 'Lord' was a courtesy title.

indicated that this was what he desired. After recounting the history of the riots Wallace called twenty-three witnesses to describe the events in detail. That the riots had taken place there was no question, but for Gordon to be convicted it had to be shown, first, that they constituted an insurrection and, secondly, that he had promoted, encouraged or participated in it. The first prosecution witness was one of the most potentially damaging.

William Hay, a printer, gave evidence that at the meeting before the riots Gordon had claimed that the King had broken his coronation oath by assenting to the Catholic Relief Bill. He went on to testify that the crowd outside the Palace of Westminster had been inflamed by the chanting of Gordon's name. Standing above the lobby of the House, Gordon had exhorted them 'to continue steadfastly to adhere to so good and glorious a cause as theirs was.' The force of Hay's evidence, however, was largely destroyed by Kenyon's skilful cross-examination. Gordon's statement at the meeting, for example, turned out when heard in full, to be not nearly as provocative as the extract quoted by Hay had suggested. On another point, Hay had claimed to be sure that Gordon had been present at a particular place in January that year. Under cross-examination, he had to admit that he could not rely on his memory. Later, he was forced to accept that he had not seen Gordon there on any occasion. The witness relied on notes which he claimed to have made at the time; and he bolstered this by claiming that making notes was 'his constant course in all occurrences of life'. When asked to 'give one instance in the whole course of your life where you ever took notes before', Hay was said to be 'thunderstruck – the sweat ran down his face and his countenance bespoke despair.' Eventually, he replied that he had previously taken notes at a meeting of the General Assembly of the Church of Scotland twenty-six years before. 'What!' exclaimed a sarcastic Erskine, 'Did he apprehend dangerous consequences from the deliberations of the grave elders of the kirk?'

Hay had also given evidence that a man he had seen carrying a flag at the burning of the Fleet Prison was the same man he had seen earlier at St George's Fields. He remembered this because the man 'looked like a brewer's servant.' Asked how he knew he was a brewer's servant, the witness broke out in sweat again and could only explain that there was something particular in the cut of his coat, the cut of his breeches and the cut of his stockings, but he could not say what it was. Kenyon asked the witness why he had gone to the House of Commons. It was, said Hays, because he thought himself in danger. 'Therefore,' responded Kenyon, 'you thrust yourself voluntarily into the very heart of danger?' Hay's credibility was destroyed.

Another witness reported that Gordon had said at St George's Fields that he was willing to 'go to the gallows' for the cause. Unable to shift him on this point, Erskine argued that the statement was open to interpretation. 'Words', he said, 'even if they can be accurately remembered, are to be admitted with great reserve and caution when the purpose of the speaker is to be measured by them. They are transient and fleeting; frequently the result of a sudden transport – easily misrepresented.' Another witness was the chaplain to the House of Commons, Rev. Thomas Bowen who gave evidence that Gordon had told the crowd that the Scotch had only got redress after they had destroyed the mass houses, but added in fairness that his memory might have been wrong on this point. Another potentially damaging witness was Richard Pond, who produced a document which Gordon had signed at his request during the disturbances. It was effectively an instruction to the rioters not to destroy his house.[38] Kenyon was unable to weaken the effect of this incriminating evidence, which left the impression that Gordon had indeed enjoyed some degree of control over the rioters.

It was late afternoon when the defence called the first of its sixteen witnesses. They were able to establish that it had been Gordon's intention to go alone to the House and for the petition to be produced in the lobby later. Evidence was given of Gordon himself having asked demonstrators marching to Westminster to turn back. Other witnesses testified to his exhortations to the crowd to be peaceable, and of the damage having been done, not by the well behaved demonstrators, but by hooligans who had joined them after they had set out. Gordon's servant came into the box to confirm that his master had spent parts of Saturday, Sunday and Monday at home and not on the streets.

---

38   It read, 'All true friends to Protestants will be particular and do no injury to the house of any true Protestant. As I am well assured, the proprietor of this house is a staunch and worthy friend to the Cause.'

Kenyon's closing speech was masterly. He declared that the prosecution had made much of the military nature of the crowd, the marshalling of them into 'divisions' or 'columns' six abreast, the wearing of blue cockades, and so on. In fact, he argued, the evidence was that the crowd in St George's Fields was peaceable, well dressed and, at first, well behaved. They had met at ten in the morning because that was an hour of sobriety, they had been urged to wear their best clothes, not to carry sticks and to give up to the magistrates anyone found misbehaving. Once the riots had begun Gordon had gone to Buckingham House to offer his assistance in ending them.

By all contemporary accounts, however, it was Erskine's summing up to the jury that carried the day. To justify a conviction, he said, the prosecution had to show, not merely that Gordon had foreseen mischief, but that 'he had wickedly and traitorously preconcerted and designed it.' Gordon was to be judged, not from the consequences of his actions, but 'from causes and designs'. Press reports at the time described the address as electrifying, not so much by the words, but by reason of 'the magic of the voice, the eye, the face, the figure, and all we call the manner with which they were uttered.' Nothing the prosecution could say in reply dispelled this impression. It only remained for the judge to deliver his summing up. Lord George objected to his partiality, but if such existed it is hard to detect it in the record. The jury took only three quarters of an hour to bring in a verdict of 'Not Guilty' to rapturous applause.

The trial had begun at 8 a.m. on Monday and ended at 5.15 a.m. on Tuesday. Everyone in court was exhausted, but had justice been done?

A century later, the great English jurist Sir James Fitzjames Stephen concluded that the acquittal was right; Lord George Gordon had been guilty of nothing more than hare-brained and criminal folly in heading an unlawful assembly.[39] Not everyone agreed, but no amount of criticism could detract from his supporters' delight in his acquittal. Congratulatory addresses were voted to him in Edinburgh and Glasgow and further sums were subscribed towards his trial expenses.

---

39   James Fitzjames Stephen, *History of the Criminal Law of England* (London, Macmillan, 1883) vol 2, p. 274.

Afterwards, Gordon remained president of the Protestant Association and published an exculpatory pamphlet, *Innocence Vindicated, and the Intrigues of Popery and its Abettors Displayed*. He even briefly considered standing as a candidate for the City of London, but his prospects of success were destroyed when there was talk of further riots. He was ostracized in establishment circles and the King turned his back on him at a royal levee. The rejection seemed to be reflected in his dress; Gordon now appeared, as he had from the first day of his trial, in sober black, carrying a Bible with him wherever he went. The process of reinvention had begun.

'GORDON AND LIBERTY'

As his interest in the Protestant cause waned, so Gordon's enthusiasm for egalitarian and libertarian causes waxed. He supported the Opposition in their attack on the nepotism of the grand Whig families and took a strong dislike to the new Prime Minister, the aristocratic William Pitt, whose taxation policies were causing discontent in Scotland. (Gordon was successful in bringing about the amelioration of a tax on the Scottish distilleries.) His interests now ranged well beyond his native country. In 1782 he visited Paris, where he was impressed by the charms of the French Queen, Marie Antoinette but horrified at the gross inequalities in French society. He also began to conduct a spirited correspondence with republican Americans and with revolutionary figures throughout Europe.

By 1783 there is evidence that Gordon's eccentricities were beginning to take their toll on his mind. In a long rambling letter addressed to the Jews of Portugal and Germany he appears (for the sense is by no means clear) to be suggesting that financiers should withhold credit from the British government in an attempt to counter Papal influence throughout Europe. Gordon's one-time secretary and first biographer, Robert Watson tells a story that at about this time the Pope sent two Jesuits to England with instructions to do away with the troublesome 'Lord', and that it was only good fortune that frustrated their plans. Whether there was any truth in this allegation or not, the fact that it could be made illustrates the strong feelings to which Gordon's criticisms gave rise.

His growing eccentricity was exemplified by his hounding of Franz Joseph, Emperor of Austria, in relation to that monarch's claim to the Austrian Netherlands. Dressed in the uniform of a Dutch naval officer with a large leather belt over his shoulder and a Highland broadsword in his belt, Gordon managed to persuade the guard at St James' Palace to cut their ribbons into Dutch cockades and raise the Dutch flag. He then awaited the arrival of the Dutch ambassador whom he had persuaded to join in his little charade. He followed this up by writing to Pitt claiming, quite untruthfully, that several hundred seamen had presented him with a petition that read 'We, the seamen whose names are underwritten, are able, ready and willing to serve the United Protestant States of Holland against the King of the Romans'. Next day he sent the Prime Minister a letter claiming, with equal mendacity, to have received an offer of a frigate of twenty-six guns and more than a thousand seamen to back the cause of Holland. Despite the improbability of these claims, a large body of seamen turned up at the Queen's House demanding employment and were persuaded to leave only by a promise that their grievances would be redressed. The government hit back by suggesting that Lord George had taken advantage of the sailors for his own purposes and an angry mob of them picketed his house in Welbeck Street. It is a tribute to Gordon's charisma that he was able to win them round and the men dispersed shouting, 'Gordon and Liberty'.

But it was the cause of penal reform which was to cost Gordon most. Appalled by the conditions he had witnessed in various prisons, Gordon resorted to his favourite stratagem, the bogus petition, supposedly from the inmates at Newgate. This time it contained a critique of capital punishment and other vicious penalties of his day. Like his address to the Jews, the document was rambling and spattered with capital letters. Unfortunately for its author, it also contained a sentence which was to bring the full force of the law down upon his head. That read, 'The just punishment ordained by God for our trespasses of thieving is altered by men like ourselves; the everlasting law of the statutes of the Almighty is changed and his true record falsified and erased by the lawyers and judges (who sit with their backs to the living God and the fear of men before their faces) till the streets of our city have run down with a stream of blood'. Even this imprudent remark might have been ignored had its author not embarked upon

yet another quixotic venture. Bizarrely, it concerned a charlatan nec-
romancer, a stolen necklace and the Queen of France.

The international confidence trickster 'Count Cagliostro' had entered Gordon's life in the summer of 1786. Giuseppe Balsamo was the
son of a Sicilian peasant. Clear facts are hard to come by, but he is said
to have been a student of medicine and chemistry at a Benedictine
monastery who ran away to join a band of thieves and cut-throats.
Saved from prison by his uncle, he developed an interest in alchemy
and the occult, claiming that he could transmute base metal into gold.
Forced to flee Italy to escape the revenge of a disappointed client,
Cagliostro travelled the world until he judged that the coast was clear.
Thereafter, he set up a fraudulent casino in Naples, was suspected
of heresy in Rome and was initiated into Egyptian Freemasonry in
England. His next move was back to France where his 'magic sup-
pers' proved popular with the King. Somehow Cagliostro became
suspected of involvement in 'the affair of the necklace', a notorious
confidence trick involving Marie Antoinette. It cost him nine months
in the Bastille before he was cleared.[40] For all his faults Cagliostro
does appear to have had a genuine concern about social inequality,
and it was this trait which endeared him to Gordon.[41]

Upon his release from prison Cagliostro was ordered to leave
France and found refuge in England. When an ambassador was sent
to inform him that he could return to France, Cagliostro declined
to meet him otherwise than in the presence of Gordon. Convinced
that the French Queen was intent on persecuting his friend, Gordon
wrote a letter to a newspaper deploring 'the Queen's faction' which
had 'brought upon the Count the hateful revenge and perfidious cruelties of a tyrannical government'. At a time of sensitive relations with
France this was too much for the British government which felt it
had put up with Gordon for too long. The result was his indictment
for the criminal libel of Marie Antoinette and the French ambassador.

40   A pretended 'count' and his wife had defrauded a cardinal of a large sum
of money for the purchase of an extravagantly costly necklace, supposedly for
Marie Antoinette.
41   Convicted of the crime of freemasonry, Cagliostro died in prison in the Cas-
tel St Angelo in Rome in 1795.

A charge of libelling His Majesty's judges by his bogus petition was thrown in for good measure.

GORDON'S LIBEL TRIALS

This time neither Kenyon nor Erskine was available to defend Gordon. (Erskine had actually undertaken to act for the prosecution.) So he decided to act for himself – with predictable results. At his arraignment before Mr. Justice Buller, Gordon made a series of objections. He objected to being called 'George Gordon Esquire' and walked out of court. The summons was reissued in the form he wished. He next claimed that the trial should be postponed until Mrs. Fitzherbert (mistress to the Prince of Wales) could be present because she had a letter he wished to produce; the application was rejected. His submission that the character of the Queen of France was as notorious as that of the Empress of Russia and could not therefore be defamed was ignored and Gordon was committed for trial, along with his publisher.

The first issue to be tried was the alleged libel of the judges. It was heard before Mr. Justice Ashurst in the Court of King's Bench on 6 June 1787 when Gordon and the newspaper publisher pleaded 'Not Guilty'. In his opening speech for the prosecution the Attorney General, after describing Gordon's visits to various prisons, asked incredulously, 'Why should a noble lord trouble about such people?' Gordon then made a long and confusing submission concerning the barbarity of the penal system, contrasting the laws of man unfavourably with the law of God, and had to be stopped by the judge. The prisoner finished with an impassioned plea against capital punishment which so bemused the jury that they promptly delivered a verdict of 'Guilty' against both defendants.

A week later Gordon reappeared before the court to answer the second charge, that of libelling the Queen of France. Once again, he tried unsuccessfully to have the hearing adjourned for no good reasons. When the Attorney General began his address with a paean of praise for 'the most high, mighty and puissant Marie Antoinette', Gordon interrupted with an audibly scurrilous aside concerning the French Queen. (It was impossible, he was to say later, to libel such a person.) His defence consisted of repeating his slander of her character ('A very *convenient* person'.) After the inevitable verdict of 'Guilty' the judge declared himself so upset that he adjourned sentence till the following day. Gordon, who had somehow been allowed to leave court without bail, promptly absconded to Amsterdam. When the French court got to hear of what had happened, pressure was applied to the Burgomeister of that city to expel Gordon. He returned to England, but was able to live there undetected for seven months. One reason for this was that in the meantime he had converted to Judaism.

What was left of Gordon's love affair with Protestantism had finally been destroyed by a ridiculous incident. He failed to attend an ecclesiastical court in connection with a disputed will and was excommunicated by the Archbishop of Canterbury. Gordon, who had been brought up as a Calvinist, commented acidly that to expel him from a society to which he had never belonged was 'an absurdity worthy of an archbishop'.[42] In the summer of 1786 Gordon applied formally for conversion to the Jewish faith. He was at first rebuffed, but later given instruction and admitted to that faith after making a generous donation of £100 to a synagogue. The conversion was genuine enough and involved circumcision, no formality in an adult. When he was eventually discovered hiding in the poor Jewish quarter of Birmingham, Gordon was living under the name, Israel bar Abraham George Gordon. Later in prison he was to attend a religious service every Saturday and scrupulously observed the Jewish dietary and clothing laws.[43] He was what the Jews call a 'righteous convert'.

Arrested by a Bow Street Runner and brought back to court to be sentenced, Gordon made a sorry sight wrapped in a greatcoat with lank hair and a three-inch long beard. He received two years imprisonment and was fined £500 for the libel of the French Queen and three years to be served consecutively for libelling the judges. But the sting came in the tail when he was also bound over to be of good behaviour for fourteen years in his own recognizances of £10,000 and ordered to find two sureties of £2,500 pounds each. Gordon had no hope of finding sureties in such large sums and on 28 January 1788 was com-

42   Hibbert, *King Mob*, p. 179.
43   He is said to have 'preserved with great care the sanguinary proofs of his having undergone the amputation'. Justin Lovell, *Notable Historical Trials* (London, The Folio Society, 1999), p. 140.

mitted in default to the very prison which only seven and a half years before the 'Gordon rioters' had burned down.[44] From prison Gordon made the gesture of producing two penniless sureties to the court; they were naturally refused. He then appealed against the order to find recognizances on the principle that, 'No man shall have a larger fine imposed upon him than his circumstances will bear'. He commented, 'As it is a mere fiction which the courts themselves chose to adopt by supposing me worth £10,000, the same fiction ought in justice to be held good in proportion to the sureties. Unless the court really intended imprisonment for life when they demanded such excessive and unprecedented bail.' The argument was sound, but the application was unsuccessful.

Shortly after entering Newgate Gordon was able, after the practice of the time, to acquire for payment a room to himself in which he lived in some comfort, even holding court to all and sundry. (He was no doubt assisted in this by the charity of his friends.) But nothing could stop his enthusiasm for liberty, and his copious correspondence continued to range around the globe. He wrote to the revolutionary French Assembly congratulating them on their new constitution, and to the founders of the American republic[45] advocating abolition of the slave trade. On 1 November 1793 the great reformer died of gaol fever (or typhoid) after three days spent in delirium. His last words were those of the French revolutionary song, the 'Ça ira'.[46]

GORDON THE MAN

Over the course of his life Gordon had developed a burning interest in a wide range of humanitarian causes, including poverty, slavery and penal reform. The writer Percy Colson described him as 'the first aristocratic Socialist in England, the first Pacifist in the modern sense, and the first to make a protest against the extreme brutality of the criminal

---

44   It is said that his family offered to stand bail for him, but their offer was refused by the prisoner as likely to be construed as an admission of guilt.
45   Including Gouverneur Morris, his stepfather's brother.
46   Loosely translated, 'All's well. All's well. Hang the aristocrats from the lamp-posts'.

laws'.[47] Gordon's secretary and biographer, Robert Watson, traced his subject's extreme sense of injustice to his early days when the young George was 'launched on the world with an annuity of £500, while [his brother] the Duke possesses more than £20,000 a year'.[48] But were his passions so great as to upset the balance of his mind? In other words, was 'the mad Scotchman' actually mad, as many such as Horace Walpole and Edward Gibbon believed?

Some have concluded from Gordon's strange odyssey that he suffered from religious monomania, but who is to say where a deep concern with spiritual and ethical matters ends and mental illness begins? During the riots of 1780 Charles Turner MP told the House of Commons that Gordon 'had got a twist in his head, a certain whirligig which ran away with him if anything relative to religion was mentioned'.[49] This was an understandable judgement on a man who began life as a Calvinist, placed himself at the head of the Protestant Association and, after flirting briefly with Quakerism, died as a Jew. Gordon's conversion to Judaism at a time in our history when Jews were widely despised was no gesture, but a long considered step wholly consistent with his religious and humanitarian outlook. As Percy Colson perceptively noted, 'The implacable God of the Calvinists and the fierce old Hebrew deity had much in common'.[50]

For all his humanity and ardent enthusiasms, however, Gordon suffered from a serious lack of judgement. The worst example of this, of course, was in 1780, when he failed utterly to appreciate the nature of the monster which his actions and rhetoric had released upon London. Legally innocent of treason he may have been, but anyone else in his position would have lived the rest of his life with a weight of moral guilt about his shoulders for the deaths and destruction which were directly due to his conduct; Gordon never displayed any such remorse. And so it came about that the actions of this charming, caring

47   Percy Colson, *The Strange History of Lord George Gordon* (London, R. Hale and co, 1937), p. xvii.
48   *The Life of Lord George Gordon with a Philosophical Review of his Political Conduct,* a rare work of 1795, quoted in Colson, *Lord George Gordon*, p. xiii.
49   Parl. Hist. Vol xxi, col. 386.
50   Colson, *Lord George Gordon*, p.131.

but unwise man, whose concerns were for the poor and the oppressed, led to the greatest disaster London was to suffer between the Great Fire of 1666 and Hitler's bombs nearly three centuries later.

ENVOI

In sixteenth-century England the threat from the temporal Catholic powers and the revanchist tendency of Rome were far from imaginary and there were not a few English Catholics who would have supported both. Two centuries later this threat was no longer real, but by then a deep mistrust of what was seen as a foreign religion had taken hold of the public psyche, fuelling the ever-potent flames of religious intolerance. Is it fanciful to suppose that the uncivilized behaviour of the Gordon rioters went some way towards preparing the public for a more liberal attitude towards followers of 'the old religion'? In any event, the riots failed to stop the inexorable process of Catholic emancipation. Further legal disabilities were removed in 1791 and 1793, and in 1829 almost all the rest disappeared. To this day, however, no Roman Catholic may sit on the throne of the United Kingdom. This is said to be because the Sovereign is, by law, head of the established church and defender of the faith, but it is a rule which is increasingly difficult to justify. The government has expressed the opinion that the Act of Settlement of 1701, which is the basis for this disqualification, is not inconsistent with the Human Rights Act 1998.[51] However that may be, one day surely the country will have to choose between a monarch's freedom of faith and an established church.

51   Reply to a Parliamentary Question, 15 October 2001. The point has never been decided in court.

THE MONKEY TRIAL
THE TRIAL OF JOHN SCOPES, 1925

*Local bigots in a sleepy Southern town were affronted when they dis-
covered that their children were being taught from textbooks which
ignored the biblical story of creation in favour of the theory of evolution. As a result, their biology teacher was arrested in his classroom,
thrown into gaol and hung in effigy for breaching a state law that
prohibited the teaching of evolution on pain of imprisonment.*

*When a gluttonous fundamentalist arrived in town to lead the pros-
ecution he was met with an enthusiastic parade singing, 'Give me
that Old Time Religion' and given the honorary title of 'Colonel' by
the mayor. The arrival in town of the teacher's attorney was greeted
only with hostility. At a prayer meeting, announced beforehand from
the bench by the judge, a hell-fire preacher asked for the teacher's
soul to be damned. In court, the prosecutor betrayed a confidence
imparted to him by the teacher's fiancé in order to badger her in the
witness box.*

*The judge wrongly favoured the prosecution by disallowing a defence
request to call scientific evidence in support of the theory of evolution.
The defence attorney then disconcerted the prosecutor by calling him
to the witness stand to give evidence. He insisted that the Bible must
be taken literally. The earth had been created by God in six days
beginning at 9 a.m. on 23 October 4004 BC. He knew this because it
had been revealed to him by God.*

*The teacher was found guilty and fined $100, which the prosecutor
asked the judge to increase. Sympathy had now turned against the
prosecutor and he was reduced to babbling the names of the books
of the Bible. As the courtroom emptied he collapsed and died. The
teacher lost his job, but the court's decision was overturned on appeal.*

Johnny Scopes (Topfoto)

W ith Spencer Tracy, Gene Kelly and Frederic March in the lead roles, Stanley Kramer's 1960 film, *Inherit the Wind,* is one of the most compelling courtroom dramas ever made.[1] Loosely based on a trial that took place thirty-five years earlier, the film, of which the above is a crude summary, has had an influence far beyond the world of entertainment. The only problem is that, as an account of the real events, most of it was inaccurate and some was the exact opposite of the truth.

The actual trial took place in Dayton, Tennessee in 1925 at a time of one of those unedifying clashes between science and religion. Its roots lay in the far-reaching social and scientific changes which were sweeping America. Industrial activity had exploded, along with a host of by-products, both good and bad, such as female emancipation, short skirts, motor-cars and organized crime, developments that were brought home to people graphically by those other novelties of their day, the radio and the cinema. America was, as it still is, a deeply religious society and many churchgoers were disturbed at what was going on around them. As Lawrence W. Levine wrote, 'Something *was* wrong with religion in the twenties; its absolute truths were being taken with a grain of salt; its prestige and appeal were declining; certainty was being replaced by uncertainty, faith by doubt, security by insecurity'.[2] Many turned for consolation to the simple verities of their youth, which they saw as validated by what was known as fundamentalism, or a belief in the literal truth of the Bible.[3] This was particularly true of the Bible Belt (broadly, the Protestant states of the

1   United Artists. The film was based on the 1955 stage play by Jerome Lawrence and Robert E. Lee which was written at the time of the McCarthy witch-hunt in which Senator McCarthy abused his office supposedly in order to eradicate communists from public life. It was set at a time 'not long ago' and contained a disclaimer that it did not 'pretend to be journalism'. Despite this, the film has been widely accepted, even taught, as an account of the 1925 trial.
2   Lawrence W. Levine, *Defender of the Faith. William Jennings Bryan; The Last Decade 1915-1925* (London, Oxford University Press, 1965), p. 259.
3   The term, 'fundamentalism' had its origins in the writings of a turn of the century Baptist minister, William B. Riley. It found its defining doctrine in a series of books published between 1910 and 1915 by the Presbyterian General Assembly which sought to re-state the basic Christian doctrines.

south-east). Tennessee was known as 'the buckle on the Bible Belt'; it stood 45th among the 48 states in order of literacy.

What worried the fundamentalists most was the theory of evolution (or Darwinism as it was pejoratively called), the idea that all species of creature developed from simple to more complex forms by means of a process of natural selection.[4] To God-fearing folk, this seemed to be contrary to the Bible which taught that the world and all the creatures on it had been created by God in the manner described in the first chapter of *Genesis,* a doctrine which has since become known as creationism. The thought that their children were being taught at public expense an explanation of the origins of Man contrary to the biblical account was particularly resented all across the Southern states, and they reacted by trying to ban the teaching of evolution in schools. Success was finally achieved by a Tennessee farmer. John Washington Butler was a man of considerable probity who had joined the Primitive Baptists because he found the Missionary Baptists too exclusive. Before coming to a view on evolution he had gone to the length of buying and studying a copy of *The Origins of Species.* (We may wonder how many evolutionists have done likewise.) In all events Butler managed to steer a bill through the State legislature that became known as the Butler Act of 1925.

THE BUTLER ACT

The Act, which was passed by a large majority, provided that:

> it shall be unlawful for any teacher in any of the Universities, Normals[5] and all other public schools of the State which are supported in whole or in part by the public school funds of the State, to teach any theory that denies the story of the Divine Creation of man as taught in the Bible, and to teach instead that man has descended from a lower

4   As first postulated by Charles Darwin in his book, *On the Origin of Species by Means of Natural Selection, or the Preservation of Races in the Struggle for Life* (1859). The word 'evolution' did not appear until the sixth edition of the work (replacing 'descent with modification'). Darwin did not speculate on the origins of man until his next great work, *The Descent of Man* (1871). In it he wrote, '...man is descended from a hairy tailed quadruped, probably arboreal in its habits'.
5   Normals were similar to teacher training colleges.

order of animals.[6]

At the time, the new law seemed unlikely to cause much difficulty. Governor Austin Peay of Tennessee, for example, pronounced, 'After a careful examination, I can find nothing of consequence in the books now being taught in our schools with which this bill will interfere in the slightest manner. Therefore, it will not put our teachers in jeopardy. Probably the law will never be applied'. He was soon to be proved wrong: a biology textbook widely in use in Tennessee schools plainly recognized evolutionary theory.

As soon as they learned of the Bill's passing, the American Civil Liberties Union (ACLU) determined to challenge it and put out a press release stating, 'We are looking for a Tennessee teacher who is willing to accept our services in testing this law in the courts. Our lawyers think a friendly test can be arranged without costing a teacher his or her job. Distinguished counsel have volunteered their services. All we need now is a willing client.' A teacher was quickly found with the aid of George Rappleyea of Dayton, Tennessee.[7] Rappleyea was a thirty-one year old coal mine manager who had become disillusioned with fundamentalist religion. (At the graveside of a child of one of his workers he was shocked to hear the minister describe the dead boy as 'awrithin' in the flames of hell' simply because he had never been baptized.)

THE DRUG-STORE MEETING

One afternoon in April 1925 Rappleyea met his friends in their usual meeting place, 'Doc' Robinson's fountain and drug-store in Main Street, Dayton, and showed them a newspaper which contained the press release. Fred E. Robinson was chairman of the local Rhea County school board and Dayton's principal supplier of school textbooks. Also present that day were his brother-in-law, the attorney Wallace C. Haggard, Walter White, the superintendent of schools, and two more attorney brothers, Sue (*sic*) and Walter Hicks. Rappleyea suggested

---

6 The Act's taxonomy was a bit fuzzy. Man is a member of a species, not an order.
7 The name is sometimes spelled Rappalyea.

that they should take up the ACLU offer, though his reasons were not entirely idealistic. Dayton was a town in decline and everyone agreed that a test case such as the ACLU proposed could put it on the map.[8] All they lacked was a teacher who would be willing to act. Sue Hicks thought that their young friend John Thomas Scopes would be the ideal candidate and a student was sent to fetch him from the tennis courts.

Scopes was the widely liked, twenty-four year old science teacher and football coach of Dayton's Rhea County High School, who had stood in for the biology teacher when he was ill. Asked in the drug-store whether biology could be taught without teaching evolution. Scopes replied that it could not, and proved the point by reading from a copy of the school textbook which happened to be on the shelves of the store. It was entitled *A Civic Biology Presented in Problems*. This textbook was for the most part a straightforward exposition of the science of biology as understood at the time, but it also contained statements such as:

> Undoubtedly, there once lived upon the earth races of men who were much lower in their mental organization than the present inhabitants. If we follow the early history of man upon earth, we find that he must have been little better than one of the lower animals...
>
> ... We have now learned that animal forms may be arranged so as to begin with the simple one celled forms and culminate with a group which contains man himself.[9]

It would be difficult to imagine statements more inflammatory to fundamentalists. After an initial reluctance Scopes agreed to play the part of the defendant in a test case; he could not have realized what a momentous event it would become and what notoriety it would bring him.

Rappleyea immediately sent a telegram to the ACLU informing them of their offer. It concluded, 'WIRE ME IF YOU WISH TO CO-

8   The idea also occurred to the nearby town of Chattanooga, but they missed their opportunity by the speed with which the grand jury was summoned in Dayton.
9   George William Hunter, *A Civic Biology: Presented in Problems* (New York, American Book Co., 1914), pp. 194, 195.

OPERATE AND ARREST WILL FOLLOW'. Their agreement came the following day. As soon as it was received, a local justice of the peace was brought into the drug-store and a warrant sworn out for Scopes' arrest. Someone sent for a deputy sheriff who told Scopes to appear before the justices the following Saturday. When he did, he was bound over to appear before a grand jury. The drug-store plotters agreed that Sue and Walter Hicks would be the prosecutors and that a former judge, John Godsey, would defend. The ACLU offered to fund the prosecution as well as the defence, but the offer was declined for ethical reasons. These cosy arrangements were to change when it was realized that a famous name would add greatly to the pulling power of the trial. At the request of Hicks and the World's Christian Fundamentals Association, William Jennings Bryan was approached to join the prosecution team and immediately jumped at the offer.

'THE GREAT COMMONER'

A tall, balding man of ample girth, the sixty-five year old William Jennings Bryan was a nationally respected politician, orator and preacher. Known as 'the Great Commoner' after the title of a newspaper he had once edited, Bryan was no political lightweight, having been three times nominated Democratic candidate for President of the United States and having held the office of Secretary of State under President Wilson. (He resigned this office in protest at the President's stand against German aggression which he saw as dragging America into an unnecessary war.) During the Spanish-American War of 1898 Bryan had been a colonel in the militia, though he never saw action.

Politically, Bryan was a social reformer who had argued for women's suffrage, world peace, independence for the Philippines, and a progressive income tax. On religion, however, he was staunchly conservative, and travelled the country using his formidable speaking skills to preach against Darwinism which he saw as being linked to atheism and the currently fashionable theory of eugenics. Scopes was to describe him as 'the most outstanding public speaker this country has produced.[10] Bryan had been enthusiastic in promoting the Butler

10   John T. Scopes & J. Presley, *Center of the Storm; Memoirs of John T. Scopes* (New York, Holt, Rinehart and Winston, 1967), p. 229. Strangely, it was Bryan

Act, though he had not wished to see it made an offence to teach evolution. His attitude to the Scopes trial can be seen from a letter he sent to Hicks, in which he wrote, 'I don't think we should insist on more (than) the minimum fine, and I will let the defendant have the money to pay if he needs it,' adding, with ill-judged optimism, 'It is a test case and will end all controversy'.[11] In another letter to the Hicks brothers he wrote, 'Now, you boys will probably live to see whether or not evolution is true. I won't'.[12] They were hardly the words of a closed mind.

Despite his towering reputation, Bryan knew that he faced great difficulties over the trial of Scopes. As an attorney, he had not practised law for twenty-eight years. As an orator, he was past his prime. He was suffering from diabetes, a condition made worse by his inability to restrain his appetite, and his mental faculties were beginning to slow. At the trial in Dayton he had the additional burden of caring for his wheelchair-bound wife, who insisted on coming into court throughout the hearing to offer moral support. For Bryan, the opportunity to strike a blow against what he regarded as militant atheism overrode all these considerations. But he wanted it to be a good fight. 'There is no reason why the Scopes trial should not be conducted on a high plane without the least personal feeling,' he wrote to a friend. 'The trial will be a success in proportion as it enables the public to understand the two sides and the reasons on both sides. Every question has to be settled at last by the public and as soon as this is understood the sooner it can be settled.'[13]

Despite Bryan's fame, it was agreed that the prosecution should be led by the thirty-one year old Attorney General for the Eighteenth Judicial Circuit and future US Senator, Thomas A. Stewart, a quietly spoken but capable lawyer. Stewart was joined by the assistant Attorney General, Ben G. McKenzie. The Hicks brothers and Hag-

---

who had given the address at Scopes' graduation in his home town of Salem, Illinois.

11   Bryan to Hicks 28 May 1925, quoted in Levine, *Defender of the Faith*, p. 335.

12   L. Sprague De Camp, *The Great Monkey Trial* (New York, Doubleday and Company, 1968), p. 45.

13   Levine, *Defender of the Faith*, p. 338.

gard completed the team, along with Bryan's son, William Jennings Bryan Jr. (who as an orator was to prove a pale shadow of his father.) Rappleyea withdrew from the prosecution, but still remained active in the case.

Bryan's involvement in what was rapidly becoming a notorious trial came to the attention of the renowned defence attorney, Clarence Darrow, who promptly volunteered to act for Scopes without any fee. (It was to cost him a substantial sum.) He was joined in this by his friend, Dudley Field Malone. Malone was an Irish-American with a flourishing international divorce practice and a formal dress sense. (He was the only advocate to keep his jacket on for most of the trial.) A reforming politician, Malone knew Bryan well and had served as third Assistant Secretary of State under him. His leader, Darrow was something altogether different.

THE 'ATTORNEY FOR THE DAMNED'

Clarence Seward Darrow was perhaps the most extraordinary man ever to practise at the American Bar. Brilliant and ruthless, high-minded and pragmatic in equal measures, Darrow had begun his career as a corporate lawyer, but achieved national recognition only after he began defending criminal cases. A romantic liberal, Darrow had been a leading opponent of the death penalty. The son of a coffin maker and the 'town atheist', Darrow regarded the existence of a God as wholly improbable, and the Christian God as particularly unattractive. Throughout his life, however, he fought shy of the term, 'atheist' which then, as now, attracted a moral opprobrium among the conventionally religious, describing himself instead as an agnostic.[14] In so far as the Scopes trial was concerned, Darrow claimed that his only object in putting himself forward was to 'focus the attention of the country on the program of Mr. Bryan and the other fundamentalists in America'.[15] Both advocates, however, shared the view that

14   Strictly, the word, 'agnostic' does not mean someone who has no view on the existence of a God (which was to be Darrow's answer to a question from Judge Raulston), but someone who believes that it is impossible to prove the existence of a God.
15   Clarence Darrow, *The Story of My Life* (New York, De Capo Press, 1932), p.

it should be the issues, rather than the guilt of the defendant, which should be uppermost in the trial, and each was confident of his ability to overcome the other.

Responsibility for leading the defence fell to a somewhat eccentric law professor, John Randolph Neal. Neal had no time for fundamentalists, who had ousted him from a teaching post. However, the prospect of conducting so prominent a prosecution was too good to miss. So anxious was he to get involved that he drove to Dayton to announce that he would be representing Scopes.

In an attempt to gain publicity for the defence Rappleyea had invited the English science writer H.G Wells to join the defence team; his approach was rebuffed. ('They must mean some other Wells. I never heard of Dayton.'[16]) He need not have worried; the press were already well alert to the case and when Scopes appeared before the grand jury to be committed for trial, bail for the young teacher was put up by the *Baltimore Sun*. The first task of Scopes and his attorney, Neil was to go to New York to meet representatives of the ACLU. These included its Director, Roger Baldwin, Norman Thomas, leader of the Socialist Party and the progressive Harvard don, later to become Supreme Court Justice, Felix Frankfurter. The news that Darrow had offered his services *pro bono* (or without charge) was met with dismay. Darrow's reputation had suffered by reason of the part he had played less than a year before in saving two of his clients, Leopold and Loeb, from the death penalty they were widely believed to deserve.[17] The ACLU also feared that the headline-grabbing attorney would allow his agnosticism to convert the defence into an attack on religion and wanted to replace him by their own man. The argument was resolved when Scopes firmly expressed his desire to be represented by Darrow. The ACLU nominee declined to act, but another of their attorneys,

---

249. Strangely, the book does not mention the key fact, of which Darrow cannot have been unaware, namely that the prosecution was a collusive one.

16   Quoted in De Camp, *The Great Monkey Trial*, p. 80.

17   Leopold and Loeb were two privileged university students whose crime spree ended in the pointless kidnap and murder of a thirteen year old boy. The defendants escaped the death penalty as a result of Darrow's defence speech of some twelve hours duration, but were sentenced to life imprisonment. Loeb was murdered by a fellow inmate. Leopold was released after serving thirty-four years.

the very able Arthur Garfield Hays, offered to serve with Darrow. In a huff, Baldwin shunned the trial. But what line was the defence going to take?

Darrow and another lawyer who dropped out before the trial started wanted to get the case before a Federal court as soon as possible. Hays and Malone disagreed; they wanted the case heard on its merits in Dayton. Whichever tactic worked, it was agreed, the others would have to resign. As it happened, the point did not arise because Neal's attempts to get the trial removed to a Federal court were to prove unsuccessful. The main thrust of the defence was to show that the Butler Act violated the constitutional separation of church and state. All eyes now turned to Dayton.

DAYTON, TENNESSEE

Dayton was a pleasant little town in east Tennessee. Its population of 1,800 was swollen for the duration of the trial by some thousands of mountain people fascinated by the forthcoming battle. Bryan's wife kept a newsletter for her friends in which she wrote of the incomers: 'They are to me a new phase of American life; tall, gaunt, thin, underfed, sad; they are both interesting and pathetic. They do not shave every day and [their] proper costume is a blue shirt, generally worn open at the neck, and a pair of blue overalls, a high crown felt hat with a wide brim... [They] have no real part in American life; marry and intermarry until the stock is very much weakened.'[18] But the mountain people were not the most bizarre visitors to Dayton: also present was an extraordinary mélange of people, from the curious to the committed, the holy roller to the conman, the exhibitionist to the salesman.[19] Evangelist tents vied for attention with ice cream merchants and sleight of hand artists. As the day of the trial approached signs went up proclaiming such messages as, 'READ YOUR BIBLE', 'SWEETHEARTS COME TO JESUS' and 'WHERE WILL YOU SPEND ETERNITY?' With commendable initiative a haberdasher

18   Quoted in Paolo E., Coletta, *William Jennings Bryan* (Lincoln, University of Nebraska Press, 1969), vol. III, p. 245.
19   A 'holy roller' was a Pentecostal Christian accustomed to 'speaking in tongues'.

named Darwin put up a notice reading, 'DARWIN IS RIGHT', followed by the word, 'inside' in small letters. Four days into the hearing two apes were brought into town, along with a fifty-one year old man with receding brow and prominent jaw who described himself as 'the Missing Link'. For the course of the trial, the town, like the courtroom, was never to lose the atmosphere of a circus.

Bryan arrived in Dayton by train on 7 July, bizarrely kitted out in morning dress with a bow tie, pince-nez and a cork helmet he had picked up on his travels. Some three hundred people turned up to greet him, but the welcoming band had to be cancelled when it was realized that most of its members were Scopes' pupils. After a motor parade through town Bryan went to a banquet which the Progressive Club had organized in his honour. Scopes and his English father had also been invited to the feast where they were welcomed by Bryan. Two days later, Darrow arrived in town and was met by a crowd of similar proportions.[20] To ensure impartiality the good folk of Dayton had laid on a reception for the great defender identical in every respect to that accorded to Bryan.

THE CROWDED COURT

The trial took place in Dayton's 1891 courthouse, a large red-brick building which still serves the same purpose today. Judge, jury, prosecution and defence all sat on a railed dais in the large second floor courtroom.[21] In front of them were 250 seats for the public, but even these were not enough for the vast crowd of people anxious to get in, and most had to stand around the walls. (Later in the proceedings the public had to be warned for walking off with the attorneys' chairs.) And there was the press. Such was the notoriety of this trial that the courtroom had had to be adapted to the needs of more than a hundred reporters and photographers from all parts of America and beyond, along with the tools of their trade, twenty-two telephones and telegraphs and radio microphones.[22] Perhaps the most prominent of

20 In his autobiography Darrow claimed otherwise, but most reports are against him.
21 First floor in UK English usage.
22 It was the first trial to be broadcast live nationwide.

the pressmen was the *Baltimore Sun* columnist and wit, Henry Louis Mencken. Throughout the trial this urban sophisticate used his columns to satirize what he saw as the narrow-minded Daytonians. But his barbed and elitist comments led to threats, and he was happy to leave town before the end of the trial.

Friday, 10 July was hot and airless and most of the attorneys in the Dayton courtroom had abandoned their jackets.[23] Many were waving fans provided by a toothpaste company bearing the legend, 'Do your gums bleed?' After a quarter of an hour of photographs and general settling down, the proceedings began, as they were to do on each day of the trial, with a prayer from a local clergyman.[24] This was very much to the satisfaction of the judge, His Honour John Tate Raulston, a conscientious lawyer with an unfortunately sanctimonious turn of phrase and a weakness for having his photograph taken. Like everyone in town, Raulston was well aware of the collusive nature of the prosecution. After welcoming the 'foreign' (that is to say, non-Tennessee) lawyers, he began the process of empanelling yet another grand jury in order to remedy a supposed technical deficiency in the indictment (or formal statement of the charge). In explaining their task, Judge Raulston found it necessary to read aloud the whole of the first chapter of the book of Genesis, which contains one of the two main biblical accounts of creation. With that out of the way, another jury had to be selected to actually try the case.[25]

Jury selection took up most of the first day. When one of the panel of potential jurymen (called veniremen) admitted that he had preached against evolution applause broke out in the courtroom and Judge Raulston had to warn against any repetition. Another potential juror, when asked whether he had heard anyone talk about evolution, answered frankly, 'Well, I have heard lots of talk against it, and some talk for it, whether either one knew what they were talking about, I

23   At the request of the jury, electric fans were installed on the fifth day of the trial.
24   A reading of the text does not bear out the defence criticism that the prayer was partisan.
25   Throughout this chapter I have used the transcript in *The World's Greatest Court Trial* (Cincinnati, Ohio, 1925). Other authorities contain slightly different chronologies.

don't know. They might have been like me, did not know.' The panel as finally chosen were mostly middle-aged farmers, all were regular churchgoers, one of them was illiterate and few were widely read outside the Bible.

'AND THE EVENING AND MORNING WERE THE SECOND DAY'

Next day, Neal rose to his feet to ask for the revised indictment to be quashed; it was the first attempt by the defence to get the case before a higher court. The jury were ordered out of the room[26] while he argued, among other things, that the Butler Act was contrary to the freedom of speech guaranteed by the constitution of the State of Tennessee, as well as against the fourteenth amendment to the US constitution.[27] It was not a strong case and Tom Stewart had little difficulty demolishing it. It was now Clarence Darrow's turn to take up the cudgels. In the course of a rambling, witty and frequently moving examination of the relation between religion and society Darrow declaimed:

> If today you can take a thing like evolution and make it a crime to teach it in the public school, tomorrow you can make it a crime to teach it in the private schools, and the next year you can make it a crime to teach it to the hustings or in the church. At the next session you may ban books and the newspapers. Soon you may set Catholic against Protestant and Protestant against Protestant, and try to foist your own religion upon the minds of men. If you can do one you can do the other. Ignorance and fanaticism is ever busy and needs feeding. After a while, Your Honour, it is the setting of man against man and creed against creed until with flying banners and beating drums we are marching backward to the glorious ages of the sixteenth century when bigots lighted fagots to burn the men who dared to bring any intelligence and enlightenment and culture to the human mind.

He added:

Can a legislative body say, 'You cannot read a book or take a les-

26   They were nevertheless able to listen to the proceedings over the loudspeakers on the lawn.
27   Which guarantees that, 'No State shall make or enforce any law which shall abridge the privileges or immunities of citizens of the United States'.

son, or make a talk on science until you first find out whether you are saying against Genesis'. It can unless that constitutional provision protects me. It can. Can it say to the astronomer, 'you cannot turn your telescope upon the infinite planets and suns and stars that fill space, lest you find that the earth is not the center of the universe and there is not any firmament between us and the heaven'. Can it? It could – except for the work of Thomas Jefferson, which has been woven into every state constitution of the Union, and has stayed there like the flaming sword to protect the rights of man against ignorance and bigotry, and when it is permitted to overwhelm them, then we are taken in a sea of blood and ruin that all the miseries and tortures and carrion of the middle ages would be as nothing.

The perceptive Mrs. Bryan left a pen portrait of Darrow in court as a man 'with light hair rapidly growing grey and a seamed face. He is smooth faced and has a weary-hopeless expression...He wears rather soiled suspenders [braces in UK English] and his favourite attitudes are shrugging and thrusting of his hands under his suspenders bringing them together and clasping his hands in front of his breasts.[28] Another observer wrote:

> The powerful shoulders writhed upwards, rippling his wet shirt, rumpling the limp collar. His left hand caught at his blue suspenders; the right arm, formerly wagging in mere wrist movements, now became the boom of a sail, and the sail whipped by an invisible tornado. The crescendo rose, and his right hand slapped the left palm in brisk staccato. Judge Raulston's grin sagged into total disbelief.[29]

The following morning Darrow began the proceedings by objecting to the minister's daily prayer. While the practice might have been unobjectionable in other circumstances, he said, it was inappropriate in a case of this nature. Judge Raulston overruled the objection, observing that the ministers had been instructed not to make reference to any issue in the case. This ruling did not stop representatives of 'various well-known religious organizations, churches and synagogues' from presenting a petition objecting to the prayers of 'fundamentalists'. The judge answered them by saying that he would in future ask the

28   Quoted in Coletta, *William Jennings Bryan,* vol. III, p. 255.
29   Ray Ginger, *Six Days or Forever* (London, Oxford University Press, 1958), p. 106.

pastor's association to nominate the minister to say prayers. Laughter in court acknowledged that this was hardly a concession, since the association in question did not include any of the objecting faiths.[30] For some onlookers the objection had merely served to confirm Darrow's well known anti-religious stance.

Judge Raulston then announced his rejection of Darrow's motion concerning the legality of the Butler Act, which meant that the trial had to proceed. By this time, a degree of asperity was beginning to creep into inter-attorney relations, which was not helped by a supposed press leak and ensuing inquiry ordered by the judge. (Embarrassingly, it turned out that the 'leak' had arisen from an injudicious remark by the judge himself.)

The prosecution then called evidence of Scopes' statement that he could not teach civic biology without teaching evolution and that he could not do that without violating the Butler Act. Former pupils confirmed that their teacher had classified humans along with other animals.[31] One of them said that man had been classed 'along with cats and dogs, horses, monkeys, lions, horses and all that'. Asked by Darrow whether Scopes had meant that a cat was the same as a man, he said, 'No, sir. He said man had a reasoning power that these animals did not'. Darrow commented dryly, 'There is some doubt about that'.

THE DEFENCE

It was not until the afternoon of the fourth day of the trial that the defendant got to enter his plea of 'Not Guilty'. In his opening statement Malone took a number of points, notably that the Butler Act required the prosecution to prove, not only that his client taught evolution, but also that he had denied the Bible story. (It was an interesting point which would eventually go to the Court of Appeal). The Bible contained a number of conflicting accounts of the origin of man; which of them was to be believed, he suggested, was a matter of faith, not science. There was no conflict between evolution and science. Malone

30   They were respectively the Unitarians, the Congregationalists and the Jews.
31   The boys had to be brought to court by Scopes as they had fled into the woods in order to avoid giving evidence against their teacher.

scored a nice point in throwing Bryan's own words back against him. (He had cited Jefferson as writing that 'the regulation of the opinions of men on religious questions by law is contrary to the laws of God and the plans of God'.) None of the defence arguments was accepted by the judge.

Although Raulston had at first ruled against the calling of expert evidence he was finally persuaded to admit it, but directed that it must be given in the absence of the jury and could not be the subject of cross-examination. (This concession was designed to allow the evidence to be available to any appeal court which might have to review the court's decision.) The defence were ready; they had assembled a team of a dozen experts, who until then, had been accommodated in a large decayed mansion outside town which came to be known, inevitably as 'the Monkey House'. The first expert to be called was Maynard M. Metcalf, a pedantic zoologist of considerable academic distinction and a deacon of his local Congregationalist church. Metcalf explained the theory of evolution and testified that all scientific opinion agreed in its truth, though individual scientists might disagree about the exact method by which it was brought about. There were audible gasps from the public gallery when he referred to the earth being many millions of years old.

The following day, Darrow sought to call the rest of his expert witnesses. The purpose of this, he explained, was that, since the Butler Act prohibited the teaching of evolution, it was necessary to establish exactly what that theory was. The Bible, he said, was not in conflict with evolution unless it was taken literally. 'There isn't a human being on earth', he added with ill-judged optimism, 'who believes it literally'. Apart from some highly technical argument about procedure, the issue came down to whether the expert witnesses would be usurping the role of the jury in determining the outcome of the case. Attorney General McKenzie argued that it would. According to the judge's ruling, he said, to teach evolution was to deny the Bible's account of the origin of man. There would be no purpose therefore in permitting the defence to seek to prove that evolution was consistent with the Bible. The prosecutor claimed that, in seeking to prove that when the Bible said that God created man in his own image 'they were actually having God say that He issued some sort of protoplasm, or soft dish rag, and put it in the ocean and said, "Old boy, if you wait around about 6,000 years, I will make something out of you"'. McKenzie could use wit as mercilessly as Darrow.

After lunch, Bryan came forward to voice his objection to the use of expert witnesses: '[I]t isn't proper', he said, 'to bring experts in here to try to defeat the purpose of the people of this state by trying to show that this thing that they denounce and outlaw is a beautiful thing that everybody ought to believe in...the Christian believes man came from above, but the evolutionist believes that he must have come from below...How dare those scientists put man in a little ring like that with lions and tigers and everything that is bad!' Darwin's *Descent of Man*, he said, asserted that man was descended from monkeys; 'not even American monkeys, but from old world monkeys!' It was a hoary jest that the defence lawyer had used many times before. Rising to his theme, Bryan said of the evolutionists, '...they cannot find a single species that came from another, and yet they demand that we allow them to teach this stuff to our children, that they may come home with their imaginary family tree and scoff at their mother's and father's Bible.... [T]hey do not explain the great riddle of the universe—they do not deal with the problems of life—they do not teach the great science of how to live... They shut God out of the world.' No one seemed to mind that he had strayed far from the legal point in order to make the case against 'Darwinism', but when he sat down the applause was polite rather than rapturous.

It fell to Malone to respond to Bryan, which he did in a highly emotional speech. It was the only occasion when he took his jacket off. His peroration ended:

> ... these gentlemen say 'the Bible contains the truth- if the world of science can produce any truth or facts not in the Bible as we understand it, then destroy science, but keep our Bible.' And we say, 'keep your Bible. Keep it as your consolation, keep it as your guide, but keep it where it belongs, in the world of your own conscience, in the world of your individual judgment, in the world of the Protestant conscience that I heard so much about when I was a boy, keep your Bible in the world of theology where it belongs and do not try to tell an intelligent world and the intelligence of this country that these books written by men who knew none of the accepted fundamental facts of science can be put into a course of science, because what are they doing here?' We

have just had a war with twenty-million dead. Civilization is not so proud of the work of the adults. Civilization need not be so proud of what the grown ups have done. For God's sake let the children have their minds kept open – close no doors to their knowledge; shut no door from them. Make the distinction between theology and science. Let them have both. Let them both be taught. Let them both live...

The truth always wins and we are not afraid of it. The truth is no coward. The truth does not need the law. The truth does not need the forces of government. The truth does not need Mr. Bryan. The truth is imperishable, eternal and immortal and needs no human agency to support it. We are ready to tell the truth as we understand it and we do not fear all the truth that they can present as facts. We are ready. We are ready. We feel we stand with progress. We feel we stand with science. We feel we stand with intelligence. We feel we stand with fundamental freedom in America. We are not afraid. Where is the fear? We meet it, where is the fear? We defy it, we ask Your Honor to admit the evidence as a matter of correct law, as a matter of sound procedure and as a matter of justice to the defense in this case.

It was generally judged to be the finest address of the trial and met with 'profound and continued applause'. A police officer on loan from Chicago pounded the table with his nightstick so hard that it broke. Scopes was later to describe the address as 'the most dramatic event I have attended in my life'.[32] Tom Stewart had the difficult task of replying for the prosecution, but he rose to the occasion. He began in his usual measured way, but towards the end began to feel his subject as strongly as his opponent:

They say this is a battle between religion and science. If it is, I want to serve notice now, in the name of the great God, that I am on the side of religion. They say it is a battle between religion and science, and in the name of God, I stand with religion because I want to know beyond this world that there may be an eternal happiness for me and for all.

It was a powerful speech which was well received, but, after the court had closed for the day and the public had gone home it was to Dudley Field Malone that Bryan came up and said in a quivering voice, 'Dudley, that was the greatest speech I ever heard.'[33]

32   Scopes & Presley, *Center of the Storm*, p. 156.
33   De Camp, *The Great Monkey Trial*, p. 343.

CONTEMPT

Before proceedings began the following day, the sixth of the trial, Darrow tried to circumvent what he assumed would be the judge's ruling to exclude the evidence of his remaining expert witnesses. (His plan was to get the experts to tell the press out of court what their evidence would have been if admitted in court.) Learning of his intention, Judge Raulston asked Darrow before the sitting began not to go down that road lest the jury got to hear evidence which had been ruled inadmissible. He refused.

In court, the Judge gave his expected ruling:

> [U]nder the provisions of the Act involved in this case, it is made unlawful thereby to teach in the public schools of the state of Tennessee the theory that man descended from a lower order of animals. If the court is correct in this, then the evidence of experts would shed no light on the issues.

He was prepared to permit the witnesses' affidavits to be read into the record for the benefit of the appeal court, but only in the absence of the jury. Exceptions (objections in UK English usage) followed thick and fast, including at one point an exception to an exception. The situation descended into acrimony when Darrow was refused the afternoon off to prepare his affidavits. He angrily snapped, 'I do not understand why every request of the state and every suggestion of the prosecution should meet with an endless waste of time and a bare suggestion of anything that is perfectly competent on our part should be immediately overruled'. This was not entirely fair, but the advocate refused to back down when challenged:

Raulston: 'I hope that you do not mean to reflect on the court?'

Darrow: 'Well, Your Honour has the right to hope.'

Raulston: 'I have the right to do something else, perhaps.'

Darrow: 'All right. All right.'

It was unnecessarily discourteous of Darrow, but in the end he got his time off and the court adjourned for the weekend.

Judge Raulston, brooded all weekend over Darrow's remarks and the adverse press comment to which they had given rise, and on the following Monday read out a prepared citation of the attorney for 'contempt and insult'. Darrow was ordered to enter into a bond of $5,000 to appear from day to day and not to depart without the court's leave. While those present were assimilating this, Arthur Garfield Hays failed in an attempt to read into the record a message from the State Governor favourable to the defence view of the law.[34] The Governor's opinion on legal matters, Judge Raulston correctly held, was immaterial. When the court resumed in the afternoon Stewart informed the judge that, following a discussion between them, the defence attorney had a statement to make. Darrow now apologized in the most fulsome terms for having 'overstepped the bounds' the previous day. His apology met with 'general applause' from the public and he was forgiven by the judge in his characteristically overblown way.[35]

Immediately after accepting Darrow's apology the judge ordered the court, its officials, the parties, the press and the public to all move outdoors. The building, he had been advised, was likely to collapse, not as a result of divine intervention, but owing to the exceptional load it was bearing. The rest of the day's hearing took place on a platform which had been hastily erected on the lawn in front of the courthouse. It began in the absence of the jury with the reading into the record of the written statements from the remaining defence witnesses. Scientists expounded Darwin's theory of evolution and explained why they thought that it was not inconsistent with Christian belief. All present knowledge, one said, was 'utterly inconsistent' with the fundamentalists' 'theory' of 'special creation'. And a rabbinical expert explained that, without the advantage of modern biblical scholarship, the King James Version of the Bible had been mistranslated.

34   The Governor had stated that 'this bill does not require any particular theory or interpretation of the Bible regarding man's creation to be taught in the public schools'.
35   'I think the Man that I believe came into the world to save man from sin, the Man that died on the cross that man might be redeemed, taught that it was godly to forgive and were it not for the forgiving nature of Himself I would fear for man.'

Before the jury could be called back, Darrow made yet another objection, this time to a ten-foot long sign on the lawn right in front of the jury box which proclaimed, 'Read your BIBLE'. Either remove it, he demanded, or put up another sign of equal size reading, 'Read your EVOLUTION'. (As Darrow was to remark in his autobiography, 'it was not a rainy day so that I was taking no chance with lightning.') The prosecution not being able to agree among themselves whether to concede the point or not, the judge ordered that the sign be removed.

There then occurred an event almost unprecedented in the history of criminal litigation; Arthur Garfield Hays called the prosecuting attorney, Bryan, to give evidence for the defence. Reading the record, Hays seems to have been almost deliberately obscure as to his purpose in calling Bryan. Accepting that the main question was whether Scopes had taught what he was said to have taught, he added gnomically, 'We think there are other questions involved, and we should want to take Mr. Bryan's testimony for the purposes of our record, even if Your Honor thinks it is not admissible in general...' The great preacher leapt at the opportunity, confident that he could stand up to Darrow's cross-examination. Darrow was equally confident; even agreeing to waive the necessity for the witness to take the oath. After a short exchange between the court and the attorneys and an assurance that the witness's privileges as a lawyer would be protected, Judge Raulston metaphorically held up his hands and said, 'Call anyone you like'. But Hay's request was no spur of the moment tactic, but had been dreamed up along with Darrow a few days before. Determined to use the trial as a platform to demolish the fundamentalist case on evolution, Darrow had spent hours rehearsing his questioning with a geologist on the team of experts.

Once again, the long-suffering jury were excluded from the hearing, thus missing what came to be regarded, rightly or wrongly, as the high point of the trial.

THE CONFRONTATION ON THE LAWN

The confrontation between Bryan and Darrow took place on the lawn outside the court beneath the shade of some young trees; it turned out to be something that neither had anticipated. What it certainly was not was an examination of the issues before the court. As an outraged Bryan was to say, 'these gentlemen have not come here to try this case. They came here to try organized religion'. An ill-tempered Darrow countered: 'we have the purpose of preventing bigots and ignoramuses from controlling the education of the United States'. Things got so far out of hand at one point that Hays had to intervene to remind everyone that the purpose of the defence was to demonstrate that, while the Butler Act spoke of 'the Bible' it was possible to have an understanding of that book which was not a literalist one. It was a perfectly reasonable line for the defence to take; however, it was a path that Darrow had deliberately chosen to eschew.

From the start of the cross-examination, Darrow sought to portray the witness as a simple-minded obscurantist, but he had misjudged the man. When asked whether he claimed that everything in the Bible should be interpreted literally, the preacher replied, 'I believe everything in the Bible should be accepted as it is given there', but qualified this immediately by adding that 'some of the Bible was given illustratively', such as the phrase, 'Ye are the salt of the earth'. Darrow scoffed at his acceptance of the biblical miracles, such as the story of Jonah and the whale.[36] Bryan replied that if God could make the whale He could make a man and make both do as he wished. Bryan said he accepted as literally true the biblical reference to God making the sun stand still.[37] Interestingly, when pressed about the physical consequences of such a miracle, he added that the Bible used language that people understood at the time. So far, his evidence had revealed a man with beliefs little different from those of many mainstream Christians of the day.

Darrow then turned to the origin of the world (despite the fact that the trial was strictly about the origin of man). Bryan answered that he could not agree that there had been civilizations dating back 5,000 years as archaeology suggested. However, he did not necessarily accept Bishop Ussher's famous calculation that the earth had been created in 4004 BC.[38] Despite persistent questioning, Bryan maintained

36 Jonah 1:17.
37 Joshua 10:12.
38 The seventeenth-century theologian and Anglican Archbishop of Armagh calculated that the earth was created on 23 October 4004 BC. At the time of the

that man could not be dated further back than the flood, whenever that happened to have been. The scientists should agree more closely with each other, he said, before he would give up his belief in the Bible.

But the real surprise was still to come. Asked whether the earth had been made in six days, Bryan called for a Bible and, turning to Genesis, replied:

> The fourth verse of the second chapter says: 'These are the generations of the heavens and of the earth, when they were created in the day that the Lord God made the earth and the heavens,' the word 'day' there in the very next chapter is used to describe a period. I do not see that there is any necessity for construing the words, 'the evening and the morning,' as meaning necessarily a twenty-four-hour day, 'in the day when the Lord made the heaven and the earth'.

This further expression of Bryan's less than literalist beliefs was met with startled gasps from the fundamentalists present. They were equally dismayed when he went on to concede that the earth might have been come into existence 'many millions of years' before.[39]

Bryan displayed a degree of self-satisfaction when forced to admit to a complete ignorance of other faiths: 'I have been so well satisfied with the Christian religion that I have spent no time trying to find arguments against it.' And, 'I have all the information I want to live by and die by'. When Darrow pressed this line of questioning too far Stewart had had enough. He jumped in to make the obvious objection: Darrow was cross-examining his own witness, a procedure impermissible without the approval of the judge. The objection went unregarded in the hurly-burly of argument. Stewart protested with justification: 'we have left all annals of procedure behind'. At one point the judge allowed matters to get so far out of hand that Bryan, the witness, was allowed to question Darrow, the attorney, without being stopped. Neither party secured any further advantage before the proceedings closed for the day.

Scopes trial it was the practice for this date, along with other chronology derived from it, to be printed in the margins of Bibles.

39   Thus putting Bryan into the camp of what was called the old creationists; as opposed to the young creationists who insisted on Bishop Ussher's date for the creation of the world.

On the eighth and final day of the trial it was drizzling with rain and the court resumed its sitting indoors, presumably preferring the risk of structural collapse to the certainty of inundation. Judge Raulston began the proceedings by belatedly conceding that he had been in error in allowing Bryan to give evidence.[40] His evidence could shed no light upon any issue that would be argued before the higher courts and would accordingly be expunged from the record. Having ruled on the legality of the Butler Act, Raulston said that the only remaining issue was 'whether or not Mr. Scopes taught that man descended from a lower order of animals.' The defence were content with the ruling. They were admitting the teaching of evolution and simply wanted to challenge the legality of the Act. Darrow asked the judge to instruct the jury to bring in a verdict of 'Guilty' so that the matter could be taken swiftly to a higher court. Attorney General Stewart agreed and Judge Raulston ruled accordingly.

After a nine-minute retirement the jury (who had heard very little evidence and hardly any relevant argument during the whole course of the trial) brought in the inevitable verdict of 'Guilty'. The judge imposed the fine of $100, but was immediately reminded by the Attorney General that he had failed to give the defendant his opportunity to address the court before sentence. Scopes now spoke up for the first time in court:

> Your Honour, I feel that I have been convicted of violating an unjust statute. I will continue in the future, as I have in the past, to oppose this law in any way I can. Any other action would be in violation of my ideal of academic freedom, that is, to teach the truth as guaranteed in our constitution, of personal and religious freedom. I think the fine is unjust.

He was given leave to appeal against the decision of the court and bail was granted pending appeal. The customary speeches of mutual congratulation then took place between the attorneys of both sides. When Bryan referred to Dayton as being 'the centre and seat of the trial largely by circumstance', Darrow countered:

40 Darrow believed that the prosecution had 'got to' the judge, and that further cross-examination of Bryan would weaken their case (Darrow, *The Story of My Life*, p. 268.) L. Sprague De Camp puts it down to police fears of violence and disorder. (De Camp, *The Great Monkey Trial*, p. 415.)

I fancy that the place where the Magna Charta was wrested from the barons in England was a very small place, probably not as big as Dayton. But events come along as they come along. I think this case will be remembered because it is the first case of this sort since we stopped trying people in America for witchcraft because here we have done our best to turn back the tide that has sought to force itself upon this, upon this modern world, of testing every fact in science by a religious dictum.

The minister pronounced a short benediction and the courtroom emptied. Dayton, as Darrow was to write in his autobiography, had had her day in the sun.

POST-MORTEM

Despite the fact that Scopes had been convicted, Bryan was disappointed at the outcome of the trial. He had been tactically blindsided by Darrow's request for what was in effect a directed verdict.[41] This meant that he could not put the defence attorney in the witness box to be cross-examined as he had been, and that he had lost the right to the final speech which he had spent so many weeks preparing.[42] (The address was to have been, he said, 'the mountain peak of my life's effort'.[43]) Despite all this, Bryan left town to embark upon a marathon tour of the area, covering hundreds of miles and speaking to thousands of people in the hot sun. Returning to Dayton five days later, he preached the Sunday morning service in church, enjoyed a heavy dinner and then lay down for a nap before taking evening service. He did not wake up.

The exact cause of Bryan's death was never discovered, but when told by reporters that he had died of a broken heart, Darrow is said to have replied, 'Broken heart nothing; he died of a busted belly.'[44] The

41 In his autobiography Darrow expressed regret at this outcome, but that he had planned it that way there can be no doubt.
42 Under Tennessee law, if the defence waived its right to a concluding speech the prosecution were similarly shackled and had no further opportunity to address the court.
43 William Jennings Bryan, *The Last Message of William Jennings Bryan* (New York, Revell, 1925), pp. 7-8.
44 It seems most likely that he died of diabetes, aggravated by the heat, his exertions at the trial and his prodigious appetite. Levine, *Defender of the Faith*,

ungenerous H.L. Mencken described Bryan as a 'charlatan... deluded by a childish theology'. But Washington declared official mourning and the ex-militiaman turned peace campaigner was buried, as he had requested, with full military honours in Arlington National Cemetery.

The trial has often been portrayed as a bitter struggle, but in fact it was conducted for the most part with courtesy, even good humour. The public gallery (if that term may be used of this overcrowded courtroom and the lawn to which it adjourned for a day) was by no means entirely partisan. If it sometimes shouted 'amen' to prosecution arguments, it also applauded well-made points from the defence, and the most enthusiastically received speech was from a defence attorney. The lawyers were usually polite towards each other, sometimes effusive. McKenzie, for example, referred to Clarence Darrow as 'the greatest criminal lawyer in America today'. Darrow returned the compliment towards 'my friend, McKenzie, whom I have learned not only to admire but to love in our short acquaintance'. The occasional tetchiness or loss of temper – whether genuine or simulated is not always clear – mostly ended with an apology. And one hot day during the trial, Scopes went swimming with William Jennings Jr., turning up late at court in consequence.

The press came out of the affair badly. Laziness and headline grabbing dictated their reports. Some reporters frankly admitted that they were producing copy which reflected their papers' circulation needs more than the events they were witnessing. As a result, the prosecution, its star performer Bryan and the residents of the town of Dayton were portrayed in the media as witless reactionaries soundly trounced by a liberal reformer, an image which they have never been able completely to shake off.

So was it a fair trial?

THE JUDGE'S RULINGS

There really was only one issue in the trial: as Tom Stewart said when objecting to one of Darrow's wilder excursions, 'It is a case involv-

---

p. 357.

ing the fact as to whether or not a schoolteacher has taught a doctrine prohibited by statute.' The defence were entitled to raise the point of the statute's constitutionality, but the question was never whether evolution or creationism was correct, however strongly lawyers on both sides wished to argue the point.

Judge Raulston was a Baptist lay preacher who sometimes found himself affronted by the unbelieving Darrow's anti-fundamentalist remarks, but it is difficult to discern any serious pro-prosecution bias in his rulings.[45] A small-town judge with no experience of a case of this magnitude, he seems to have done the best he could. He was right to rule that Governor Peay's view on the legal effect of the Butler Act was irrelevant and his controversial exclusion of the expert witnesses was also unimpeachable. However, his decision to allow Bryan to be called as a defence witness was a grievous mistake, as he himself admitted. What is sometimes overlooked is that because Bryan was Darrow's witness, not the prosecution's, he could not be cross-examined unless the court was satisfied that he was hostile to the defence.[46] (He was, but the point was never ventilated, a shortcoming for which Raulston must share the blame.)

But there was worse: most of the questions which Darrow put to Bryan on the lawn were totally irrelevant to the issue before the court and should have been disallowed.[47] (It cannot be too strongly stressed that a witness's willingness to answer questions put to him is no reason to admit them in evidence when they are otherwise inadmissible.) Darrow was allowed to pour scorn on fundamentalist beliefs concerning the creation of the earth, the story of the flood and the miracles, but dealt hardly at all with the biblical story of the creation of man, de-

45 Contrary to the impression given in the film, *Inherit the Wind*, Judge Raulston referred to Darrow as 'colonel' throughout the proceedings in accordance with local custom. The attorney declared jocularly that he would take the title back north with him. By an unintended irony of Tennessee court practice, the Attorney General was referred to throughout the proceedings as 'General'.
46 Even then, the witness's evidence would carry no probative weight except to counter his earlier testimony.
47 Darrow's cross-examination followed a set of questions which he had put to Bryan in an article in the *Chicago Tribune* two years before. The questions had not been answered and had led to a breakdown in relations between the two men.

nying which was the only teaching that the Butler Act prohibited. One is tempted to think that the judge must have been so fascinated by the drama of the occasion (perhaps even the glory reflected on himself) that he simply gave no thought to the legal issues involved, at least until reality broke in upon him. Unfortunately, a technical error on the part of the defence (see below) has denied to us for ever the opinion of the appeal court on the propriety of the Judge's rulings.

In the famous battle on the lawn Darrow successfully exposed the limitations of Bryan's knowledge of science and his ignorance of other beliefs, but he failed in his main objective of exposing Bryan as a narrow-minded literalist. Bryan's views may not have been those of the East Coast intelligentsia, but they were not all that different from those of many Christians of his day – or since; indeed, many of his supporters were shocked at their relative liberality. Darrow's tricky,[48] sometimes facetious,[49] questioning of Bryan got him nowhere; the preacher gave as good as he got. Possibly in an ill-judged attempt to demonstrate his fairness the judge allowed Darrow to get away with some remarkable slurs on Bryan's faith, such as his reference to the witness's 'fool religion' and to 'fool ideas that no intelligent Christian on earth believes', language that would have been out of place in a debating chamber, let alone a court. And when he came to deal with the trial in his autobiography, Darrow was not above downright misrepresentation of his opponent's views.[50]

Some commentators have described Bryan as a man broken by Darrow's questioning, an image which his death shortly after only served to reinforce. Bruised he certainly was, and dismayed by his lost opportunities, but 'broken' is an adjective too far. For all the

48   For example, 'Do you know anything about how many people there were in Egypt 3,500 years ago, or how many people there were in China 5,000 years ago?
49   For example, when Bryan mentioned having met a Buddhist, Darrow asked, 'What did he look like, how tall was he?'
50   He quoted Bryan as saying, 'I am more interested in the Rock of Ages than the age of rocks', a neat apophthegm, but a long way from what the witness actually said, which was: 'It is desirable to know the physical sciences, but it is necessary to know how to live. Christians desire that their children shall be taught all the sciences but they do not want them to lose sight of the Rock of Ages while they study the age of rocks'.

verbal fireworks during this head-to-head clash between the nation's two most famous orators, the battle on the lawn succeeded neither in advancing the prosecution's reputation, nor in damaging that of the defence. More to the point, it contributed nothing to the outcome of the trial.

THE APPEAL

Scopes' appeal came before the Supreme Court of Tennessee on 17 January 1927, a year and a half after the trial. Dissatisfaction with Darrow's performance had led to his being dropped from the defence team. Some even suggested that his confrontational approach had actually reinforced fundamentalist views. The only issue before the court was the legality of the Butler Act. Chief Justice Green, giving the judgment of the court, dismissed the appellant's arguments one by one.[51] As to the question of whether the prosecution had to prove both the teaching of evolution *and* denial of the Bible story, he held that the Butler Act, while 'not drafted with as much care as could have been done', was clear. It represented a form of rhetoric exposition by iteration which simply implied that 'to forbid the denial of the Bible story would ban the teaching of evolution'. (To at least one English lawyer this seems contrary to the plain words of the Act.) Nor, he held, did the Act impose any unconstitutional restriction on Scopes' liberty. He was free to teach the theory of evolution in any school outside the state system. Finally, the Chief Justice turned to the establishment clause of the constitution, which provides that 'no preference shall ever be given, by law, to any religious establishment or mode of worship'. The court was not able to see how prohibiting the teaching that man descended from a lower order of animals gave preference to any religious establishment or mode of worship.

Having rejected all the appellant's arguments of substance the court nevertheless reversed the conviction on a technical point. Under the Tennessee constitution a fine in excess of $50 had to be assessed by a jury, whereas the $100 fine on Scopes had been fixed by the judge.[52]

51 Only one of the two dissenters would have struck down the Act.
52 The constitution provided that 'No fine shall be laid on any citizen...that shall exceed fifty dollars, unless it shall be assessed by a jury of his peers, who

The defect could not be remedied, the court held, but, since Scopes was no longer in the employment of the State of Tennessee, nothing was to be gained from prolonging the life of 'this bizarre case'. The court therefore suggested to the Attorney General that he should enter a *nolle prosequi* ('unwilling to pursue'), a legal device which would have had the effect of discontinuing the prosecution. Which is exactly what he did, thus closing the door to any hope of getting the case before the US Supreme Court.

THE IRONIES OF THE TRIAL

There are two ironies concerning the 'Monkey Trial' deserving of note.[53] First, Scopes may never have taught evolution at Rhea County High School and, secondly, the evolution that was taught there was not the simple science it was assumed by all concerned to be, but something far more sinister. When asked at that fateful meeting at the drug-store whether, when he filled in as biology teacher, he had covered evolution, Scopes replied, 'We reviewed for final exams, as best I remember'. But in his autobiography, *Center of the Storm*, the former teacher wrote: 'To tell the truth, I wasn't sure I had taught evolution. Robinson and the others apparently weren't concerned about this technicality. I had expressed willingness to stand trial. That was enough'.

Even that may have been an exaggeration. Immediately after the trial was over Scopes is said to have told a young reporter:

> There's one thing I must tell you. It's worried me. I didn't violate the law ... I never taught that evolution lesson. I skipped it. I was doing something else the day I should have taught it, and I missed the whole lesson about Darwin and never did teach it. Those kids they put on the stand couldn't remember what I taught them three months ago. They were coached by the [defence] lawyers. And that April twenty-

shall assess the fine at the time they find the fact, if they think the fine should be more than fifty dollars'. Despite an objection from the Attorney General, Judge Raulston had mistakenly taken this somewhat confusing provision to mean that the judge could impose the fine, particularly since the jury in the case had actually left it to him to fix the fine. The Court of Appeal strained the construction of the Act by holding that it vitiated the conviction.

53   It was so named by H.L. Mencken.

fourth date was just a guess. Honest, I've been scared all through the trial that the kids might remember I missed the lesson. I was afraid they'd get on the stand and say I hadn't taught it, and then the whole trial would go blooey. If that happened they would run me out of town on a rail.[54]

It seems probable that Darrow was aware of the true position and it has been suggested that this was why he did not call Scopes to give evidence. A more likely reason is the one which the attorney himself gave, namely that there was nothing that Scopes could have said which would have affected the outcome of the trial. After the trial a fund was set up for the teacher by the expert witnesses. It paid for Scopes' first year of a geology course at Chicago University. Denied the opportunity of a fellowship (which would have paid for a second year) on the ground of his 'atheism', Scopes went into the oil industry, in which he remained for the rest of his life. He married in 1930 and died in 1970.

Civic Biology was not the simple school text that it seemed to be. It certainly taught evolution as it was understood at that time, but it used that theory to advance the racist and eugenist views which were then fashionable throughout much of the Western world. (Hence, *Civic Biology*.) The book inveighed against the perpetuation of inferior stock and adopted the view that intermarriage between the superior and the 'low and degenerate' races should be stopped:

> Just as certain animals or plants become parasitic on other plants or animals, these families do harm to others by corrupting, stealing or spreading disease, but they are actually protected and cared for by the state out of public money. Largely for them the poorhouse and asylum exist. They take from society, but they give nothing in return. They are true parasites.

It was a theory that two decades later was to lead to the most tragic consequences in Europe. It is ironic that a book containing views such as these should have been held up as a banner of liberal thought.

---

54   De Camp, *The Great Monkey Trial*, p. 432.

BACK TO THE COURTS

A few years after the Butler Act was passed in Tennessee, the State of Arkansas enacted their own version. It became unlawful for a teacher in any state-supported school or university 'to teach the theory or doctrine that mankind ascended or descended from a lower order of animals,' or 'to adopt or use in any such institution a textbook that teaches' this theory'. The law gave rise to no difficulties until the mid sixties when a public school in Little Rock adopted a new textbook. A tenth-grade biology teacher alleged that the law required her to teach a view of the origins of life contrary to the views of the textbook from which she had to teach it. Her claim was upheld by the US Supreme Court as being contrary to the First Amendment to the American constitution.[55] The Butler Act had at long last (effectively) been overruled.[56] The fundamentalists returned to the attack nearly two decades later with a new formulation of words. A Louisiana Act forbade the teaching of the theory of evolution in public schools unless it went alongside instruction in the theory of what the legislators were pleased to call 'creation science'. Justice William Brennan, speaking for the majority of the Supreme Court, had no difficulty in holding that 'the pre-eminent purpose of the Louisiana legislature was clearly to advance the religious viewpoint that a supernatural being created humankind.'[57]

'Creationism' obviously had no future and it was time for the fundamentalists to change tack. Shortly after the Louisiana judgement, an entirely novel concept emerged, which on the face of it made no reference to divine intervention in the origins of mankind.

---

55   *Epperson v Arkansas* 393 US 97 (1968). The first amendment reads: 'Congress shall make no law respecting an establishment of religion, or prohibiting the free exercise thereof; or abridging the freedom of speech, or of the press; or the right of the people peaceably to assemble, and to petition the Government for a redress of grievances.' The origins of this clause are far from clear, though the likeliest purpose was to prevent the oppression of dissenters in the way that they had suffered under the established church in England.
56   In fact, it had been repealed in Tennessee only weeks before the Little Rock case got to the Supreme Court.
57   *Edwards v. Aguillard* 482 US 578 (1987). Justice Scalia and Chief Justice Rehnquist expressed a minority view when they said that it was for the State to determine whether creationism was a science.

'INTELLIGENT DESIGN'

'Intelligent design', its exponents will tell you (for it is still very much alive), holds that 'various forms of life began abruptly through an intelligent agency, with their distinctive features already intact: Fish with fins and scales, birds with feathers, beaks and wings, et cetera'.[58] The more cynical suspected from the start that this new concept was merely creationism under another name.

It was not long before the new doctrine was challenged in the American courts, and with triumphant success. In 2004, the Dover Area School District Board of Pennsylvania required a statement to be read aloud to students in the ninth grade biology class, which included assertions such as, '[Darwin's] Theory is not a fact. Gaps in the Theory exist for which there is no evidence. … Intelligent design is an explanation of the origin of life that differs from Darwin's view'. Despite the fact that students were invited to keep an open mind, the ACLU filed suit on behalf of a number of parents, contending that the statement violated the Establishment Clause of the First Amendment to the constitution.

Their claim was upheld after a six-week trial before Judge John E. Jones III of the US District Court for the Middle District Court of Pennsylvania. In a devastating 139-page judgment he noted that not one witness had been able to explain how the supernatural action suggested by intelligent design could be anything other than an inherently religious proposition. The secular purposes claimed by the school board, he held, amounted to a pretext for the board's real purpose, which was to promote religion in the public school classroom. Criticizing the 'breathtaking inanity' of those responsible for the policy and the untruthfulness of some of their witnesses, this Republican appointed, church-going judge held that intelligent design was not science and 'cannot uncouple itself from its creationist, and thus religious, antecedents'.[59]

---

58 Quoted in Percival Davis and Dean H. Kenyon, *Of Pandas and People, the Central Question of Biological Origin* (Foundation for Thought and Ethics, 1989). It is a key document setting out the creationists' case.
59 *Tammy Kitzmiller et al. v. Dover Area School District et al.* (2005). Case no. 04cv2688.

For over a century now, few educated people have had reason to doubt the outlines of the theory of evolution. While people are entitled to believe otherwise for reasons of faith, we have long passed the point at which it is possible to contemplate the dissemination to the young of any alternative explanation of the origin of man. Yet religious opposition to the teaching of evolution in schools is far from dead, and not only in America. At the time of writing at least three state[60] schools in England offer the creationist 'theory' to their pupils as having equal weight with the theory of evolution and dozens of schools are said to be using creationist teaching materials. As the distinguished American lawyer Alan M. Dershowitz has written, 'We live in an age of increasing fundamentalism among all faiths. It affects our politics, our schools, our laws and almost certainly our juries. The Scopes trial may not be an anachronism. It may be a portent.'[61]

60 'Public schools' in American usage.
61 Alan M. Dershowitz, *America on Trial: Inside The Legal Battles That Transformed Our Nation* (New York, Warner Books, 2004), p. 267.

The arrest of Alice Lisle (Topfoto)

THE BLOODY ASSIZES

THE TRIAL OF DAME ALICE LISLE, 1685

*This is the story of an old lady condemned to be burned at the stake
for harbouring a minister of religion, of the notorious judge who tried
her, and of the King who denied her mercy.*

T he tiny invasion fleet of three ships, eighty-three fighting men,
a few guns and an assortment of muskets landed at Lyme Regis
in Dorset on 11 June 1685.[1] They were lucky to get that far
because, in the words of a local historian, 'a Barbados vessel near the
Cobb[2] had powder and Lyme had cannon, but the two could not be
brought together…'.[3] Once on shore, the invaders unfurled their banner of Leveller[4] green on which were inscribed the words, 'Fear nothing but God', while their leader, the Protestant Duke of Monmouth,
knelt to give thanks to the Lord. England's last rebellion had begun.

James Scott, Duke of Monmouth, was the eldest, though illegitimate, son of Charles II. He was born in 1649 to his father's mistress,
Lucy Walters, during the King's exile in The Hague. James Scott has
been described as possessing 'in full measure the full charm of the
Stuarts, and much of their fickleness'.[5] His father recognized his talents by making him a Duke and marrying him to the Countess of
Buccleuch. What he would not do, however, was acknowledge his
son's legitimacy, and it rankled. When fears were expressed at the

---

1   Lyme Regis had been chosen because of its supposed sympathy with 'the
old cause', a term implying a combination of political radicalism and religious
non-conformism.
2   The Cobb is the small, man-made harbour at Lyme Regis.
3   Robert Dunning, *The Monmouth Rebellion: A Complete Guide to the Rebellion and the Bloody Assize* (Wimborne, Dovecote Press, 1984), p. 23.
4   The Levellers were a loose group of people whose aims included a more
equal society.
5   G.W. Keeton, *Trial for Treason* (London, Macdonald, 1959), p. 91.

possibility of the King being succeeded by his Catholic brother James, Monmouth began mixing with people who saw him as the future king. A series of blatant 'progresses' around the West Country and the North[6] coupled with popular manifestations of support for Monmouth led to his arrest. He was released on entering into a bond for his good behaviour, but it did not take much to persuade the aggrieved Duke to become one of the leaders of a planned uprising to put him on the throne.[7] It was not the only conspiracy going round; a much more dangerous enterprise (the 'Rye House Plot') aimed to assassinate both Charles and his brother James. When both conspiracies were betrayed Monmouth went into hiding, but eventually made his peace with the King by betraying his accomplices and agreeing to go into exile in Holland. Here, he lived comfortably with his Protestant mistress, Henrietta Wentworth, leaving his wife and children in England; meanwhile his fellow conspirators were tried and sentenced to death by the King's trusted judge, George Jeffreys.

When King Charles II died in February 1685 his Catholic brother came to the English throne as James II.[8] Monmouth, now in Brussels, allowed himself to be persuaded by his fellow exiles that this was the time to act. Henrietta pawned her jewels to finance the enterprise and the last invasion of England got under way.

Once his little force had landed at Lyme Regis, Monmouth's first task was to raise an army. It did not prove difficult in a part of the country where the people had long been strong supporters of Parliament and fierce opponents of papism. Very soon, 6,000 men had rallied to his cause, but even before they left town bad news arrived from the North. It had been intended to coincide the landing in Dorset with a rising of the clans in Scotland, but the plan had been betrayed to the government and its leader swiftly captured and executed.

On 18 June the Duke and his army arrived in Taunton where he proclaimed himself king (thus giving England two kings called James

6 During which he was reported, significantly, to have cured a woman of 'the king's evil', a power thought to be peculiar to the king.
7 The plot found support from a fanciful story put about by Monmouth to the effect that Charles had confessed to having married his mother and that proof of this could be found in a mysterious black box.
8 He was already James VII of Scotland.

at the same time). He promised toleration for dissenters, annual parliaments and abolition of the standing army, all in other words that the West Countrymen wanted. But at this point Monmouth seems to have lost the plot and marched, counter-marched and fought his way inconclusively through three counties. On 6 July the rebels found themselves at Sedgemoor, low-lying marshland near the Bristol Channel in what is known as the Somerset Levels. Here, he attempted a daring night attack on the royal forces. While the rebel soldiers were floundering around an unexpected drainage ditch someone, possibly one of their officers, discharged his pistol, alerting the King's troops. An effective resistance and counter-attack were quickly organized that soon put paid to the numerically superior but badly trained and inadequately armed rebel forces. By dawn and despite fierce resistance, Monmouth's army had been routed. The Duke fled the field, only to be captured two days later hiding in a ditch at Ringwood in Hampshire, unshaven but still in possession of the Order of the Garter. He was hastily convicted of treason and on 15 July beheaded in the Tower of London, somewhat clumsily, by Jack Ketch.

Some 1,300 rebels had been killed and over 300 captured. The rest were hunted down by the soldiers and parish constables, who hanged many of them summarily on trees and makeshift gibbets. The rest of the rebels, some 1,500 in all, found themselves in gaols up and down the West Country awaiting their fate. Our tale concerns two members of Monmouth's defeated army who managed at first to escape death or capture only to be caught in the home of a sympathizer, the seventy year old, Dame Alice Lisle.

ALICE LISLE

Alice Lisle was born around 1614, the daughter of Sir White Beckenshaw. At the age of sixteen she became the second wife of John Lisle, barrister of the Middle Temple and Member of Parliament for Winchester in the Parliamentary cause. At the outbreak of the civil war, Lisle became a Colonel in Cromwell's army. When King Charles I was defeated and put on trial, Lisle was appointed one of the Commissioners who tried him, sitting next to the President of the court and advising on legal matters.[9] For this and other services he was made Lord President of Cromwell's High Court of Justice and elevated to the rank of Viscount. When the Commonwealth was established, Lisle became a member of the Commission which framed the new, republican constitution.

But the world continued to turn and, following the restoration of the monarchy, Lisle was one of the few not to be granted mercy by the Act of Indemnity and was attainted traitor. Along with his wife Alice he fled to Switzerland, where three years later he was murdered on his way to church by royalist extremists. After her husband's death Alice retired to her late father's home, Moyle's Court in Ellingham,[10] a few miles north of Ringwood in Hampshire, which she had been permitted by King Charles II to keep. Although married as Anglicans, Alice and her husband had become Dissenters, that is to say, people who refused to accept the doctrines of the established church. Dissenters had little in the way of freedom of worship and the pious Alice felt deeply for the sufferings of the dissenting ministers. One of them she knew was fifty-three year old John Hickes (or 'Hicks'). He had been one of Monmouth's army and when he asked for shelter she readily agreed to give it. However, when he arrived at Moyle's Court he was accompanied by a stranger, Richard Nelthorpe (or 'Nelthorp'). Nelthorpe was a wealthy barrister who had been proclaimed an outlaw for his part in the 'Rye House Plot'.[11] Like Hickes, Nelthorpe was a fugitive from the rout at Sedgemoor.

The two men had been taken to Moyle's Court by a labourer called John Barter. He became suspicious when he overheard their conversation and went to the authorities. Next day, a party of soldiers arrived at Alice Lisle's home under command of the royalist Colonel Thomas Penruddock. No one at the house answered his knocking for 'a pretty while', but eventually Alice's elderly bailiff, Carpenter, came to the door. Asked who was in the house, he admitted that there were 'strangers present' and indicated where Hickes and a Warminster baker called James Dunne were to be found, asking only that his mistress

9   His name does not appear on the death warrant.
10   Some believe that Moyle's Court was the manor house on which Bramshurst Court in Hardy's novel *Tess of the D'Urbervilles* was based.
11   Nelthorpe's age is not known but he was admitted to Gray's Inn in 1669.

118

should not be told who had betrayed them. (He kept quiet about the presence of the notorious outlaw, Nelthorpe.) The pair were duly discovered in the malthouse, Dunne hiding under 'some sort of stuff'. At this point Alice arrived on the scene. Accused of harbouring rebels, she replied 'I know nothing of them. I am a stranger to it.' She went on to deny that anyone else was hiding in the house, but a further search revealed Nelthorpe 'hid in a hole by the chimney'. Alice could only repeat, 'I know nothing of them.' This was not true and the lie was to be her undoing.

Hickes, Nelthorpe and Dunne were arrested along with Alice and committed to prison to stand trial before King James II's most trusted and feared judge, George Jeffreys.

THE 'BLOODY ASSIZE'

On 8 July 1685, two days after the Battle of Sedgemoor, a Commission of five judges was appointed to try the captured rebels. The senior judge was George Jeffreys, the Lord Chief Justice, who for the occasion was made Lieutenant-General in command of the King's forces in the West, surely a unique appointment for one of His Majesty's judges. Jeffreys was left under no illusions by King James II; his task was to deal with those responsible for a rebellion that had nearly overturned the lawful government, gravely upset society and had cost the lives of hundreds of men and the maiming of many more. (At that time the idea of judicial independence was one that remained largely in the future.) The Assizes opened on 27 August in the dimly lit great hall at Winchester Castle. The first trial was that of Alice Lisle. She appears to have been deliberately chosen to be made an example of, for no other trial was held at Winchester on that Assize, even the trials of Nelthorpe and Hickes being reserved until later.

The indictment alleged that Mrs. Lisle[12] was guilty of treason on the ground that she did 'traitorously entertain, conceal and comfort... John Hickes and cause meate and drink to be deliver'd to him...' She pleaded not guilty and asked to be tried 'by God and my country',

12   Throughout the proceedings she was referred to as Mrs. Lisle since her husband's title had lapsed upon the Restoration.

the ancient formula which had once distinguished jury trial from trial by ordeal. The prosecutor was the leader of the Western Circuit and Jeffreys' friend, Sir Henry Pollexfen.[13] After Pollexfen had opened his case Alice, fearful of going unheard, interrupted the proceedings to say how much she abhorred the rebellion. Jeffreys stopped her, explaining that 'we must observe the common and usual methods of trial in your case, as well as others. ... You shall be fully heard when it comes to your turn to make your defence... ' It is,' he said, 'a business that concerns you in point of life and death; all that you have or can value in the world lies at stake, and God forbid that you should be hindered in time or anything else, whereby you may defend yourself...'

Pollexfen's first three witnesses established that Hickes had been a member of Monmouth's army; Alice did not attempt to deny it. Far less straightforward, however, was the evidence of his next witness, James Dunne, the man who had been arrested along with Nelthorpe and Hickes. His tortuous struggle in the witness box to give away as little as possible about Alice Lisle's guests, while admitting even less about his own role in their attempted escape, was to be the dramatic highlight of the trial. Pollexfen, well aware of Dunne's sympathies, asked Jeffreys in court to examine the witness strictly. Before Dunne said a word, therefore, he was given a lengthy warning by the judge of the peril to his immortal soul if he were to lie to the court. Despite this, Dunne went on to tell a manifestly improbable story.

Dunne's first version of events was that a 'short, black man' of swarthy complexion had come to his house on 24 July asking whether he would be willing to take a message to Mrs. Lisle on behalf of a Mr. Hickes; he would be well-rewarded for his pains. Dunne agreed, and on the following day rode some twenty-six miles to Moyle's Court, where he met Mrs. Lisle's bailiff, Carpenter. Carpenter would have

13   The lawyer Alan Wharam suggests that Pollexfen, a 'known favourer of the Presbyterian party,' had been deliberately appointed prosecutor instead of the Attorney General in order to moderate the expected excesses of Jeffreys. (Alan Wharam, *Treason: Famous English Treason Trials* (Stroud, Sutton Publishing, 2005), p. 93.) He suggests that this could have been the reason for the various incompetences in the conduct of the prosecution, such as the failure to take Hickes' trial before that of Lady Lisle, the calling of Dunne as a prosecution witness and the failure to charge Alice with harbouring Nelthorpe. This theory seems improbable for various reasons, not least the King's refusal of mercy to Alice.

nothing to do with him and referred Dunne to his mistress. Asked whether she would agree to entertain Hickes, Alice replied that she 'did not know but she might'. Dunne returned home the following day and told Hickes that he would be received on the Tuesday evening. Jeffreys swiftly picked up the inconsistency between 'might' and 'would' and demanded an explanation from Dunne. The witness had to take time to compose himself, but eventually admitted that Alice had, indeed, directed that Hickes should arrive on the Tuesday, and at night.

When he resumed his evidence, Dunne said that at 7 a.m. the following morning the 'short black man' had returned to his house, bringing with him two others, Hickes and a 'tall black man', (whom we now know to be Nelthorpe). Dunne professed ignorance of the identities of both, but nevertheless took them to Moyle's Court. As on the Saturday, he was guided by John Barter, but before they got there, Hickes and Nelthorpe discharged Barter because they wanted to go by a different route. (Whitaker suggests that this was because the fugitives suspected that Barter would inform on them, as indeed he did.[14]) Another guide was found who took them the rest of the way. At first, Dunne claimed that Barter had acted without reward, but, on being pressed by Jeffreys, agreed that he had been promised five shillings for his pains.

Arriving at Moyle's Court between nine and ten that evening, Dunne's party were met at the door by Carpenter the bailiff. Dunne claimed that, after stabling his horse and having been shown to a room by a young woman he saw nothing more of his companions that night; it was not a story that he could maintain long. His evidence did not flow freely, but had to be drawn out of him painfully by prosecutor and judge, question by question. Jeffreys, whose scepticism of Dunne's veracity had been obvious for some time, asked what he had had for his pains. Dunne ruefully replied, 'Nothing but a month's imprisonment, my Lord'. Jeffreys expressed his disbelief of the witness as follows (his words have been rendered into modern English):

You must be a kind and good natured fellow when someone you had

14 Antony Whitaker, *The Regicide's Widow* (Stroud, Sutton Publishing, 2006), p. 200.

never met before can come to your house and persuade you, simply because he had a black beard, to ride 26 miles to Moyle's Court, to pay someone £25[15] out of your own pocket to guide you there; and all this in order to carry a message from a man you had never known before to a woman you had never seen before.

It is very odd that you should spend two nights away from home and return to entertain these people for three or four hours and then ride for miles with them again to Moyle's Court without anything to eat except a piece of cake and cheese that you had brought with you. And all this without any reward for your pains, even though you did not know any of the people you did it all for!

Jeffreys caustically asked the now visibly discomfited witness whether he baked his bread at the same easy rates as he had helped his companions. Dunne offered a desperate explanation, 'All the reason that induced me to it was, they said they were men in debt, and desired to be concealed for a while'. He protested that he knew no more, but it no longer seemed convincing. Once again, Mrs. Lisle declined the opportunity to cross-examine.

Next on the stand was the guide and informant, Barter, who gave evidence of having seen Dunne produce the letter to Alice Lisle. On the way home, he said, Barter had asked Dunne why he and Alice had looked in his direction and laughed; Dunne's answer was that she had asked whether Barter 'knew anything of the concern'. On the first visit, he added, Dunne had given him half a crown and said that he would be very well paid. Dunne claimed to have received 'a very fine booty for his part and would never want again'. He had also boasted of his companions enjoying 'twenty thousand [pounds] a year apiece'. On the second journey Dunne had given the witness a Crown[16] and repeated the promise that he would be very well paid. Troubled by his visit to Moyle's Court (he 'could not eat nor drink, nor sleep for trouble of mind'), Barter had gone to Colonel Penruddock with his story.

Jeffreys now recalled Dunne to the stand and asked him about the letter which Barter said he had given to Alice Lisle: Dunne denied any knowledge of it, or of his companions' claim of having twenty

15   In present-day values.
16   That is, five shillings.

thousand a year. The astute Jeffreys had also picked up on Dunne's statement that he 'knew nothing of the business'. 'What business?', the judge asked sharply. When Dunne professed not to remember, Jeffreys roundly abused him for a liar. This was the point at which Dunne finally fell apart. Under stiff questioning from the judge he variously 'made no answer but stood musing a while', 'stood silent for a good while', 'made no answer', 'seemed to turn his head on one side but returned no answer', 'stood for a good while, but made no answer', and so on. At one point there was a pause of 'half of a quarter of an hour' – presumably some seven to eight minutes – before Dunne owned that he could not answer and asked the judge to repeat the question. In the end the witness suggested unconvincingly that 'the business' (of which he knew nothing) was whether Alice knew that Hickes was a nonconformist; it was a manifest lie and Jeffreys called for a candle to be held in front of Dunne's face all the better to see him. At this, the witness protested pitifully, 'I am so baulked, I know not what I say myself; tell me what you would have me say, for I am cluttered out of my senses.'

Resuming his evidence, Barter claimed that Dunne had admitted having hidden Hickes and Nelthorpe in his house ten days before. He had 'kept them in a chamber all day and they walked out at night, for the houses were usually searched at night.' Dunne interrupted the witness to deny the claim, but his credibility had been destroyed and Jeffreys directed that he should be prosecuted for perjury.

Colonel Penruddock then stepped forward to describe the arrests at Moyle's Court. He was the son of Sir John Penruddock, who had been sentenced to death for organizing the royalist Sealed Knot revolt of 1655, and it was widely believed that Alice's late husband was among the judges of the Cromwellian court which had condemned him.[17] This fact was to be alluded to obliquely more than once in the proceedings.

17 Certainly, the *State Trials* report of Penruddock's trial – written by Penruddock himself – refers to one of the judges as Commissioner Lisle, but it seems that this judge may have been from another branch of the family. See Seymour Schofield, *Jeffreys of the Bloody Assize* (London, Thornton Butterworth, 1937), pp. 176, 289n.

When Alice failed to challenge Penruddock's evidence, Jeffreys turned to Dunne and asked him why he had been in hiding in the house. Clutching at straws, Dunne said that he had hidden because he had heard 'a stir and bustle' and was 'frighted at the noise'. Asked whether he took the others to be rebels, a visibly shaken Dunne prevaricated, saying once again, 'I am quite cluttered out of my senses. I don't know what to say.' The candle was held to his face once more, but he remained mute. At this point Alice Lisle could not contain herself, 'I hope that I shall not be condemned without being heard.' 'God forbid', answered Jeffreys. 'The king's courts never condemn without hearing.' This infelicitous remark appears to have been a sneering reference to a case which her husband had tried.

The next witness was a soldier called Dowding who said that he had found Hickes in his hidey-hole and confirmed Alice's denial of knowing that the fugitives were in her house. Hearing this, the prisoner indignantly cried out, 'This fellow broke open my trunk, and stole great part of my best linen. And sure, a person who robs me is not a fit evidence against me because he prevents his being indicted for felony by convicting me.' It was a fair point, and one which Jeffreys failed to remind the jury of at the end of the case.

Dunne now made a dramatic intervention; he asked to go into the witness box again. 'Let him tell the truth and I am satisfied', said Jeffreys. Dunne had changed his story; though still denying that he had harboured Hickes in his own house, he now admitted that Alice Lisle had asked him if Hickes had been in the army. (He said he told her that he did not know.) He confirmed that she had ordered food and drink to be brought in which all four had consumed together. Jeffreys interrupted Dunne to warn him that, before the beginning of the Assize, Nelthorpe had revealed to him under questioning exactly what had taken place at Moyle's Court. Hearing this, Dunne conceded that there had indeed been talk among them of the army and of fighting. Armed with this admission, the prosecution closed its case.

It was now Alice Lisle's opportunity to present her case, which according to the law as it was then could only be by way of a simple unsworn statement:

My Lord, I knew of no body's coming to my house, but Mr. Hickes; and for him I was informed that he did abscond by reason of war-

124

rants that were out against him for preaching in private meetings, but I never heard that he was in the Army, nor that Nelthorpe was to come with him; and for that reason it was that I sent to him to come by night; but for the other man, Nelthorpe, I never knew that it was Nelthorpe. I could die upon it, nor did not know what name he had till after he came into my house; but as for Mr. Hickes, I did not in the least suspect him to have been in the army, being a Presbyterian minister that used to preach and not to fight.

She asked permission to call a witness to prove that she was unaware in advance of Nelthorpe's coming, but Jeffreys refused to hear him on the ground that it was only her harbouring of Hickes that was alleged in the indictment. Alice then attempted to deal with her incriminating denials of the fugitives' presence in her house. They had been made, she said, 'in great consternation and dread of the soldiers, who were very rude, and could not be restrained by their officers from plundering my house.'

Alice had, she admitted, been willing to shelter Hickes, but only 'knowing him to be a dissenting preacher and that there were warrants out against him upon that account' and not for any other reason. As for Nelthorpe, she was unaware of his identity before he arrived. More than that, she abhorred the principles and practices of the late rebellion and 'would have been the most ungrateful person living should I have been disloyal, or acted anything against the present king, considering how much I was obliged to him for my estate...I shed more tears for [King Charles I on his execution] that any woman then living then did'.[18] She concluded:

My Lord, I know the King is my Sovereign, and if I would have ventured my life for anything, it should have been to serve him; I owe all that I have in the world to him; and though I could not fight for him myself, my son did; he was actually in arms on the King's side in this business; I instructed him always in loyalty, and sent him thither: It was I that bred him up to fight for the King.

18   Other sources doubt her on this.

Had she been tried in London, she claimed, she could have called Lady Abergavenny, Lord Chancellor Hyde and other persons of quality to give evidence of her dislike of the rebels' cause.[19]

Almost at the last minute Alice clutched at a point of law. The village of Keynsham, she pointed out, where Hickes was said to have been in arms, was not in Hampshire where her trial was taking place. (This was significant because in those days there was a rule that a prisoner could be prosecuted only in the county in which the crime was committed, and Hickes had committed no crime in Hampshire.) 'That is nothing', dismissed Jeffreys, 'But the treason you committed was in this county'.

All the evidence having been given, Jeffreys now had the task of 'charging' the jury, that is to say, of instructing them how they should approach their decision. He began with an injunction that they should not be moved 'by compassion to the prisoner, or her allegations or protestations of innocence; nor on the other hand were they to be influenced by anything that came from the Court, or is insinuated by the prosecutor, but should be guided by the evidence alone'. He warned them, particularly and more than once, not to be influenced by John Lisle's part in the execution of King Charles I. Cynics have suggested that this was a sly way of reminding, or informing, the jury of her late husband's role as a regicide,[20] but his past was well known in the area and a failure to give the warning would no doubt have been criticized just as much. The rest of the judge's summing up was more controversial.

English judges, unlike their American cousins, have always enjoyed the privilege of indicating to the jury their view of the strength of the evidence, and in those days they were accustomed to doing so in a manner far more forceful than today. Before getting down to the facts of the case, therefore, Jeffreys reminded the jury, at length and in the strongest of terms, of the wickedness of the late rebellion, of its pernicious attacks on the King and the established church, and of the harm it had done to the country as a whole. Turning to the facts, he led

19   The order of this distressed lady's argument has been rearranged by the present writer in order to make it more coherent.
20   Because no evidence had been called about it.

them through Alice's repeated protestations that she knew nothing of the fugitives' presence in her house and of her instructions that they should arrive at night. 'Works of darkness,' he said, 'always desire to be in the dark.' In summary, he said, 'The proof that had been given of the fact she was charged with was as plain as the sun at noonday.'

Before the jury retired, one of their number asked for guidance on whether Alice could be convicted for harbouring a traitor before that traitor had been adjudged as such. (The point had been raised by Alice herself earlier, no doubt on the advice of her lawyer friend.) Jeffreys dismissed the objection. Any other rule, he said, would have meant that if Hickes had been wounded in the rebellion and had died of his wounds after the prisoner had taken him in it would have been impossible to prosecute her at all. Jeffreys has been much criticized for this ruling. However, three hundred years later the great Sir James Stephen observed of the point that 'this is another example of the numerous instances in which there really was no law at all... .'[21] Shortly after this, His Majesty's judges adopted Jeffreys' understanding of the law; and that is how it stands to this day.

THE JURY'S DOUBTS

The jury retired. Half an hour or so later their foreman came back into court, saying, 'My Lord, we have some doubt whether she knew Hickes had been in the army'. Jeffreys replied cogently:

> Was there not proved a discourse of the battle and of the army at supper-time? Did she not enquire of Dunne if Hickes had been in the army? And when he told her he did not know she did not say she would refuse him, but ordered him to come by night, by which it is evident that she suspected it? ... Come gentlemen, it is a plain proof.

The juryman insisted, 'My Lord, we do not remember that it was proved that she did ask any such question when they were there.' Jeffreys answered:

> Sure, you do not remember anything that passed? Did not Dunne tell you that there was such discourse, and she was by and Nelthorp's

21   Sir James Fitzjames Stephen, *A History of the Criminal Law of England* (London, Macmillan & Co., 1883), vol. 1, p. 413.

name was named. But if there was no such proof the circumstances and management of the thing is as full of proof as it can be. I wonder what it is that you doubt of?

After the jury had 'laid their heads together' for a further quarter of an hour they returned a verdict of 'Guilty'. In a comforting gesture of the sort that judges sometimes make to juries after conviction, Jeffreys declared that the proof of Alice's guilt was so plain that 'had I been among you and she had been my own mother, I should have found her Guilty.'

It was now about 11 p.m. and the court adjourned until the following day. In passing sentence Jeffreys lamented that Alice, 'a gentlewoman of quality and fortune, so far stricken in years… ought to have had more discretion'. After the usual diatribe against Dissenters ('the canting, whining, Presbyterian, phanatical profession') he passed the sentence demanded by law, namely that the prisoner should be burnt alive.[22] With a surprising gesture, he went on to intimate that if Alice would only confess her guilt her execution might be respited. Pen and ink, he said, would be provided for her, presumably to allow her to petition for a pardon.[23] At the request of the Winchester clergy Jeffreys deferred execution for a week; it was not open to him in law to do more. Alice's friends, Sir John and Lady Abergavenny, made representations on her behalf, but King James II declined to extend mercy to her, 'having left it all', he wrote untruthfully, 'to the Lord Chief Justice'. A petition from Alice herself merely ensured that the form of execution was changed from burning to the block, her head and body being 'graciously' granted to her family.

All avenues of appeal now having been exhausted, Alice Lisle was beheaded in the Market Square at Winchester on 2 September 1685.[24] An observer commented, '… she was old and dozy and died

22 Burning was the sentence prescribed for women; for men, it was to be hung, drawn and quartered.
23 Whitaker suggests, more cynically, that Jeffreys simply wanted the consolation of a written confession. (Whitaker, *The Regicide's Widow*, p. 176.)
24 Local tradition has it that she stayed the night before her execution in what is now the Eclipse public house, stepping onto the scaffold by an upstairs window.

without much concern.'[25] 'Dozy' does not sound like the defendant whose clear speech is reported in the *State Trials* and one wonders if Alice had not been administered some merciful potion. She was buried in a tomb on the right hand side of the porch at St Mary's Church, Ellingham, under the style and title, 'Alicia Lady Lisle'. The men whom Alice had given shelter to fared no better. Hickes was tried for treason at Taunton and executed at Glastonbury on 6 October. Shortly after, Nelthorpe was hung, drawn and quartered 'before Graies Inn foregate' on the old warrant of outlawry. His attainder was reversed in the next reign.

THE AFTERMATH

Jeffreys continued with his bloody commission. From Winchester the judges rode to Dorchester, dragging their miserable train of prisoners behind them. At Taunton, which had been the centre of the rebellion, 139 men were hung, drawn and quartered in the space of a few days. The heads of some of the condemned were nailed to the doors of churches. 'The smell from gibbeted and mangled corpses', wrote Keeton, 'infected the entire countryside'.[26] The commission went on to complete its bloody work at Salisbury, Exeter, Wells and Bristol.

It is difficult to estimate the numbers dealt with by the Bloody Assize, but it seems likely to have been over two thousand in all. Nearly half of them confessed, many in consequence of an offer of leniency from the Solicitor General. What they did not know was that for a good many of them leniency was to mean transportation to Barbados, where they were worked virtually as slaves in atrocious conditions. Between two hundred and fifty and five hundred of the rest were executed in the usual barbarous fashion. Some cheated the executioner by dying of the smallpox or gaol fever (typhus) in the overcrowded prisons. The rest had their sentences reduced to hanging (in those days, a form of slow strangulation), imprisonment or whipping. A few were pardoned and a handful escaped. Perhaps the most venal aspect of the whole business, to modern eyes at least, was the profit made by some out of this human traffic. About eight hundred and fifty pris-

25   P.J. Helm, *Jeffreys* (London, Robert Hale, 1966), p. 138.
26   Keeton, *Trial for Treason*, p. 102.

oners were made the subjects of gifts to King James II's supporters and royal hangers-on, such as the Governor of Jamaica, the Queen's secretary, even her ladies-in-waiting; they realised about £10 to £15 a head.[27] Jeffreys wrote to the King complaining that the money would have been better spent compensating those who had fought the rebels, but his protest was ignored and he was given, in addition to his fee, a condemned rebel who subsequently bought his pardon for the princely sum of £14,760, perhaps £1.5m in today's money.

The Bloody Assize deserves its reputation. Justice was summary at best and punishment was brutal in the extreme. Throughout the proceedings Jeffreys wrote to the government recommending names that deserved pardon. The *Dictionary of National Biography* comments, 'That so few pardons were forthcoming, and that so much vigour was used in trying them in the first place, resulted principally from the energy with which James wanted the rebels pursued'.

At the request of her two married daughters, Alice Lisle's attainder was reversed in 1689 by a private Act of Parliament, on the ground that 'the verdict was injuriously extorted and procured by the menaces and violences and other illegal practices' of Judge Jeffreys. But was this a fair assessment of what had happened?

'BLOODY JEFFREYS'

To English schoolchildren the words, 'Bloody' and 'Jeffreys' go together like 'cheddar' and 'cheese'. James himself, when later exiled in France, found it convenient to blame all his errors on his former Chancellor. But there was to be was a far more potent source for his evil reputation. It lay in what P.J. Helm called 'the seductive brilliance of Macaulay's style'.

Thomas Babington Macaulay was England's most renowned historian. In his magisterial *The History of England from the Accession of James the Second* (1848) Macaulay described Jeffreys in these terms:

> Tenderness for others and respect for himself were feelings alike unknown to him. He acquired a boundless command of the rhetoric in

27   Between £1,400 and £2,100 in today's money.

which the vulgar express hatred and contempt. The profusion of mal-
edictions and vituperative epithets which composed his vocabulary
could hardly have been rivalled in the fishmarket or the beargarden...
Impudence and ferocity sate upon his brow. The glare of his eyes had
a fascination for the unhappy victim on whom they were fixed. Yet his
brow and his eye were less terrible than the savage lines of his mouth.
His yell of fury, as was said by one who had often heard it, sounded
like the thunder of the judgment day... There was a fiendish exulta-
tion in the way in which he pronounced sentence on offenders. Their
weeping and imploring seemed to titillate him voluptuously; and he
loved to scare them into fits by dilating with luxuriant amplification
on all the details of what they were to suffer.[28]

Macaulay based his view of Jeffreys on two principal sources,
Lord Campbell's *Lives of the Lord Chancellors*, and a mass of pamphlets. Whatever his legal merits, Campbell was far from a scrupulous
historian and few would now rely on the *Lives*. The actor/barrister,
H.B. Irving, for example, described its author as 'undeterred by the
absence of authority'.[29] The great lawyer Sir James Fitzjames Stephen
took a similar view.[30] But if Campbell was ill-informed and careless,
others were positively malicious.

As soon as King James II had fled the country a host of pamphlets
appeared vilifying the man in charge of the 'Bloody Assize'; indeed,
the very term is taken from the title of one of them.[31] The story of
this ephemeral 'literature' is complex, but much of it was republished
under the title, *The Western Martyrology*.[32] The following extract con-

28   Thomas Babington Macaulay, *The History of England from the Accession of
James II,* vol. 1 (United Kingdom, The Folio Press, 1985), p. 342.
29   H.B. Irving, *Life of Judge Jeffreys* (London, W. Heinemann, 1898), p. 182.
30   Stephen, *History of the Criminal Law of England*, vol. 1, p. 323.
31   A number of them were collected together in a volume entitled, *The Bloody
Assize, or a complete history of the life of George, Lord Jeffries, etc.*
32   The full title tells it all: *The Western Martyrology or Bloody Assizes containing the Lives, Trials, and Dying-Speeches of all those Eminent Protestants that
Suffer'd in the west of England, and Elsewhere From the Year 1678, to this Time
Together with the Life and Death of George L. Jeffreys. The Fifth Edition. To
which is now added, to make it complete, An Account of the Barbrous Whippings
of Several persons in the West. Also the Trial and Case of Mr. John Tutchin (the
Author of the Observator), with the Cruel Sentence pass'd upon him; and his
petition to K. James to be hang'd: never before Printed. With an Alphabetical*

cerning Jeffreys is representative of its style: 'A certain barbarous joy and pleasure grinned from his brutal soul through his bloody eyes whenever he was sentencing the poor souls to death and torment...'. After Jeffreys had passed, it went on, he left:

> some places quite depopulated, and nothing to be seen in 'em but forsaken Walls, unlucky Gibbets and Ghostly Carcasses. The Trees were laden almost as thick with Quarters as Leaves. The Houses and Steeples covered as close with Heads as at other Times frequently in that Country with Crows and Ravens. Nothing could be liker Hell than all those parts, nothing so like the Devil as he. Caldrons hissing, Carcasses boyling, Pitch and Tar sparkling and glowing, Blood and Limbs boyling, and tearing, and mangling.

The pamphlets were the work of a small but influential coterie of anti-Jacobites based in Axe Yard, Westminster. Their principal author was the Whig writer, John Tutchin. Expelled from school for theft, Tutchin was well-qualified to write of the Bloody Assize because he himself had been brought before Jeffreys at Dorchester for spreading false news of the success of the insurrection. For this, the record shows, he was sentenced to a fine of five marks or imprisonment in lieu and ordered to be whipped.[33] When he came to write the *Martyrology*, however, Tutchin inflated his sentence to one of seven years' imprisonment and a whipping throughout all the market towns of Dorset. This flagrant falsehood, which was repeated by Macaulay and many others, was characteristic of much of his writings.[34] The most notorious of the pamphleteers, however, was the renegade Jesuit and serial perjurer, Titus Oates, in whose lodgings the writers were based. Oates had made his fortune by his denunciation to the authorities of a wholly fictitious 'Popish Plot' to assassinate the King and replace him with the Duke of York. It resulted in the execution of thirty-five wholly innocent Roman Catholics and the imprisonment of many more. Subsequently convicted of perjury, Oates was sentenced by Jeffreys to be imprisoned for life, pilloried and whipped, describing him

---

Table to the Whole. London Printed for John Marshall at the Bible in Grace-Church-Street. MDCCV.

33   See J.G. Muddiman (ed.), *The Bloody Assizes* (Edinburgh, William Hodge & Co., 1929), pp. 136-146.

34   Tutchin contracted the smallpox and was never whipped. He died in a debtors' prison.

justly as 'a shame to mankind'.[35] With his character in the hands of chroniclers like these, Jeffreys' reputation was doomed.

Writing in the 1890s, H.B. Irving was among the first to doubt the accuracy and impartiality of the pamphlets. He described their publisher, the bookseller Dunton, as 'a low class publisher of obscene and sensational literature who, to use his own words, "had been infected with the itch of printing and had indulged his humour to excess"'.[36] In recent years, with growing evidence of the Axe Yard clique's libel industry, it is now possible to make a more balanced judgement of Jeffreys the judge.

THE REAL JEFFREYS

George Jeffreys was born in 1645, the son and grandson of royalist judges. He left university without taking a degree but was called to the Bar at the Inner Temple in 1668 and practised at the Old Bailey and Middlesex sessions, where he was renowned as a skilled cross-examiner. Such was his success that he could afford to buy himself estates in Buckinghamshire, where he played host to Charles II. He married happily and had seven children before his wife's death in 1678. He married again, less happily, the following year. Jeffreys was a hard-drinking man at a time when people drank fiercely, but he was not constantly the worse the wear for drink, as his detractors have suggested.

The Stuart kings were determined to bring the judiciary to heel and Jeffreys proved to be their willing servant.[37] As a result, he rose rapidly through the judicial ranks, being knighted in 1677 and appointed Recorder of London at the age of thirty-three.[38] After a brief period as Chief Justice of Chester, he was made Chief Justice of the Court of King's Bench and, a few months later, a Privy Councillor. Just be-

35   He was released from prison in 1688 and for a few years given a royal pension for his services to government. He died in obscurity in 1705.
36   Irving, *Life of Judge Jeffreys,* p. 265. J.G. Muddiman described Dunton as 'a crack brained Whig'. (Muddiman, *The Bloody Assizes*, p. 6.)
37   They were not to be the last government to want to do so.
38   He lost the appointment in 1680 after his royalist leanings alienated the Whig City.

fore the Monmouth rebellion the new King, James II, appointed him first Baron Jeffreys of Wem. Shortly after the 'Bloody Assize' he was rewarded with the Lord Chancellorship, a post he was to hold for only four years. A firm Anglican, Jeffreys served his Catholic master faithfully, but his influence at court began to wane in proportion to the growth in the number and influence of James' Catholic appointees. In the end, he was one of the few who left his post only after the King had fled his country.

Putting aside the malicious falsehoods of his enemies, how does Jeffreys measure up as a judge?

The seventeenth century was not a vintage era for the English bench. Even Coke, [39] the greatest of the judges of the day, behaved in ways which would horrify us today, while Jeffreys' predecessor, the notorious Scroggs[40] was described by Keeton as touching 'depths of venality and ignorance which have not been passed before or since'.[41] Some critics have taken a similar view of Jeffreys. One of them, for example, wrote that he 'had a limited knowledge of the law and had risen to prominence because of his strict adherence to the court party'.[42] Only the latter part of this sentence was justified; Jeffreys was well-read and maintained a fine library. Contemporary opinion regarded the younger Jeffreys as one of the finest of courtroom advocates and the older man as a popular and witty judge who won particular admiration for rooting out abuses, whether among court clerks, counterfeiters, fraudulent attorneys or the rascally burghers of Bristol.[43]

In his own day, the barrister Roger North, a life-long enemy of Jeffreys, acknowledged that 'when he was in temper and matters indifferent came before him [Jeffreys] became his seat of justice better

39   Sir Edward Coke, Chief Justice of the Common Pleas (1606-13), Chief Justice of the King's Bench (1613-16).
40   Sir William Scroggs, Lord Chief Justice (1678-1681).
41   Keeton, *Trial for Treason*, p. 93.
42   Alfred F. Havighurst, 'The Judiciary and Politics in the Reign of Charles II' *Law Quarterly Review*, 66 (1950), p. 246.
43   The mayor and aldermen had a nice racket going. They offered petty criminals the option of transportation (from which these worthies benefited) instead of hanging, even in cases which did not carry the death sentence.

than any other I saw in his place'.[44] Despite subsequent criticism, Jeffreys was admired in his time for his conduct of the trial of Colonel Algernon Sidney, the republican convicted in 1683 for his undoubted part in the Rye House Plot.[45] And it is difficult to find any criticism of Jeffreys' conduct of civil cases. In modern times J.G. Muddiman even went so far as to write that, 'he was a great lawyer, a great judge, and a great man... [though] by no means exempt from the defects of the judges of his day...'.[46]

As Alfred F. Havighurst has observed, '[T]he determining factors in treason trials [in those days] were the ignorant and easily influenced juries, the immature notions of judicial evidence which then prevailed, the limited defence open to the accused, and the advantages enjoyed by crown counsel'.[47] Given that he had to administer a largely inchoate criminal procedure and impose the bloody sentences that the law then required, a balanced judgement would regard Jeffreys as no worse, perhaps even a little better than most other judges of his era.

How then did Jeffreys deal with his most notorious case?

DID ALICE GET A FAIR TRIAL?

Few trials have been so cloaked in myth as that of Alice Lisle.

---

44   North was the brother of Sir Francis North, Chief Justice of the Common Pleas and Lord Chancellor until his death in 1685.

45   Criticism has been directed at Jeffreys' summing up in that case, but H.B. Irving described it as showing only 'that degree of bias which is usually found in the summings up of strong judges'. It had in any event been agreed by his brother judges. (Irving, *Life of Judge Jeffreys*, p. 177.) In his (unsuccessful) petition for mercy Sidney complained that Jeffreys had interrupted him frequently while he gave evidence; Schofield dismisses the complaint as unfounded: Schofield, *Jeffreys of the Bloody Assize*, p. 85.

46   Muddiman, *The Bloody Assizes*, p. 191. For a contrary view see Whitaker's otherwise excellent study of the Lisle case, *The Regicide's Widow*, which in the present writer's respectful view takes insufficient account of the political dynamics of Jeffreys' day and is inclined to judge seventeenth-century judicial conduct by the standards of the twenty-first century.

47   Havighurst, 'The Judiciary and Politics in the Reign of Charles II' *LQR*, 66, p. 251.

We are fortunate in having what purports to be a complete record of the proceedings, but how accurate is it? It first appeared three decades after the events in question in one of the earliest series of law reports known as Howell's *State Trials*.[48] The materials for this series were collected by John Derby, a dissenting Whig, and edited by Thomas Salmon, a high Tory, for which reason some have seen it as marred by political prejudice. It was on the basis of this report that Macaulay claimed that Jeffreys 'stormed, cursed, and swore in language which no well-bred man would have used at a race or a cockfight.' The *State Trials* report certainly quotes Jeffreys as making lurid denunciations of Dissenters, imprecations and invocations of the Deity, even at one point an invitation to prayer. And he was quick to condemn the witness, Dunne in the most threatening of terms, but were these his very words and, if so, how should we view them?

The *State Trials* fall far short of contemporary standards of law reporting. However, most now agree that their account of Alice Lisle's trial has the ring of truth. George Keeton, for example, wrote that the 'character [of the report] strongly suggests that it was written by an eye-witness, possibly one of the junior counsel for the Crown, and, although the unknown author may have touched up or even exaggerated Jeffreys' interventions, there is a strong air of authenticity about it.'[49] Seymour Schofield claimed that 'the usual garbled utterances are put in Jeffreys' mouth'.[50] And J.G Muddiman flatly denied that Jeffreys used abusive language from the bench, concluding that it was probably an invention.[51]

The present writer, while accepting the possibility of malicious interpolations in the record designed to put Jeffreys in the worst possible light, is inclined to accept the report as it stands, verbal warts and all. Although his reported language in the Lisle case is less temperate than in any of his other trials, Jeffreys, like most judges of his day, felt bound to condemn in vehement terms people he believed to be evildoers and lying witnesses, particularly when their crimes were against the state and its established religion, which the courts were under a

48 (1685) 11 St. Tr. 298.
49 Keeton, *Trial for Treason*, p. 104.
50 Schofield, *Jeffreys of the Bloody Assize*, p. 289.
51 Muddiman, *The Bloody Assizes*, p. 28.

particular duty to uphold. H.B. Irving may have got it right when he wrote that Jeffreys' tone and language, 'were always those of a passionate and irritable man, easily stirred to indignation by the presence of those he disliked...' There were, however, two other reasons for his irritability and intemperate language at Winchester.

First, the Assize judges were under great pressure to get through an extensive list in a ridiculously short space of time. As Whitaker notes, 'five judges had four weeks, including traveling time and weekends, in which to dispose of not merely 1,500 cases from the rebellion, but another 300 or so of everyday crime.'[52] The trial of Alice Lisle took only six hours from arraignment to finding of guilt, but courts were more expeditious in those days. What is not generally known is that Jeffreys had to work in considerable physical discomfort. For many years he had suffered from an excruciatingly painful illness, the side effects of which often include nausea and vomiting. The condition seems to have been particularly distressing during the Bloody Assize. Writing to Secretary of State Sunderland from his lodgings at Dorchester, Jeffreys implored, 'I am at this time so tortured with the stone that I must beg your Lordship's intercession to his Majesty for the incoherence of what I have advertised to you and his Majesty and the trouble of'. He asked leave for his letter to be written by his servant.[53] And at Bristol, he declared himself to be 'mortified by a fit of the stone'.[54] Jeffreys could be justly criticized for failing to disqualify himself from sitting when suffering from such a debilitating condition, but that it added to his natural intolerance of liars and rebels there can be little doubt.

How then did Jeffreys actually conduct the trial of Alice Lisle?

The most notorious calumny, still repeated in some publications and web sites, is the suggestion that Jeffreys bullied the jury into returning a guilty verdict. It is said that they returned a verdict of 'Not Guilty' on three occasions, each of which was rejected by Jeffreys with threats and imprecations, until in desperation they brought in a verdict of 'Guilty'. The only problem with this dramatic story is

---

52   Whitaker, *The Regicide's Widow*, p. 45.
53   Irving, *Life of Judge Jeffreys,* p. 289.
54   *Ibid.,* p. 302.

that it has absolutely no basis in the record.[55] It seems to have had its origin in the writings of Bishop Burnet, another unreliable historian,[56] who may have confused the trial with one which took place at the Old Bailey in 1670, where exactly these events are recorded as having occurred.[57]

By far the commonest criticism of Jeffreys is his supposed brow-beating and abuse of witnesses and defendants.[58] Some of it is obviously fanciful. Macaulay, for example, was to write of Jeffreys' angry countenance when addressing prisoners. Now, it is famously difficult to find the mind's construction in the face, but, as P.J. Helm has pointed out, Kneller's engraving of Jeffreys in London's National Portrait Gallery does not bear out this picture of the man. (Neither, it must be added, do the paintings of Jeffreys by John Michael Wright and William Wolfgang Claret in the same collection.) The only basis, on which Macaulay's comment could possibly have been made, were sources now wholly discredited.[59]

Jeffreys has been widely condemned for 'taking over the prosecution' of Alice Lisle. If the only report of the trial available to us is to be believed (and it first appeared thirty-four years after the event) there is force in this criticism, at least when judged against present-day standards. Former prosecutors when elevated to the bench have often been tempted to injudicious interventions in the questioning of witnesses, and Jeffreys was no exception. It would be wrong however to transpose modern scruples onto an age in which they would scarcely have been recognized. Whitaker suggests that 'such behaviour was barely acceptable in Jeffreys' day', but the key question is whether it affected the outcome of the trial.

---

55   It is true that Jeffreys is reported as having expressed impatience at the time the jury were taking, but they returned to court before he could do anything about it. Trials moved much more swiftly in those days.
56   The bishop may also have been the source of the suggestion that Alice fell asleep during the trial.
57   The trial of William Penn and other Quakers, Samuel Starling presiding.
58   See, for example, Stephen, *History of the Criminal Law of England*, vol. 1, p. 413.
59   Macaulay himself acknowledged that 'some stories which have been told concerning [Jeffreys] are false or exaggerated'.

It is certainly the case that Jeffreys did not hesitate to let the jury know his opinion of the witness Dunne in terms which we would today regard as extravagant. (This 'strange, prevaricating, shuffling, sniveling, lying rascal'). But florid language of this sort was common in the seventeenth century and, even if accurately recorded, the verbal abuse of a transparently lying witness is an entirely different matter from abuse of the accused; and that is something to which Jeffreys never stooped. He has, it is true, been criticized for shouting at Alice Lisle,[60] but this was probably due to the fact, as clearly recorded in the *State Trials*, that she was hard of hearing.

It is to Jeffreys' credit that he displayed a proper concern that this elderly lady should understand how the trial was going to be conducted and be given a fair opportunity to present her case. Realizing that the prisoner might be 'ignorant of the forms of law', Jeffreys went to the trouble of explaining to her exactly how a trial proceeds by way of the examination and cross-examination of witnesses and the making of speeches. Furthermore, the report states that at the commencement of the proceedings:

> … the prisoner desiring, by reason of her age and infirmities (being thick of hearing) some friends of hers might be allowed to stand by her and inform her of what passed in the court; one Matthew Browne was named, and allowed of by the court to give her all assistance that he could in that matter.

Browne was a deputy clerk of the peace whose legal knowledge Alice appears to have drawn on more than once during the trial. (It may have been he who suggested that she should use nineteen of her thirty-five peremptory challenges to remove from the jury persons she believed to have been ill-disposed towards her.)

Jeffreys can justly be criticized for his less than even-handed charging of the jury. At one point he referred wholly improperly to the supposed role of Alice's late husband in the conviction of Penruddock's father. Interestingly, the author of the report in the *State Trials* appends a footnote to this reference, 'This was an unjust insinuation only to prejudice the Jury, being, *as the Chief Justice owned*, nothing to the purpose for which it should have been left alone, and tho'

---

60   No contemporary basis for this criticism can be found.

he said, it ought not to influence the Case, yet he knew it was very likely to do so.' (Emphasis added.) Every bit as prejudicial was what Jeffreys failed to say. Twenty years later, *The Bloody Assize* reported that, on the scaffold, Alice handed to the sheriff a paper containing her 'last words'. Though probably fictitious,[61] this 'speech' contained the following complaint:

> I have been told, That the Court ought to be Council [*sic*] for the Prisoner: Instead of Advice, there was Evidence given from thence, which (tho' it was but Hearsay) might possibly affect my Jury. My Defence was such as might be expected from a weak Woman; but such as it was, I never heard it repeated again to the Jury.

There was force in this criticism, whoever made it. Jeffreys failed in charging the jury to address Alice Lisle's principal defence, namely that she was unaware of Hickes' status as a rebel, but thought him to be merely a fugitive Dissenter. The summing up was also deficient in that it took the jury themselves to pick up on another issue, namely whether Alice had given food and shelter to Hickes *after* she had become aware that he had been among the rebel soldiers. In the end it mattered not a jot since the jury, after having been properly though tardily instructed by the judge, returned a verdict of 'Guilty', which implied their disbelief of her version of the events at Moyle's Court. Ultimately, while Jeffreys' conduct of the trial was not faultless, it was not the judge's conduct but the strength of the evidence against Alice which secured her conviction.

'A WEAKNESS VERY NEARLY ALLIED TO VIRTUE'

Alice Lisle had certainly given refuge to a fugitive traitor, but that was not an offence then, any more than it is now, unless it could be proved that she was also aware of his status as such. It is not possible to be certain from the evidence given at the trial that Alice knew of Hickes' rebel activities – as distinct from his nonconformist views – when she agreed to take him in, nor is there much reason to doubt Alice's claim that she was unaware that when he came to her house

---

61   Muddiman, *The Bloody Assizes*, pp. 28-29. Whitaker in *The Regicide's Widdow* suggests otherwise.

he would be accompanied by Nelthorpe. However, once the two of them were safely ensconced in Moyle's Court, it was not long before she was made aware that both were soldiers fleeing from Monmouth's defeated army. (It is difficult to believe that she failed to enquire of Nelthorpe's identity and pick up on his notorious outlawry). By giving them food and continuing to give them shelter knowing them to be traitors sought by the law, Alice committed the offence with which she was charged. But is that all there is to be said?

Let us assume that Alice's account of what she knew of her guests is correct up to the time of their arrival; and the evidence does not contradict her on this. She had agreed to give refuge to a fellow Dissenter. It was only when she quizzed him and his unexpected companion that she became aware that they were both fugitive traitors. In a world where the law is always observed in strictest detail she would then have promptly kicked out both her guests, or at the very least reported them to the authorities. She did neither, believing no doubt that they would be under her roof for only a short space of time and that, anyway, it was only a minor transgression. In this she would have been seriously mistaken, but how many of us would have done what the law required, and evicted or betrayed a fellow believer and his friend once they were under our roof?

And that brings us to the question of sentence.

The law traditionally discriminates in punishment between the actual criminal (the principal in the first degree) and those who assisted him (the accessories). But this has never been the case with high treason. In Alice's day the law required that all parties to the crime should be sentenced to a horrible death, no matter the degree of their participation. Macaulay commented on this barbaric rule:

> The feeling which makes the most loyal subject shrink from the thought of giving up to a shameful death the rebel who, vanquished, hunted down, and in mortal agony, begs for a morsel of bread and a cup of water, may be a weakness; but it is surely a weakness very nearly allied to virtue, a weakness which, constituted as human beings are, we can hardly eradicate from the mind without eradicating many noble and benevolent sentiments.

Alice's tragedy was, not her conviction, but her sentence of death. This was not Jeffreys' choice; it was the law of the land and only one person could amend it. Jeffreys went out of his way to suggest that Alice should seek the King's pardon. It was the King, not Jeffreys, who refused it. And so it was that this pious old lady was sent to her death by a monarch fearful of losing his throne for an act of mercy which few compassionate people could have resisted making. But history sometimes balances the bad with the good. Three years later James II was swept off his throne with not a hand lifted in his defence and was to spend the rest of his life in bitter exile. Jeffreys died in the Tower of London awaiting trial on charges of treason. He was a month short of his forty-fourth birthday.

THE CHATTERLEY AFFAIR
THE TRIAL OF PENGUIN BOOKS, 1960

In high-Victorian England, sex was viewed officially as a function of the animal kingdom, permitted to human beings only within the marriage bond and provided that neither party derived much pleasure from it. Practice, of course, was different. This attitude took half a century to wither, its final passing being marked by the well-known lines of England's most sex-obsessed librarian:

Sexual intercourse began
In nineteen sixty-three
(which was rather late for me) -
Between the end of the "Chatterley" ban
And the Beatles' first LP.

Annus Mirabilis, Philip Larkin (1967).

The 'Chatterley ban' was of course the prosecution of Penguin Books for publishing D.H. Lawrence's novel, *Lady Chatterley's Lover*. Strictly speaking, it was not a ban since, as explained in the introduction, censorship of the press had been abandoned in England for over three hundred years. Nevertheless, this *cause célèbre* marked the end of an era.

Lady Chatterley's Lover is the story of a love affair between the wife of a Derbyshire mine owner and the gamekeeper on her husband's estate. Twenty-three year old Connie Reid – no virgin – had married twenty-nine year old Clifford Chatterley in 1917 while he was on leave from the war. He returned to the front, but was 'shipped over to England again six months later, more or less in bits'. Clifford became a baronet on the death of his father and when her husband was released from hospital in 1920 Connie had to keep house in the gloomy family seat of Wragby Hall in reduced circumstances. Impotent, paralyzed from the hips down and in a wheel chair, the only arousal Clifford can obtain is through the ministrations of his nurse

D.H. Lawrence circa 1910 (Topfoto)

and companion, Mrs. Bolton. Sexually frustrated and longing for a child, Connie throws herself briefly into the arms of a young playwright, and then her husband's gamekeeper, Mellors. Oliver Mellors was formerly a blacksmith who had left an unhappy marriage to join the army. Despite being commissioned, he had retained his local dialect when he wished to use it. Their relationship, both spiritual and sexual, is the central feature of the book. When Connie becomes pregnant by Mellors she goes to Venice in an attempt to conceal the paternity of her child. The ruse does not succeed and Sir Clifford refuses to give her the divorce she desires. Connie's father, Sir Malcolm was at first offended by Mellors' humble birth, but on meeting him found common cause in their open attitude to sex. Mellors is dismissed from his job and at the end of the book is waiting for a divorce in order to be united with his lover.

Clifford is portrayed throughout the book as a cold and insensitive intellectual, interested only in money, in contrast to the uncouth but earthy Mellors. In a final letter to Connie, Mellors describes Clifford's miners in language which sums up one of the book's main themes: 'They're a sad lot, a deadened lot of men: dead to their women, dead to life. The young ones scoot about on motor-bikes with girls, and jazz when they get a chance. But they're very dead. And it needs money. Money poisons you when you've got it, and starves you when you haven't ... If things go on as they are, there's nothing lies in the future but death and destruction for these industrial masses.'

Ignoring for the moment the difficulty of believing in a gamekeeper who can describe his fellow men as 'these industrial masses', Lawrence manages to pack a load of significance into this graphic tale of love between the classes, lambasting at the same time the evils of war, the English class system, the ill-effects of industrialization and, most famously, the need for frankness in matters of sex. It was the last that was to get him into trouble.

CENSORSHIP IN ENGLAND

For centuries, the courts in England had treated erotic 'literature' as a form of criminal libel. At first, it was necessary to prove that the 'libel' could give rise to a breach of the peace, but this was effectively done away with in 1727 when the notorious pornographer Edmund Curll was convicted of publishing *Venus in the Cloister*, an imaginary conversation between two nuns. The dubious distinction of being the first novel to be prosecuted is held by *Fanny Hill or Memoirs of a Woman of Pleasure*. *Fanny Hill* was written in 1748 by John Cleland while in debtor's prison and sold for £20 to pay his debts. The prosecution seems to have lapsed after the book was withdrawn from publication. Nowadays, the *Dictionary of National Biography* describes the book as 'a stylistic tour de force'. At the time of writing, it is being serialized on television.

The prosecution of 'dirty books' was made easier by The Obscene Publications Act of 1857. It was known as Lord Campbell's Act after its promoter, the Lord Chief Justice, who famously described pornography as 'poison more deadly than prussic acid, strychnine or arsenic'. Even at the time it was recognized that there would be difficulties in defining obscenity, but the problem was soon to be resolved. Henry Scott, a Protestant zealot, published a virulently anti-Catholic booklet entitled, *The Confessional Unmasked; Shewing of the Depravity of the Romish Priesthood, the Iniquity of the Confessional, and the Questions Put to Females in Confession*. Copies were seized and ordered to be destroyed by the Wolverton magistrates. Scott appealed to the Recorder,[1] Benjamin Hicklin, who declined to confirm the order on the ground that the book had been written in order to expose the Catholic church and not for reasons of obscenity. His decision was overturned by a Divisional Court of the Queen's Bench. Giving the judgment of the court, Sir Alexander Cockburn, Chief Justice of the Common Pleas, held that intent was irrelevant because a man is presumed to intend the results of his actions. His judgment is best remembered, however, for what was to become known as the Hicklin test: 'I think the test of obscenity is this: whether the tendency of the matter charged as obscenity is to deprave and corrupt those whose minds are open to such immoral influences, and into whose hands a publication of this sort may fall.'[2]

The need to judge obscenity against those whose minds are open to immoral influences led the writer John Chandos to observe that 'for

1 In England a judicial appointment.
2 *R v Hicklin* (1868) LR 3 QB 360.

the next ninety-one years' after Hicklin, 'literature in England and for almost as long in America was subject to a control designed to preserve the innocence or ignorance of a hypothetical adolescent girl, and at times it would seem, a feeble-minded one.'[3]

While few jibbed with the law being used to seize and destroy pornography plain and simple, the suppression of serious factual works gave increasing concern. When in 1877 Charles Bradlaugh and Annie Besant published *The Fruits of Philosophy*, a pamphlet arguing the case for birth control, they were charged with 'unlawfully and wickedly devising and intending to vitiate and corrupt the morals of youth and of others, and to bring them into a state of wickedness, lewdness and debauchery'. The formidable Annie spoke in court for nearly two days in defence of the pamphlet and was rewarded with cheers from the public gallery. Chief Justice Cockburn expressed sympathy for the authors' motives: 'A more ill advised and more injudicious prosecution never was instituted.' Nevertheless, he felt bound to take a strict view of the law; if the pamphlet was of an obscene character the authors' motives were irrelevant. The debates in the jury room were so energetic that they could be heard in court. The ensuing verdict was an obvious compromise: the jury found that the pamphlet was calculated to deprave public morals, but entirely exonerated the defendants from any corrupt motive in publishing it. Cockburn ruled that this gnomic utterance should be treated as a verdict of 'Guilty' and sentenced each of the two authors to six months imprisonment and a fine. Despite the fact that their convictions were later overturned on a technicality,[4] serious writings continued to be condemned. Twenty years after *The Fruits of Philosophy*, the first medical study of homosexuality, Havelock Ellis's *Sexual Inversion*, had to be withdrawn from publication to avoid prosecution.

Nor did serious fiction escape. In 1915 police seized a thousand copies of Lawrence's novel, *The Rainbow*. The prosecution described it as 'a mass of obscenity of thought, idea and action throughout', and

3   John Chandos (ed.), *'To Deprave and Corrupt' – Original Studies in the Nature and Definition of 'Obscenity'* (New York, Association Press, 1962), pp. 27-28.
4   The indictment failed to specify which words were 'indecent'. *Bradlaugh v R.* (1878) QBD 607.

the Bow Street magistrate ordered its destruction. It is not surprising that Lawrence was unable to find a publisher for his next novel, *Women In Love*.[5] Perhaps the most notable proceedings, however, concerned Radclyffe Hall's novel, *The Well of Loneliness*, which, like *The Rainbow*, dealt sympathetically with the issue of lesbianism. In 1928, despite generally favourable reviews, copies of the book were seized at Dover and application made to the Bow Street Magistrate for a destruction order. Norman Birkett KC, acting for the publishers, Jonathan Cape, sought to tender thirty-nine witnesses to attest to the book's merits, but the magistrate refused to hear them: 'A book may be a fine piece of literature,' he observed, quite correctly within the law as it then was, 'and yet obscene.' An appeal to Quarter Sessions was of no avail.

But literature did have its occasional victories, and one of them showed just how far the judges were prepared to go within the confines of the law. In 1953 the publishing house Secker & Warburg and its radical chairman Frederic Warburg were prosecuted for publishing Stanley Kaufmann's novel, *The Philanderer*.[6] The judge, Mr. Justice Stable, delivered a judgment which, like the judge himself, was notable for its clarity and compassion. After reviewing the changing attitudes to sex throughout the ages he said:

> The charge is not that the tendency of the book is either to shock or to disgust. That is not a criminal offence. The charge is that the tendency of the book is to corrupt and deprave. Then you say: 'Well, corrupt and deprave whom?' to which the answer is: those whose minds are open to such immoral influences and into whose hands a publication of this sort may fall. What, exactly, does that mean? Are we to take our literary standards as being the level of something that is suitable for the decently brought up young female aged fourteen? Or do we go even further back than that and are we to be reduced to the sort of books that one reads as a child in the nursery? The answer to that is: Of course not. A mass of literature, great literature, from many angles, is wholly unsuitable for reading by the adolescent, but that does not mean that a publisher is guilty of a criminal offence for making those works available to the general public. I venture to suggest that you

5   *The Rainbow* and *Women in Love* were originally intended to form one novel entitled, *The Sisters*.
6   Published in the United States as *The Tightrope*.

give a thought to what is the function of the novel. I am not talking about historical novels when people write a story of some past age. I am talking about the contemporary novelist. By 'the contemporary novelist', I mean the novelist who writes about his contemporaries, who holds up a mirror to the society of his own day. The function of the novel is not merely to entertain contemporaries; it stands as a record or a picture of the society when it was written. Those of us who enjoy the great Victorian novelists get such understanding as we have of that great age from chroniclers such as Thackeray, Dickens, Trollope, Surtees, and many others of that age.

The Philanderer, he pointed out, had been written in America:

If we are going to read novels about how things go in New York, it would not be of much assistance, would it, if, contrary to the fact, we were led to suppose that in New York no unmarried woman or teenager has disabused her mind of the idea that babies are brought by storks or are sometimes found in cabbage patches or under goose-berry bushes? ... You may agree that it is a good book, or a bad book, or a moderate book. It is at least a book. It is the creation of a human mind and it depicts people created by the author in the environment in which that portion or portions of their lives with which the book deals were spent. You may agree or you may not—I do not know—that it is not mere pornographic literature, the filthy, bawdy muck that is just filth for filth's sake... the Crown say: 'Well, that is sheer filth.' Is it? Is the act of sexual passion sheer filth? It may be an error of taste to write about it. It may be a matter in which, perhaps, old-fashioned people would mourn the reticence that was observed in these matters yesterday, but is it sheer filth? That is a matter which you have to consider and ultimately to decide.

He concluded:

The literature of the world from the earliest times when people first learned to write so far as we have it today—literature sacred and pro-fane, poetry and prose—represents the sum total of human thought throughout the ages and from all the varied civilizations the human pilgrimage has traversed. Are we going to say in England that our contemporary literature is to be measured by what is suitable for the fourteen-year-old schoolgirl to read? You must consider that aspect of the matter. And there is another aspect of the matter which I should like you to consider before you come to your conclusion. I do not suppose there is a decent man or woman in this court who does not wholeheartedly believe that pornography, filthy books, ought to be stamped out and suppressed. They are not literature. They have got no message; they have got no inspiration; they have got no thought. They have got nothing. They are just filth, and, of course, that ought to be stamped out; but in our desire for a healthy society, if we drive the criminal law too far, further than it ought to go, is not there a risk that there will be a revolt, a demand for a change in the law, so that the pendulum will swing too far the other way and allow to creep in things that under the law as it exists today we can exclude and keep out? Remember what I said when I began. You are dealing with a criminal charge. This is not a question of what you think is a desirable book to read. It is a criminal charge of publishing a work with a tendency to corrupt and deprave those into whose hands it may fall.

The jury of nine men and three women returned a verdict of 'Not Guilty'.[7] Stables had pushed the Hicklin judgment to its limits; only legislation could do away with it altogether. Fortunately, there were people willing to work for it.

THE LAW REFORMED

In an imaginative attempt to liberalise the law the Society of Authors set up a committee consisting of representatives of the Home Office, the Director of Public Prosecutions, the police, the Public Morality Council, publishers, writers and printers, chaired by its president, the redoubtable Sir Alan Herbert. The draft Bill which the committee drew up would have allowed prosecutions only where the 'dominant purpose' of the authors was an intention to corrupt or a recklessness as to whether the readers were corrupted or not. Evidence of artistic merit, they recommended, should be allowed.

The Act as it finally emerged was an unhappy compromise. It retained the Hicklin test of a 'tendency to deprave and corrupt', but required the effect of the work to be judged by reference to its likely audience rather than the most vulnerable members of society. There is a logical contradiction here, as the Court of Appeal later acknowledged in proceedings involving Hubert Selby Jr.'s book, *Last Exit to Brooklyn*: 'The legislature can hardly have contemplated that a book

7   *R v Martin Secker Warburg Ltd* [1954] 1 WLR 1138.

which tended to corrupt and deprave the average reader or the majority of those likely to read it could be justified as being for the public good on any ground.' The court got round this by holding that the test should be whether the effect of the book was to tend to deprave and corrupt a significant proportion of those persons likely to read it.[8]

The Act also introduced a requirement that the work should be judged as a whole, rather than by its isolated parts. Most importantly, however, it introduced a new defence of justification whereby the publisher would be acquitted if he could prove that publication is 'in the interests of science, literature, art or learning, or of other objects of general concern'. For this purpose, 'the opinion of experts as to the literary, artistic, scientific or other merits of an article' was made admissible in court.

It did not take long for the new law to be tested, and the case involved one of the most famous writers of the twentieth century.

'BERT'

David Herbert Lawrence, known to his family as 'Bert', was born on 11 September 1885 in a colliery village in Nottinghamshire, the fourth child of Arthur John Lawrence and Lydia Lawrence, née Beardsall. Arthur was a coal miner who spent much of his wages on drink, Lydia a former school teacher from Kent who had married for love. Determined that her son should not go down the pit like her husband and his three brothers, she ran a small clothes shop to make ends meet.

Bert, never happy at home, won a scholarship to Nottingham High School but did not fit in with the middle-class pupils and left at the age of sixteen to became a clerk at a surgical appliances factory. In the same year his older brother Ernest died of erysipelas; it was a traumatic loss and Bert went down with pneumonia. From then on, Lydia pinned all her hopes on Bert. A young friend, Jessie Chambers, introduced him to literature and he became a pupil teacher, ultimately obtaining a teaching diploma from Nottingham University. After winning a short story competition Lawrence went to London where he taught at an elementary school and wrote poetry in the evenings. His

---

8   *R. v Calder and Boyars* [1968] 3 All ER 644.

first novel, *The White Peacock* was published in 1910; shortly afterwards, he was devastated by the death of his mother, with whom he had always been close. In 1912 he met thirty-three year old Emma Maria Frieda Johanna Weekley, née von Richtofen, then the unhappily married wife of his former professor at Nottingham. When she visited her relations in Germany Lawrence went along as well and persuaded her to leave her husband. In 1913 he published his first major novel, *Sons and Lovers*, which was based on his childhood and early loves. The couple returned to England at the outbreak of the Great War and, after Frieda's divorce, got married. During the winter of 1914 he met the society hostess Lady Ottoline Morrell and began moving in literary circles. After *The Rainbow* had been seized by police Lawrence and Frieda retreated to Cornwall, where they hoped to find privacy from censorship and the war, which he found repugnant. He did, but it did not last long.

Lawrence had been twice declared unfit for military service and suspicions were rife about him and his German wife who were living near the shipping lanes. The result was a military exclusion order which meant that the couple had to leave Cornwall. On his thirty-third birthday Lawrence was finally declared fit to be 'conscripted for light non-military duties', but peace supervened before he could be called up. After the war, and for Lawrence, a bad bout of influenza, the nearly penniless couple left England to embark on what was to prove a lifelong perambulation around the world, finally settling in Taos, New Mexico. In 1925 his congenital chest weakness was diagnosed as tuberculosis and the couple returned to Europe.

As well as being a novelist Lawrence was also a gifted poet and painter. In 1929 the manuscript of his volume of poems, *Pansies* was seized by the Post Office. (They protested that it had been in the course of a routine investigation, but the journalist Alan Travis claims that all Lawrence's post was being opened as a matter of course.) On the advice of the Director of Public Prosecutions, his publisher Martin Secker omitted fourteen poems from the published work. Later that year, police seized a number of Lawrence's paintings which were being displayed at a London gallery. The eighty-two year old magistrate before whom they were brought refused to hear evidence on the merit of the paintings, observing, 'The most splendidly painted picture in the universe might be obscene'. Of this decision Lawrence wrote – with perhaps less than his usual flair:

Ah my nice pictures, let me sponge you very gently
to sponge away the slime
that ancient eyes have left on you, where obscene eyes have crawled
leaving nasty films upon you every time.

Later that year Lawrence became ill and went abroad in search of a healthy climate. He died in the South of France on 2 March 1930 at the age of forty-four and his ashes were taken to Taos for interment in a memorial chapel.

Lawrence had been a literary and artistic radical throughout his life, but his scandalous reputation rests almost entirely on one book.

THE BOOK

The first draft of *Lady Chatterley's Lover* was written during a brief visit to England in 1926. It was revised later that year, when much of the controversial content was added. The final version was written in just five weeks. Unable to find a publisher, Lawrence had the book printed privately in Florence in July 1928 and sold through friends at £2 a copy. By December, the first print of a thousand copies had been sold out. Pirated editions were produced abroad and grew in numbers after Lawrence's death. Two versions of the book were published in England and America in 1932. The jacket sleeve of one of them contained an endorsement by Frieda, claiming that it 'suggests to the greatest possible extent the original's strength and vigor'. Suggest it might, but in fact, every description of the sex act and all four-letter words which could have been regarded as remotely objectionable had been left out. Lawrence's reputation went into decline after the war until 1956 when England's foremost paperback publisher, Penguin Books, published a biography of him by the greatly respected critic, F.R. Leavis.

Penguin followed this up in May 1960 by announcing that they were going to bring out both *Women in Love* and *Lady Chatterley's Lover* in order to mark the thirtieth anniversary of the author's death. Their intention was to print 200,000 copies of the unexpurgated text at 3*s*. 6*d*. a copy. Questions were asked of the Attorney General and the printers took fright. When Penguin turned to another printer the trade was informed and the Director of Public Prosecutions, Sir Theobald (Toby) Mathew, sent a police officer to Penguin to find out their intentions. Sir Allen Lane, the company's founder and chairman, duly confirmed their plans and supplied the Director with a dozen copies of the book. Both sides were content to see it used as a test case of the new Act. It only remained for the Director to obtain counsel's opinion and this was provided by Mervyn Griffith-Jones QC, senior Treasury counsel at the Old Bailey. He advised that, 'In my opinion the unexpurgated version of *Lady Chatterley's Lover* – a proof copy of which I have read – is obscene and a prosecution for publishing an obscene libel would be justified. Indeed if no action is taken in respect of this publication it will make proceedings against any other novel very difficult.' The Attorney General, Sir Reginald Manningham-Buller, was asked if he agreed with the decision to prosecute; he replied that he had only read the first four chapters, 'but if the remainder of the book is of the same character I have no doubt you were right to start proceedings – and I hope you get a conviction'. Documents recently unearthed by Alan Travis suggest that the Home Office were also consulted on the decision. Some have seen this degree of consultation as incompatible with the Director's duty to decide whether to prosecute or not, but in fact it is not because that decision often involves dimensions beyond the merely legal.

The prosecution was received with incredulity in literary circles; after all, the 1959 Act was thought to have done away with the possibility of serious writing being condemned as pornography. The much respected commentator Bernard Levin wrote in *The Spectator*, 'The case promises to be one of the most splendid and uproarious shows ever put on at public expense... It is surely going to be difficult for the prosecution to find anybody taken seriously by the literary or academic worlds to swear that publication of *Lady Chatterley's Lover* is not in the public interest as a literary event and that its tendency would be to deprave and corrupt those who might read it.' Documents only recently released from the National Archives reveal that in August 1960 Manningham-Buller wanted to prosecute Levin for these remarks.

Fortunately, Sir Jocelyn Simon, the Solicitor General, had more sense and nothing came of the Attorney's ridiculous suggestion.[9]

Griffith-Jones, to whom the conduct of the prosecution was entrusted, had prosecuted many high profile cases with distinction. He was an experienced advocate of orthodox views with a strong line in sarcasm. Gerald Gardiner QC was engaged for the defence.[10] The sixty year old Gardiner had enjoyed a conventional career, from Harrow School and the Coldstream Guards to Oxford and the Bar. It is worth noting, however, that he had been rusticated at university for publishing a pamphlet attacking restrictions on women undergraduates, subsequently became chairman of the legal campaigning body, 'Justice' and ended his career as one of the great reforming Chancellors of recent times.[11] Gardiner's first task was to consider how best to make use of the new power to call expert witnesses. He and his instructing solicitors, Rubenstein, Nash and Co. assembled seventy people of distinction in the literary, political, legal, religious and sociological spheres to give evidence for the defence; it was a veritable line-up of the literati.

As Bernard Levin had correctly anticipated, the prosecution did not have as easy a time, in fact, their efforts to find reputable witnesses for the prosecution ended in total failure. Alan Travis describes in *Bound and Gagged* how, when Helen Gardner FRA, Reader in Renaissance Literature at St. Hilda's College, Oxford, and a much respected literary critic, was invited to give evidence for the Crown she replied:

> I am strongly in favour of the completion of the Penguin edition of the works of D.H. Lawrence by the publication of the full text of *Lady Chatterley's Lover*. I should therefore be unwilling to give any assistance to those who are desirous of suppressing the work. I do not consider the literary merit of this particular work is an important or indeed relevant, consideration. It is in my view a serious work of literature which merits serious consideration. Its merits and defects as a work of literature present a critical problem to which I am not prepared to give a hasty answer... .'

9   *The Times*, 29 June 2007.
10   His juniors were Jeremy Hutchinson and Richard Du Cann.
11   The Lord High Chancellor was then head of the judiciary.

In the result only one witness was called for the prosecution, and he was a police officer who gave formal evidence of having received the books from Penguin. (It is an interesting question, not ventilated at the trial, whether this amounted to 'publication' within the meaning of the law.)

THE OLD BAILEY

The trial began on 20 October 1960 in Court Number 1 at the Old Bailey before Mr. Justice Byrne. Two of Penguin's directors were seated at counsel's table, but the dock was empty, since only the company and not its directors had been charged. This fact was to be a source of friction between counsel when early on in the proceedings Gerald Gardiner appeared to suggest that the prosecution had refrained from prosecuting any director solely in order to avoid the jury having to convict a human being. Griffith-Jones denied the suggestion indignantly and it still rankled at the end of the trial. (Can you imagine the comments, he asked in his closing speech, if he had put Sir Allen Lane, one of England's most respected publishers, in the dock?)

Griffith-Jones opened the proceedings with a meticulously fair description of the law, referring to Stable's judgment in *The Philanderer* case, in which he had appeared for the prosecution. Without any expert witnesses to contradict the experts on the other side, he decided to direct all his efforts to disproving the defence that publication of the book was 'in the interests of literature, art, science, learning or other object of general concern'. He was willing to concede that Lawrence was 'a well-recognized and indeed a great writer', but claimed that *Lady Chatterley's Lover* 'sets upon a pedestal promiscuous and adulterous intercourse. It commends, indeed it sets out to commend, sensuality almost as a virtue (Gardiner would later put this phrase to his witnesses with monotonous regularity). It encourages, and indeed advocates, coarseness and vulgarity of language.' Then, in a passage for which the name of Griffith-Jones will always be remembered, he asked the jury, 'Would you approve your young sons, young daughters – because girls can read as well as boys – reading this book? Is it a book you would have lying around in your own house? Is it a book you would wish even your wife or your servants to read?'

It is difficult to comprehend all the inappropriate preconceptions inherent in this simple question. As the writer and ex-policeman, C.H. Rolph, was to observe, '[it] had a visible – and risible – effect on the jury and may well have been the first nail in the prosecution's coffin.'[12]

Griffith-Jones drew attention to two elements of the book. First, the frequency and pleasure with which Connie and Mellors had had intercourse: 'You may think that this book, if the descriptions had been confined to the first occasion on which sexual intercourse is described would be a very much better book than it is'. The book, he went on, contained thirteen descriptions of sex in which only the locus in quo was different. '[T]he emphasis,' he said, 'is always on the pleasure, the satisfaction and the sensuality of the episode'. To most of those in court he must have seemed to be suggesting that sexual satisfaction was something to be deplored, and that if it had to take place the fewer the occasions the better. He must have exercised great restraint not to have mentioned rabbits.

He particularly objected to the language that Mellors and Connie used to each other in referring to sex. The prosecuting team had gone through the book meticulously counting the number of times each four-letter-word had been used and Griffith-Jones spelled them out to the jury one by one in all their Anglo-Saxon glory, a performance which must have seemed distinctly odd in the sterile surroundings of the Old Bailey. Why this tactic was not objected to by the defence is difficult to understand because the 1959 Act required the effect of the book to be 'taken as a whole'.

Replying for Penguin Books, Gerald Gardiner claimed that, far from promoting adultery, Lawrence was a supporter of marriage, anxious to make clear that promiscuity does not lead to satisfaction. Lawrence's Anglo-Saxon words were the language that someone like a gamekeeper would have used. He suggested that in the 'attitude of shame ... which very large numbers of people have towards sex in any form, the jury might think that 'it is not at all easy for fathers and mothers to find words to describe that which, most properly, they

12   C.H. Rolph, *The Trial of Lady Chatterley* (Harmondsworth, Penguin, 1961), p. 17.

want to describe to their children.' It was a curious tactic to suggest that parents would find it helpful to employ words which were then regarded as the language of the gutter to instruct their little ones in matters of sex. The day ended with the jury going to read the book in the retiring room.

The first defence witness was called the following day. He was Graham Hough, a lecturer in English and Fellow of Christ's College, Cambridge. The book, he said, was concerned with the relations between men and women, with their sexual relations, with the nature of proper marriage. The sexual passages, although the centre of the book, occupied no more than thirty pages in a book of three hundred pages. They were not repetitive and were necessary to its purpose. Under cross-examination Mr. Hough conceded that there were a number of passages in the book which 'did not come off at all'; some, he admitted, were failures, some 'utterly, disastrously bad'. Under gentle re-examination from Gerald Gardiner Mr. Hough described how it was Lawrence's practice to repeat a key word in order to gain emphasis. Gardiner also managed skilfully to elicit a number of quotations from other literary critics praising Lawrence before Griffith-Jones intervened to stop him. Next in the box was a far more heavyweight witness.

Helen Gardner, who had turned down the offer to give evidence for the prosecution, declared that Lawrence was 'certainly among the six greatest, the five or six greatest writers in English literature of this century, taking the first sixty years of the twentieth century.' She did not regard '*Lady Chatterley's Lover*' as a wholly successfully novel. 'I wouldn't rank it among the greatest of the works that Lawrence wrote, though I think that certain passages of it have very great literary merit, and indeed are among the greatest things he wrote.' The Anglo-Saxon words were not disgusting in themselves. By using them so frequently Lawrence had gone far to redeem the word from low and vulgar associations. 'His intention was to make us feel that the sexual act was not shameful, and the word used in its original sense therefore was not shameful.' Griffith-Jones surprised everyone in court by asking only two questions:

Griffith-Jones: 'Was Lawrence a great writer?'

Gardner: 'Yes.'

Griffith-Jones: 'Was this one of his greatest books?'

Gardner: 'No, but it contained some of his greatest writing.'

Miss Gardner was followed by Mrs. Joan Bennet, a lecturer in English at Cambridge. The book, she said, did not support promiscuity, but the same could not be said of adultery: '[A] marriage can be broken when it is unfulfilled.' Griffith-Jones suggested that Lawrence 'shows the woman breaking [marriage] without any conditions at all, without even telling her husband, does he not?' Mrs. Bennet had to concede that he did:

Griffith-Jones: 'And ... that is exactly what he himself had done? He had run off with his friend's wife, had he not?'

Bennet: 'Yes.'

Griffith-Jones: 'The whole book is about that subject?'

Bennet: 'Yes'.

And Griffith-Jones sat down. It almost seemed as if Lady Chatterley herself was on trial for adultery.

The courtroom sat up once again when the popular author Dame Rebecca West CBE entered the witness box. Lawrence, she said, considered a good marriage to be perhaps the most important thing in the world. 'The baronet and his impotence were a symbol of the impotent culture of his time, and the love affair with the gamekeeper was a calling, a return of the soul to the more intense life that he felt when people had a different culture, such as the cultural basis of religious faith.' She accepted that the book was 'full of sentences of which any child could make a fool, because they were badly written. Furthermore, the author had a great defect which marred the book: 'He had absolutely no sense of humour.' Griffith-Jones had no questions of the witness; it was an augury of things to come.

John Robinson, Bishop of Woolwich, was the next witness. Despite a protest from Griffith-Jones, he was allowed to give evidence on the ethics of *Lady Chatterley's Lover*. The book was not intended, he said, to exalt immorality but portrayed the sex relationship as something essentially sacred. Asked, 'Is this a book which in your view Christians ought to read?', the Bishop replied, 'Yes, I think it is,' thus ensuring an easy headline for the evening papers. After the Cloth came the Dons.

Dr Vivian Pinto, Professor of English at Nottingham University, told the court of an interesting comment by Lawrence himself in his essay, *A Propos of Lady Chatterley*. Explaining how he had been tempted to expunge the four-letter-words from the Italian edition of his book, Lawrence had written, 'Impossible! I might as well try to clip my own nose into shape with scissors. The book bleeds.' The effect of Pinto's evidence was blunted somewhat when, after Griffith-Jones had read out one of the more lurid passages in the book, the witness began to say, 'I think that this should be read in Nottingham dialect to get the…', before being silenced by laughter in court.

The next big gun was the academic writer on popular culture, Richard Hoggart, who, like Lawrence, had his roots firmly in the working class.[13] Griffith-Jones could not believe his ears, however, when the witness praised Lady Chatterley as 'highly virtuous and if anything puritanical'. He asked, 'I thought I had lived my life under a misapprehension as to the meaning of the world 'puritanical. Will you help me?' Hoggart did. 'In England today the word "puritanical" has been extended to mean someone who is against anything which is pleasurable, particularly sex. The proper meaning of it, to a literary man or to a linguist is somebody who belongs to the tradition of British puritanism generally, and the distinguishing feature of that is an intense sense of responsibility for one's conscience. In that sense, the book is puritanical.'

Edward Morgan (E.M.) Forster then took the oath. England's most distinguished living author confirmed Hoggart's view by saying that Lawrence was the greatest imaginative novelist of his generation and could legitimately be described as part of the great Puritan stream of writers in this country. He was not cross-examined. But when Roy Jenkins MP, chief sponsor of the Obscene Publications Bill, began to suggest that the prosecution was contrary to the spirit of the legislation he was stopped by the judge. (This was because in the English courts the intent of the legislature is normally something for the court alone to construe.)

---

13   His book, *The Uses of Literacy*, had recently been a great popular success.

The evidence of an educational psychologist, Dr James Hemming, was the occasion for lengthy discussions on the law, leading to a number of legal rulings from the judge. When the witness was finally allowed to give his evidence he claimed that the educational value of *Lady Chatterley's Lover* 'would act as an antidote to the coarseness and the dehumanizing influences that [people] meet in relation to sex and their relation to sex.' 'You are being serious in your evidence, I suppose?' sneered Griffith-Jones. There then followed what C.H. Rolph described as a 'prolonged, embarrassing and somewhat ludicrous colloquy' about a particular sentence in the book. After prosecuting counsel had asked the witness for the umpteenth time what the sentence meant, a juryman was seen to roll his eyes to heaven.

The distinguished critic and writer Raymond Williams drew attention to an observation which was made by one of the book's minor characters, 'It's the one insane taboo left: sex as a natural and vital thing.' Norman St. John-Stevas, the lawyer, Catholic and student of moral theology, had written a book on the law of obscenity and had drafted the original Bill. He claimed that Lawrence was 'essentially a writer in the Catholic tradition'. He had 'no hesitation in saying that every Catholic priest and every Catholic would profit by reading this book.' (The Catholic judge made no comment.) There was a great gulf, said St John Stevas, between Lawrence's book and works of pornography.

The literary editor of the *Sunday Times* told the court how the book had been brought to his school by a friend, and that he had read it, 'because it was a dirty book.' (Quite how this advanced the defence is difficult to understand.) Sir Allen Lane of Penguin Books described the high reasons which had led his company to publish *Lady Chatterley's Lover* (in which, strangely, a concern for profit seems to have played no part). Dilys Powell, the noted book and film reviewer of the *Sunday Times*, claimed that in *Lady Chatterley's Lover* sex was 'taken as being something to be taken seriously and as a basis for a holy life.' 'Did I hear you aright?' said an astonished Griffith-Jones. But even her fame was overshadowed by the poet Cecil Day Lewis, who from the witness box described the book as recommending 'a right and full relationship between a man and a woman'. Griffith-Jones asked if it was 'perfectly natural for Lady Chatterley to 'run off to the hut in the forest to copulate with her husband's gamekeeper'. Day Lewis replied that such conduct was in her nature as 'an averagely sexed woman.'

The Rev. Donald Tyler, director of Religious Education in Birmingham, got short shrift from prosecuting counsel when he offered the opinion that *Lady Chatterley's Lover* would help youngsters to grow up as mature and responsible people, and was 'a most impressive statement of the Christian view of marriage'. When he observed that Mellors was very much attracted by Connie, Griffith-Jones could not refrain from commenting, 'Of course he is. Everybody who commits adultery is presumably very much attracted by the man or woman with whom they do it.... And not only was he committing adultery but he was committing adultery with somebody else who was committing adultery.'

Other witnesses included the director of the Industrial Christian Fellowship (who expatiated on the book's 'moral purpose' and claimed that he would not object to his children reading it), the headmaster of Alleyn's School (who claimed that children used 'plain Anglo-Saxon words'), the headmistress of Keighley Grammar School (who said that her girls 'were acquainted with these words by the time they were ten'), the popular historian, C.V. Wedgewood (who said that the book would be distorted without the descriptions of sex), the television personality and one-time controller of News and Censorship at the Ministry of Information, Francis Williams (who said much the same thing), the journalist, Anne Scott-James (who spoke of the book's 'immense merits') and Walter Allen, literary editor of the *New Statesman* (who described *Lady Chatterley's Lover* as a 'work of genius' and a moral book to boot). The novel was also praised by Stephen Potter, then the author of a book about D.H. Lawrence, though better known since for his humorous writings, and Noel Annan, Provost of King's College, Cambridge (who like so many others had declined to give evidence for the prosecution).

After the editor of the *Guardian* had tendered his laudatory views on *Lady Chatterley's Lover* without challenge, Gerald Gardiner announced to a surprised, and perhaps relieved, courtroom that in view of the 'decrease in the amount of cross-examination' he proposed to call only one of his remaining thirty-six witnesses. It was an ironic moment in court when the twenty-one year old graduate, Bernardine

Wall, gave her judgement on the novel, while the author of *The Waste Land* and *Murder in the Cathedral*, T.S. Eliot OM, waited in vain for his name to be called.

Summing up to the jury on the fifth day of the trial, Gerald Gardiner said that no higher class of experts could have been called in any similar case. It would, he said, be difficult to deny that Chaucer's *Canterbury Tales* was obscene, but if made the subject of prosecution, it would, like *Lady Chatterley*, be open to the defence of literary merit. He drew attention to the prosecution's failure to call a single witness. He poured scorn on the idea that the book could have been published in its expurgated version. And the charge that it was about adultery, he said, could be made as easily against *Anthony and Cleopatra*. As to the four-letter words, he asked, 'Do you really suppose anyone would really be depraved by reading words they know very well?'

In reply, Griffith-Jones declared, untruthfully, that he had not called witnesses because he was conceding that Lawrence was a great writer. It was the jury's task, he said, 'to weigh in the balance the obscenity … and on the other [hand] the literary merit and the other merits, any other merit you can find, and say, does that weigh it down in the interests of the public?' There must, he said in language more redolent of the smoking room than the Old Bailey, be standards which we are to maintain, some standards of morality, some standards of language and conversation, some standards of conduct which are essential to the well-being of our society. He was on stronger ground when he drew attention to some of the more extravagant claims of the experts concerning the supposedly high-minded message of the book. Did it really condemn promiscuity? Was it really a 'treatment of sex on a holy basis'? Could it truly be said to be 'a book of moral purpose'? Did it offer a 'positive antidote to the shallow, superficial values of sex which are widely current today'? The relationship between Connie and Mellors, Griffith-Jones suggested, was concerned with only one thing, as witnessed by the fact that, '…[d]uring the time they were having their thirteen first bouts [*sic*], there is not a single word spoken between them at any other time than just before, during or afterwards, or about anything other than sex.' What else did he suppose people spoke of during such moments?

It was Mr. Justice Byrne's task to direct the jury on the law. If they were not satisfied that the book was obscene they must acquit; but if the prosecution had satisfied them that it was obscene they must go on to examine the question of whether its publication was justified by its literary or other merits. After three hours of deliberation the foreman of the jury announced their verdict of 'Not Guilty'. Under the English legal system there is no way of knowing whether they had found the book not obscene, or obscene but justified by its literary merits.

The judge declined to order the prosecution to pay Penguin their costs, which amounted to some £13,000, but gave no reasons for this decision. Afterwards, the judge's wife, Lady Byrne, was heard to say, 'I call that an absolutely disgusting verdict.'[14] The publicly funded Arts Council saw fit to celebrate the victory with a party, and the book sold three million copies in the next twelve months. The prosecution had been a resounding success – for Penguin. With one blow they had increased both their liberal credentials and their profits.

The trial of *Lady Chatterley's Lover* was certainly a well-deserved poke in the eye for an obscurantist establishment. But was the book as creditable a work of literature as some of the defence witnesses so sanctimoniously claimed? Mellor's language is often stilted and more concerned with promoting the author's social views than advancing the story. While Lawrence makes a good case for frankness in matters of sex not everyone will agree with his assertion in *A Propos of Lady Chatterley's Lover* that 'sex is the one thing you really cannot swindle'. Nor is it easy to work up much sympathy for the wife of a badly wounded soldier who jumps into bed with a number of men behind his back. And the use of 'dirty words' makes many passages positively toe-curling to read. F.R. Leavis, one of England's most perceptive (if occasionally eccentric) literary critics, writing only a few years before the trial, put the book into perspective as:

> a courageous, profoundly sincere, and very deliberate piece of work; if it errs, it is not through lack of calculation. The trouble lies in its being in certain ways too deliberate – too deliberate, at any rate to be a wholly satisfactory work of art, appealing to imaginatively sensitized feeling. What may be called the hygienic undertaking to which it is

14   Muriel Box, *Rebel Advocate: A Biography of Gerald Gardiner* (London, Victor Gollancz Ltd., 1983), p. 118.

devoted commands one's sympathy – the undertaking to cleanse the obscene words and to redeem from the smirch of obscenity physical facts. But the willed insistence on the words and facts must, it seems to me, whatever the intention, have something unacceptable, something offensive, about it; it offends, surely, against Lawrence's own canons – against the spirit of his creativity and against the moral and emotional ethic that he in essence stands for.[15]

But the Old Bailey trial of 1960 was not the first time the book had been 'acquitted' in court, and England not the first country.

LADY CHATTERLEY IN NEW YORK

In 1930 a Massachusetts bookseller and his clerk were sent to prison for selling a copy of *Lady Chatterley's Lover*. Over two decades later another publisher decided to take the risk again. Grove Press, a small independent publishing house, had been bought by Barney Rosset in 1951 and turned into the foremost alternative imprint in America. In the spring of 1959, Rosset printed 30,000 copies of the unexpurgated version of the book with a preface by a former librarian of Congress and an introduction by a distinguished English professor. The decision was taken to distribute it through a book club; it was not a good call. The Postmaster General had been charged by Congress with the task of removing obscene matter from the postal system. Acting under the Comstock Act of 1873, which made it illegal to send 'obscene, lewd, and/or lascivious or filthy' material through the mail, twenty-four packages containing 164 copies of the book were seized in the post and brought before a Post Office employee known as the judicial officer. The Postmaster's lawyer, while acknowledging Lawrence's literary merits, argued that 'the inclusion of filthy and obscene terms, together with the repetitious discussions and descriptions of the sex act upset the balance, so that the literary merit is submerged and outweighed by the obscenity'.

The publisher called a witness to testify that the advertising agency had no difficulty in placing advertisements for the book, and a literary critic to state that Lawrence's descriptions of sexual encounters

---

15 F.R. Leavis, *D.H. Lawrence: Novelist* (Harmondsworth, Penguin Books with Chatto and Windus, 1955), p. 73.

were germane to the expression of his ideas. Fulfilment in the marriage state, the witness said, was an idea that was finding expression in magazines as respectable as the *Ladies Home Journal*. Another expert anticipated some of the Old Bailey comments by describing *Lady Chatterley's Lover* as 'a religious novel'. Perhaps the most convincing case was made by Barney Rosset himself:

> ... Since the book was written in 1928 the emotional maturity of the American people has undergone a great change... it would be incomprehensible if this book were published today that the public would be shocked, offended or would raise any outcry against it; but rather they would welcome it as the republishing, the bringing back to life, of one of our great masterpieces ...

In the end the judicial officer took the easy way out and ruled that, 'To hold the book to be mailable matter would require a reversal of rulings of long standing by this Department and to cast doubt on the rulings of a coordinate executive department.' The decision was now down to the Postmaster General himself. On 11 June 1959 *Lady Chatterley's Lover* was banned from the mail. When this decision was challenged in the Federal court, Judge Frederick van Pel Bryan held that the Postmaster's decision was contrary to law and clearly erroneous. There was 'no question about Lawrence's honesty and sincerity of purpose, artistic integrity and lack of intention to appeal to the prurient interest of the average reader.' He ordered that the book be allowed all the privileges of the mail.[16] The Federal government appealed, and on 25 March 1960 Judge Bryan's decision was affirmed by the Second Circuit Court of Appeal.[17] The book, the court held, was a polemic against crass industrialization, the British caste system and inhibited sex relations between men and women. The four-letter words to which the Postmaster had objected were subordinate, but highly useful elements in the development of the author's purpose. The Post Office wisely decided to take the case no further.

The punishing costs of these legal battles brought the publishing house to the brink of financial disaster. But the American authorities

16   *Grove Press v Christenberry,* 175 F. Supp. 488 (S.D.N.Y. 1959).
17   *Grove Press, Inc. v Christenberry* 276 F.2d 433 (2d Cir. 1960).

had not yet done with *Lady Chatterley's Lover* and this time the case went all the way to the top.

LADY CHATTERLEY ON THE BIG SCREEN

It all began when a motion picture entitled *Lady Chatterley's Lover* was denied a licence by the motion picture division of the Education Department of New York on the ground that three isolated scenes were 'immoral' within the intent of an Education law. The Regents of the University of the State of New York upheld the denial, but on the broader ground that 'the whole theme of this motion picture is immoral ..., for that theme is the presentation of adultery as a desirable, acceptable and proper pattern of behavior.' On judicial review the decision of the Regents was annulled and a direction made that a licence be issued. This ruling was in turn reversed by a sharply divided Court of Appeal, a majority of whom found that the picture as a whole 'alluringly portrays adultery as proper behavior'. A by-now mystified distributor took the case to the US Supreme Court.

On 29 June 1959 the Supreme Court held that, 'What New York has done... is to prevent the exhibition of a motion picture because that picture advocates an idea – that adultery under certain circumstances may be proper behavior [*sic*]. Yet the First Amendment's basic guarantee is of freedom to advocate ideas. The State, quite simply, has thus struck at the very heart of constitutionally protected liberty.' The constitutional guarantee of free speech, the court held, 'is not confined to the expression of ideas that are conventional or shared by a majority. It protects advocacy of the opinion that adultery may sometimes be proper, no less than advocacy of socialism or the single tax. And in the realm of ideas it protects expression which is eloquent no less than that which is unconvincing.' Without conceding that 'the State is entirely without power to require films of any kind to be licensed prior to their exhibition', the Court struck down the denial of a licence to *Lady Chatterley's Lover*.[18]

---

18 *Kingsley Pictures v Regents* 360 U.S. 684. The present test for obscenity in America, laid down since Rembar's case is, (a) whether the average person, applying contemporary community standards, would find that the work, taken as a whole, appeals to the prurient interest; (b) whether the work depicts or describes,

It was a great victory for freedom of the press and a long way in advance of English law.

WHERE DO WE GO FROM HERE?

Charles Rembar, the fighting attorney who had defended *Lady Chatterley's Lover* in the New York courts, has argued that the question of the book's obscenity was decided on better grounds in America than in England. One reason, he suggested, was the willingness of the American publisher to stake the case on the issue of freedom and to relinquish whatever other legal argument or tactic might give him victory.[19] There is force in this argument, though of course the lawyers in each country had no option but to defend the book in the ways permitted by their countries' laws. Another reason for the superiority of the American treatment of the issue, Rembar contended, was the US constitution.

The First Amendment to the constitution provides that: 'Congress shall make no law … abridging the freedom of speech, or of the press.' On the face of it this right allows of no exceptions, but as the great Justice Oliver Wendell Holmes observed, 'The most stringent protection of free speech would not protect a man falsely shouting fire in a theater and causing a panic.'[20] Exceptions to the right have been recognized in relation to such matters as defamatory words, the incitement to violence, and, of course, obscenity.

In the past an English lawyer could have argued proudly that an American citizen has to consult his constitution in order to discover whether he enjoys a particular freedom or not, whereas an Englishman can do what he will unless the conduct is prohibited by law. All that changed, alas, in 1951 when the United Kingdom ratified the

---

in a patently offensive way, sexual conduct specifically defined by the applicable state law; and (c) whether the work, taken as a whole, lacks serious literary, artistic, political or scientific value: *Miller v California* (413 U.S. 14 [1973]). The judgment recorded that the court had seen 'a variety of views among the members of the Court unmatched in any other course of constitutional adjudication.'
19   Charles Rembar, *The End of Obscenity* (London, Andre Deutsch, 1968), p. 154.
20   *Schenck v United States* 249 US 47.

European Convention on Human Rights and Fundamental Freedoms, and in 1998 when the Convention was incorporated into English law. Whatever the shortcomings of the Convention, it is at least an improvement on the US constitution in that it recognizes that freedom of speech 'carries with it duties and responsibilities'.[21] It is in this way that the English obscenity laws creep in under the fence.[22] But is the Act of 1959 the best that we can do?

D. H. Lawrence himself accepted the need for censorship, but only of the right sort: '... even I would censor genuine pornography, rigorously. It would not be very difficult. In the first place, genuine pornography is almost always underworld, it doesn't come into the open. In the second, you can recognize it by the insult it offers invariably, to sex, and to the human spirit. Pornography is the attempt to insult sex, to do dirt on it. This is unpardonable.'[23] Nowadays, this will be seen as a simplistic view of the problem. As Rembar wrote, pornography 'is in the groin of the beholder.' The book that one person wishes to see burnt another believes to be redeemed by its literary merit, while yet a third sits by wondering what all the fuss is about. Furthermore, what was unthinkable one day may be tolerated the next and applauded the day after. So it was with *The Golden Ass*,[24] *The Decameron*,[25] Casanova's *Memoirs*,[26] *Sexual Inversion*[27] and *The Naked Lunch*.[28] 'Time,' wrote H.L. Mencken in *A Book of Prefaces* (1917), 'is a great legalizer, even in the field of morals.'

It is probably due in part to Lawrence that few but the more cloistered spirits nowadays would question our right to enjoy sex in what-

---

21   Article 10 of the Convention allows exceptions for 'such formalities, conditions, restrictions or penalties as are prescribed by law and are necessary in a democratic society in the interests of...public safety, for the prevention of disorder or crime, for the protection of health or morals, protection of the reputation or rights of others....'
22   See *Handyside v UK* (1976) EHRR 737.
23   D. H. Lawrence, *Pornography and Obscenity* (London, Faber & Faber, 1929), pp. 12-13.
24   By Lucius Apuleius in the first century A.D.
25   By Boccacio (1350).
26   Which Casanova was still writing at the time of his death in 1798.
27   By Havelock Ellis (1896).
28   By William S. Burroughs (1959).

ever way we please, so long as it does no harm to others. It is a bad law which requires the pornographer to justify his work by unwarranted and often specious claims to literary merit. Surely, the only possible justification for banning books, plays or movies is that they promote crime, or some other equally undesirable outcome like the corruption of children. As Rembar wrote, 'We had defended *Lady Chatterley* not on the ground that it promoted morality, but rather that it presented a view on the subject... The fact that a book is on the side of the angels should never be crucial. Else we may find ourselves suppressing the devil's proposals, the precise negation of free speech.'

In this, as in so many things, Thomas Jefferson got it right when he wrote, 'It is so difficult to draw a clear line of separation between the abuse and the wholesome use of the press, that as yet we have found it better to trust the public judgement, rather than the magistrate, with the discrimination between truth and falsehood.'[29]

---

29   Letter to M. Pictet, 5 February 1803.

FEASTING WITH PANTHERS

THE TRIALS OF OSCAR WILDE, 1895

All trials are trials for one's life, just as all sentences are sentences of death, and three times I have been tried. The first time I left the box to be arrested, the second time to be led back to the house of detention, and the third time to pass into prison for two years. Society as we have constituted it, will have no place for me, has none to offer; but Nature, whose sweet rains fall on just and unjust alike, will have clefts in the rocks where I may hide, and secret valleys in whose silence I may weep undisturbed. She will hang with stars so that I may walk abroad in the darkness without stumbling, and send the wind over my footprints so that none may track me to my hurt: she will cleanse me in great waters, and with bitter herbs make me whole.

Oscar Wilde, *De Profundis* (1905).

Much of Wilde's character was prefigured in his childhood. Oscar Fingal O'Flahertie Wills Wilde was born in Dublin on 16 October 1854, the second of three children. His father William was a prominent eye and ear surgeon who, when Oscar was ten years old, had been knighted for his work on the medical aspects of the census. His mother Francesca was a tall, Junoesque woman of theatrical temperament who hosted a literary salon and wrote poetry under the pen name *Speranza* ('hope' in Italian). Both were strong Irish nationalists and Oscar's middle names reflected his parents' love of Irish literature and culture. Sir William's professional success concealed a propensity to sexual philandering which was to lead to one of the most scandalous libel actions of his day.[1] When one of his patients went around complaining publicly that the doctor had chloroformed her for immoral purposes the doughty Lady Wilde published a pamphlet accusing her of lying. The somewhat unhinged patient reacted by suing for libel. Sir William failed to give evidence at the trial and

1   Before his marriage William had fathered three illegitimate children. He provided properly for them and the extended family spent the summers together.

Oscar Wilde and Lord Alfred Douglas in 1894 (Topfoto)

the plaintiff won. However, she received only nominal damages, leaving both sides to pay their own costs. As Wilde's biographer Hesketh Pearson commented, '… it appears to a layman that the jury charged [Sir William] Wilde from two to three thousand pounds for seducing a girl whose virtue they valued at a farthing.'[2] When Oscar was twelve his ten year old sister Isola died; the bereavement was to be writ large in his writings. Shortly after, the boy was sent as a boarder to a school at Enniskillen, but his years at this Protestant institution were not the happiest.

Everything changed for Oscar Wilde in 1871 when he obtained a scholarship to Trinity College, Dublin. Here, he outshone all his contemporaries in Classics, winning the coveted Berkeley gold medal for Greek (which he was to pawn more than once in later life). From Trinity he gained a demyship[3] to Magdalen College, Oxford, where he was to distinguish himself in poetry and the classics. His heroes were John Ruskin, the Slade Professor of Art, and the essayist, critic and Fellow of Brasenose, Walter Pater, who between them were rekindling interest in the Renaissance which gave rise to the aesthetic movement, or *decadence*, as it was known in France. 'The realization of oneself', Wilde was to declare in court, 'is the prime aim of life, and to realize oneself through pleasure is finer than to do so through pain. I am on that point entirely on the side of the ancients, the Greeks.' One of Wilde's most memorable experiences was in 1877 when he visited Greece along with three friends. Among his set the word, 'Greek' became code for 'homosexual', just as the words, 'uranian'[4] and 'antinomian'[5] were used to describe anyone rejecting conventional morality.

After winning the prestigeful Newdigate prize for poetry[6] and a double first in Greats[7] in 1878, Wilde left Oxford and moved to London where his recently widowed mother had re-established her salon.

---

2   Hesketh Pearson, *Oscar Wilde, His Life and Wit,* (New York and London, Harper Brothers, 1946), p. 13.
3   The name of a scholarship peculiar to Magdalen.
4   The origin of the word is disputed.
5   From the sixteenth-century sect which held that Christians were released from observing the moral law.
6   Which Ruskin had won some years before.
7   The Classics course at Oxford.

His Dublin accent disappeared and he soon established a reputation as a wit, adopting the 'aesthetic' image of floppy hat, loose shirt with wide turn-down collar and bow tie, knee britches and black silk stockings. The 'aesthete' was an easy butt for ridicule, and in W.S. Gilbert's opera, *Patience or Bunthorne's Bride* (1881), the eponymous Bunthorne 'walked down Piccadilly with a poppy/or a lily in his Mediaeval hand'. But it was gentle fun and Wilde was glad to accept an offer from Gilbert's impresario, Richard D'Oyly Carte, to publicize the new work by undertaking a lecture tour of the United States. On entering America he is said to have told a Customs official, 'I have nothing to declare ... except my genius.' The tour was a roaring success and introduced Wilde into the literary and theatrical circles.

'URANIAN' INTERESTS

It is difficult to know just when Wilde became aware of his true sexual nature. His mother had brought Oscar up as a girl for the first ten years of his life, but this was not entirely unusual at that time and there is no reason to believe that it was in any way connected with his later sexual inclinations. Wilde's friend, the talented writer and scoundrel Frank Harris, reports him as having been kissed unexpectedly on the lips by another boy at school;[8] otherwise his schooldays seem to have been unexceptional from a sexual point of view. 'Boy worship' was certainly around during his period at Oxford and Wilde was not immune from it, but any interests he may have developed in this direction had to compete with his fascination with Roman Catholicism. Wilde's biographer Richard Ellman quotes 'an unfriendly witness' as saying that Wilde 'boasted of having as much pleasure in talking about the subject of homosexuality as others in practising it.'[9]

Wilde's first lover was probably the tall, blonde portrait painter, George Francis ('Frank') Miles whom he met in 1876. The two of them shared an apartment off the Strand which became a sort of literary/artistic salon. Miles was a man of varied interests. On one occasion when police officers arrived with a warrant for his arrest for molesting

8   Frank Harris, *Oscar Wilde* (Lansing, Mich., Michigan State University Press, 1959), p. 21.
9   Richard Ellmann, *Oscar Wilde* (London, Hamish Hamilton, 1987), p. 59.

young girls Wilde stalled them while his companion escaped over the rooftops. The affair finally ended in a violent quarrel.[10]

CONSTANCE

At the same time, as his relationship with Miles, Wilde was displaying a conventional interest in the opposite sex and flirted with, even courted, more than one woman. (One of these was the beautiful Francis Balcombe, who later broke off their affair to marry Bram Stoker.) Eventually, he informed his friend, the actress, Lilly Langtry, 'I am going to be married to a beautiful girl called Constance Lloyd, a grave, slight, violet-eyed little Artemis, with great coils of heavy brown hair which make her flower-like head droop like a blossom, and wonderful ivory hands which draw music from the piano so sweet that the birds stop singing to listen to her'. Constance was a Protestant barrister's daughter he had met some two years before in Dublin. Their marriage on 29 May 1884 was a grand affair with both men and women in 'decadent' dress. After a honeymoon in Paris the couple established their home at 16 Tite Street, Chelsea.

After his father's death the newly married Oscar's frugal circumstances were further depleted by the contributions he was making to his widowed mother.[11] To supplement his income he became editor of a monthly magazine, *Lady's World* (which he renamed *Woman's World),* but tired of it after less than a year. Outwardly, his marriage had all the appearance of happiness. The couple had had two children, Cyril in 1885, and Vivian, later changed to Vyvyan, the following year. (*The Happy Prince* was written especially for them.) But in Richard Ellman's words, '[Wilde] required stronger seasoning than his adoring wife and his adoring sons could provide.'[12] And he found it in 1886 when he met and was captivated by Robert Baldwin Ross, known as Robbie.

10   Miles died in an asylum four years later.
11   Fortunately, Constance enjoyed £900 a year from her grandfather's will.
12   Richard Ellmann, *Oscar Wilde.* (London. Hamish Hamilton, 1987), p.259.

Ross was a grandson of a former Governor General of Canada and a son of Canada's Attorney General. He was a short boyish-looking lad with, in Wilde's words, 'the face of Puck'. The two became close and it was not long before the seventeen year old Robbie seduced the thirty-four year old Wilde. (Both were to tell friends that it was their first homosexual encounter, but both were lying.) Although Wilde was to move on to many other relationships his love affair with Ross was to continue on and off throughout his life. Ross was a 'liberated' homosexual who frequently resorted, as many homosexuals did in those days, to commercial sex. Wilde enthusiastically explored the illicit delights of this new world in hotels and anywhere else he could. His constant absences from home called for increasingly improbable explanations. (On one occasion he even expressed an unlikely interest in golf!) Ellman speculates that in order to explain his loss of sexual interest in Constance, Wilde may have pretended the recurrence of a venereal disease[13] We are unlikely ever to know exactly what she thought or suspected.

Wilde's name first became known to a wider audience with his collection of short stories, *Lord Arthur Savile's Crime and other Stories* (1887). The delightful fairytale *The Happy Prince* was published the following year along with other stories, but his first commercial success was his novel, *The Picture of Dorian Gray* (1890). The 'decadence' of this work, with its undercurrent of homosexuality proved too much for the W.H. Smith chain of bookshops, who refused to sell it, thus increasing its notoriety. The following year Wilde dabbled with social criticism in *The Soul of Man under Socialism*, but real fame only came with his plays: *Lady Windermere's Fan* (1892), *A Woman of No Importance* (1893), *Salome* (1894), and in 1895, *An Ideal Husband* and *The Importance of Being Earnest*. It is seldom that such literary riches fall from a single hand in so short a time. Hesketh Pearson described the author at this stage of his life: 'Picture a tall, broad, thickset, slow-moving man, inclined to corpulence; with a large, bloodless, coarse skinned face, clean shaven at a time when moustaches were in vogue, a powerful, well-shaped nose, thick,

13 It is possible that Wilde contracted syphilis from a local prostitute while up at Oxford, but, if so, the disease appears to have been cured.

purple tinged sensual lips, long crowded, uneven discoloured teeth, fleshy cheeks, heavy jaw, firm mouth, fine brow, long, dark, carefully waved hair, and expressive, heavy lidded eyes.'[14]

'BOSIE'

The grand and fateful passion of Wilde's life began in January 1891 when the poet Lionel Johnson (who only the previous year had been his lover) introduced him to his twenty year old cousin, Lord Alfred Bruce Douglas.

Douglas, known by his family name of 'Bosie' (a corruption of 'Boysie'), was a Magdalen undergraduate and budding poet anxious to meet the author of *The Picture of Dorian Gray*. He possessed in Ellman's words, a 'pale alabaster face and blond hair.' Unfortunately, he was also 'totally spoiled, reckless, insolent and, when thwarted, fiercely vindictive,' traits which were not to become apparent to Wilde until it was too late. The two men were immediately attracted to each other; the juvenile Bosie with Oscar's wit and charm, the snobbish Oscar with this most beautiful sprig of the aristocracy. From the start Wilde craved for a physical relationship; even presenting the younger man with one of his sonnets as if it had been written especially for him. At first Douglas rejected his advances, but fate was soon to intervene.

In the spring of 1892 Douglas found himself being blackmailed over an indiscreet letter he had written to a young man and sought his friend's help. Wilde rushed to Oxford, where he stayed in Bosie's rooms and got his solicitor Sir George Lewis to pay off the blackmailer. A grateful Bosie duly succumbed, and one of the most famous love affairs of the century was born. Relations between the two were intensely close, but necessarily secret. Wilde was diplomatically charming to all concerned, and in October, Douglas' mother, Lady Queensberry, even invited him to her house at Bracknell[15] in order to seek his help over Bosie's extravagance and neglect of his studies.

14 Pearson, *Oscar Wilde, His Life and Wit*, p. 144.
15 Wilde could not resist using the place name for a character in *The Importance of Being Earnest*.

Douglas later claimed to have been an innocent when he met Wilde. In *De Profundis* Wilde was to describe him at this stage in quite different terms: 'The gutter and the things that live in it had begun to fascinate you. That was the origin of the trouble in which you sought my aid, and I, unwisely, according to the wisdom of this world, out of pity and kindness, gave it to you.' As to the nature of their physical relations, Douglas acknowledged that, 'I did with him and allowed him to do what was done among boys at Winchester and Oxford,'[16] but protested that he had never liked these intimacies and denied that they had ever gone beyond public school gropings.[17] In his *Autobiography* of 1929 Douglas pledged his 'solemn word before God' that he had not committed buggery with Wilde, but was this true? The biographer Neil McKenna suggests that by this he may have meant merely that he had not allowed himself to be buggered *by* Wilde; in other words that he had not assumed the female role. This seems an unlikely explanation because Douglas was quite specific in a letter to Harris that, 'sodomy never took place between us.' Now, this may have been a lie, but it was certainly not ambiguous.

THE BOYS

Wilde's sexual interests were never exclusive. Even after meeting Douglas he continued his long standing affair with the twenty-five year old John Gray, after whom *The Picture of Dorian Gray* had been named. At the same time he was making frequent use of male prostitutes. Just before the first night of *Lady Windermere's Fan*,[18] for example, he had sex with an eighteen year old publishing house clerk called Edward Shelley whom he had met the year before. (Though Shelley later claimed to have been shocked by the experience, it was not his first.) He was to remain Wilde's favourite rent boy until the poet's

---

16   This careful periphrasis seems to have allowed the possibility of intercrural sex and fellatio (by Oscar of Bosie). See Neil McKenna, *The Secret Life of Oscar Wilde* (London, Arrow Books, 2004), p. 248.

17   H. Montgomery Hyde, *The Trials of Oscar Wilde* (London, William Hodge and Co., 1948), New Ed edition (1974). Revised as *Oscar Wilde: A Biography* (Harmondsworth, Penguin, 2001), p. 248.

18   5 March 1892.

arrest, often spending the night with Wilde at his club, the Albemarle, off Piccadilly.

In the autumn of 1892 Douglas introduced Wilde to 'a fat, talkative queen with a pronounced giggle'[19] by the name of Maurice Schwabe. Schwabe in turn introduced Wilde to Alfred Taylor, an old Marlburian, who was to play a central role in his tragedy. Taylor had a top floor flat in Little College Street, just behind Westminster Abbey, at which he held 'tea parties' in a room kept permanently shuttered and scented with pastilles. It was in effect a high-class male brothel at which Wilde (and doubtless many others) was introduced to rent boys. One of the first of these was a twenty year old ex-public schoolboy, Sidney Mavor, known to his friends as 'Jenny'. A few days after Wilde first had sex with him Mavor received a silver cigarette case inscribed, 'Sidney from O.W. October 1892.' It was to be the first of many such gifts. In February of the following year Wilde took Mavor with him to Paris for the performance of his new play, *Salomé*.[20] Taylor then introduced him to yet another rent boy, the sixteen year old Frederick Atkins.[21] Wilde was so smitten by this lad that he took him to Paris for a few days as his 'secretary'. There, they were joined by Mavor in a suite with interconnecting bedrooms.

THE LETTERS

By now, Wilde's sexual predilections were hardly a secret in society and it was not long before someone realized the money-making potential of them. In January 1893 at the Café Royal off Piccadilly, Douglas introduced Wilde to Alfred Wood, a seventeen year old unemployed rent boy.[22] After dinner, the playwright took the lad back to his home at Tite Street for sex. It was a purely commercial arrangement at £2 a night. One day, Douglas, who had not relinquished his own interest in the lad, summoned Wood to the hotel at which he was staying in Oxford and lent him a suit so that they could dine together. In one of

19 McKenna, *Secret Life of Oscar Wilde*, p. 279.
20 The Lord Chamberlain's ruling against the depiction of biblical characters on stage prevented the play being produced in London.
21 Estimates of his age vary.
22 Once again, estimates of age vary.

the pockets of the suit Wood came across what he immediately realized was an incriminating letter to Douglas from Wilde. A search of the room revealed more of Wilde's letters, all of which he pocketed. When he got back to London, Wood made a copy of one of them, later to become notorious as the 'Hyacinth Letter', and sent it to the actor/manager Herbert Beerbohm Tree who was then rehearsing *A Woman of No Importance*. Tree sent the copy of the letter to Wilde with a warning that its terms were open to misconstruction. Later in Taylor's rooms Wood showed Wilde three or four of the letters, claiming that they had been stolen from him by a 'friend', William Allen and that he had had to pay £15 to a detective to get them back. He was, he said, afraid of Allen and wanted money to go to America. Wilde handed over the money and was given the bundle of letters; what he did not realize until later was that the bundle did not include the Hyacinth Letter.

What seems to have happened is that Wood had shown the stolen letters to two of his less savoury acquaintances, William Allen and Robert Cliburn, who were notorious as blackmailers in the homosexual underworld and were most likely the people Wood wanted to get away from. Armed with what was probably the Hyacinth Letter, Allen approached Wilde at the stage door and asked ten pounds for it. As he tells it, Wilde replied, 'Ten pounds! You have no appreciation of literature. If you had asked me for fifty pounds I might have given it to you.' Shortly afterwards, Allen came to Wilde's house with the letter. Wilde's first reaction was, 'I suppose that you have come about my lovely letter to Lord Alfred Douglas. If you had not been so foolish as to send a copy to Mr. Beerbohm Tree I would gladly have paid you a very large sum of money for the letter as I consider it to be a work of art.' When Allen said that 'a curious construction' could be put on the letter Wilde sneered, 'Art is rarely intelligible to the criminal classes.' Allen then claimed that someone had offered him fifty pounds for the letter, to which Wilde replied with his customary wit, 'If you take my advice, go to him at once and sell it for sixty pounds. I myself have never received so large a sum for any prose work of that length ...' Allen left, having received only half a sovereign from Wilde for his cab fare. Five minutes later Cliburn appeared at the door proffering the missing letter and saying that Allen had had a change of heart. Wilde accepted the letter, but complained that 'this original manuscript of 'mine' had been badly soiled. Cliburn said he was sorry, but it had passed through many hands. And that, for the time being, was that.

With the success of his plays, Wilde was now enjoying a healthy income which Douglas was delighted to help him spend. At the beginning of March 1893 he took adjoining rooms for the two of them in the fashionable and expensive Savoy Hotel in London, where the food was prepared under the direction of its famous chef, Escoffier. When they left at the end of the month Wilde had run up a huge bill which he could not afford to pay. Much of this had gone on a series of rent boys brought to the hotel by Taylor for the mutual enjoyment of the two lovers.

Douglas could not continue with this lifestyle and pursue his studies at the same time, and when he was admonished for failing to turn up for an examination he left college in a tantrum; it was a move he was to come to regret. In June, Wilde rented a large house at Goring-on-Thames, known as 'The Cottage' for himself and Douglas and a succession of sexual partners. It was an expensive venture; as well as paying the rent, he was maintaining a butler, two parlour maids, a cook and a scullery maid. The 'under-butler' was in fact a young servant lad named Walter Grainger who occupied the bedroom next to Oscar's. Wilde's relationship with Douglas had never been a tranquil one and after a particularly spiteful row an exasperated Wilde complained, 'We are spoiling each other's lives. You are absolutely ruining mine and evidently I am not making you really happy.' Douglas left in a sulk, but three days later he was back again and agreed to translate *Salomé* into English. His French was not up to the job and another row ensued. As Neil McKenna observed, 'A pattern of behaviour was beginning to emerge. A period of simmering tension would erupt in a terrible scene, or series of scenes. Bosie would flounce out, sending Oscar vituperative telegrams and letters. Oscar would decide that the friendship must end. As they both cooled off, each realized that they could not live without the other.'[23] Lady Queensberry became so concerned with Bosie's state of mind that, at Wilde's suggestion, she packed him off to friends in Cairo. He came home, apparently in disgrace, in February 1894, only to be sent to Turkey as honorary attaché

23   McKenna, *Secret Life of Oscar Wilde*, p. 350.

to the British Ambassador. He never took up the post but rushed back to London instead for yet another reconciliation with Oscar.

Nothing could seemingly stop Wilde's indiscriminate passions. Later that year while he and Constance were staying at a house in Worthing for a few weeks, he was seeing Douglas intermittently, but it was never an exclusive relationship. One day he met an eighteen year old youth, Alphonse Conway, selling papers on Worthing Pier and took him back to a hotel for lunch. He too was given a cigarette case and other presents and later taken to Brighton. The two men stayed in a two-bedroom apartment at the Albion Hotel where Wilde bought the lad a suit and a straw hat. He must have known that he was playing with fire, but could not guess that his real nemesis was about to burst on the scene in the form of Douglas' father.

THE 'MAD' MARQUESS

John Sholto Douglas, ninth Marquess of Queensberry, was an extraordinary character. Having left Cambridge without graduating, he became a formidable steeplechaser, huntsman and cyclist, but it was the art of boxing with which his name will forever be linked.[24] Unfortunately, he was not reluctant to put his skill to work outside the ring and was once fined for assaulting a man who had attempted to prevent him attacking a hotel porter. Queensberry seems at first blush to be almost a caricature of an eighteenth-century aristocrat, but he was also given to writing poetry and thought deeply on the subject of religion. He married in 1866, but treated his wife abominably and his children negligently. When the marriage finally foundered, Queensberry set up a separate establishment at which he enjoyed the company of a succession of mistresses, eventually divorcing in 1877. His second wife was a seventeen year old girl who left him the day after they wed. Their marriage was annulled in 1894 because of his being 'wholly unable to consummate [the union] by reason of the frigidity and impotence of his parts of generation ... incurable by art or skill'.[25]

---

24   He endorsed, but did not write, the rules of boxing which still bear his name.
25   *Dictionary of National Biography.*

182

Queensberry was no more successful in his relations with his sons than with his wives. His second son, Percy, married the daughter of a Cornish rector. Queensberry considered the girl to be beneath his family and told his daughter-in-law so in a series of obscene letters. Bosie, his third son, was a weedy youth with little appeal to his sporting fanatic father, but it was the tragedy of Francis, his eldest son, that was to throw a shadow over both their lives.

Francis had been private secretary to the British Foreign Secretary, Archibald Philip Primrose, fifth Earl of Rosebery. Rosebery engineered a Peerage for his young protégé who duly became Lord Drumlanrig. Queensberry resented the fact that, while Francis was entitled to sit in the House of Lords, he, as a mere Scottish peer, was not. Imagine his anger therefore when he heard rumours that Francis had been seduced by his employer in Germany. The indignant Marquess went immediately to that country with the avowed intent of horsewhipping the older man, a scandal that was averted only by the intervention of the Prince of Wales. Francis died the following year, his death being recorded as a hunting accident; even at the time people assumed that it had been nothing of the sort, but suicide in fear of exposure of his relationship with Rosebery.[26]

On learning that Bosie was being 'corrupted' by an older man, both Queensberry and his wife wrote begging him to break off his friendship with Wilde. Douglas ignored all their letters. When at the end of March 1894 the Marquess came across the two of them lunching together at the Café Royal he sat down glowering nearby. In an attempt to defuse the situation Douglas rose and invited his father to join them, which he did reluctantly. Against all expectations Queensberry was captivated by the dramatist's conversation and stayed on talking with him even after his son had left, later telling Bosie, 'I don't wonder you are so fond of him.' But it did not take the choleric Marquess long to have second thoughts; on 1 April he wrote to his son complaining about his wasted years at Oxford and of his 'loafing about', and ending:

> ... I come to the more painful part of this letter – your intimacy with this man Wilde. It must either cease or I will disown you and stop all

26 Rosebery's true sexuality is still disputed.

money supplies. I am not going to try and analyse this intimacy, and I make no charge; but to my mind to pose as a thing is as bad as to be it. With my own eyes I saw you in the most loathsome and disgusting relationship, as expressed by your manner and expression. Never in my experience have I seen such a sight as that in your horrible features. No wonder people are talking as they are. Also I now hear on good authority, but this may be false, that his wife is petitioning to divorce him for sodomy and other crimes.[27] Is this true, or do you not know of it? If I thought the actual thing was true, and it became public property, I should be quite justified in shooting him on sight. These Christian English cowards and men, as they call themselves, want waking up.

Your disgusted, so-called father,
Queensberry

Douglas chose to reply to the letter by telegram; its terms could not have been more calculated to offend. 'WHAT A FUNNY LITTLE MAN YOU ARE'.[28] Wilde was horrified: 'It was a telegram of which the commonest street boy would have been ashamed.' Queensberry replied to the 'impertinent young jackanapes' and threatened to cut off his allowance unless he ceased his relationship with Wilde. Douglas decided that it would be prudent to leave for Florence, where he was soon joined by Wilde.

Wilde at least had the sense to be disturbed at the developing situation and sought to consult his solicitor, the experienced George Lewis. Unfortunately, he was unavailable, having by an unfortunate coincidence agreed to act for Queensberry on his annulment of marriage suit. At Ross's suggestion Wilde consulted another solicitor, Charles Humphreys, but before anything could be done Queensberry turned up at Wilde's Tite Street home unannounced and accompanied by a prize fighter. Wilde ordered the visitor out of his house after the latter had waved 'his small hands in the air in an epileptic fury' and screamed loathsome threats. Douglas poured oil on the flames by writing to his father saying that he intended to annoy him by appearing in public whenever he could accompanied by Wilde. He added ominously, 'If O.W. was to prosecute you in the criminal courts for libel,[29] you

27 This was untrue.
28 At five foot eight inches, Queensberry was an inch shorter than his son.
29 Simple libel is and was a civil matter; however, at that time it could found

184

would get seven years' penal servitude for your outrageous libels.' If his father assaulted him he was prepared to defend himself and Wilde with a loaded revolver. Humphreys also wrote to Queensberry demanding that he withdraw the libels in his letters to his son; it got a dusty reply. The situation was only made worse by the publication in September of a scandalous novel, *The Green Carnation*,[30] which was an obvious satire on Wilde's relationship with Douglas.

During this upset, Douglas had contracted a bad bout of influenza which Wilde, with whom he was then living, nursed him through. When Douglas recovered, it was Wilde's turn to succumb, but the younger man had no intention of returning the kindness and departed, leaving behind a note which ended, 'When you are not on your pedestal you are not interesting. The next time you are ill I will go away at once.' Their subsequent reconciliation only angered Queensberry further and he resolved to get his revenge by disrupting the opening night of *The Importance of Being Earnest*.[31] (It would not have been the first time he had employed this tactic; he had once interrupted a play by Tennyson which offended his 'agnostic' convictions.) Queensberry's plan became known and the best he was able to do was to leave a bunch of vegetables at the stage door. Wilde consulted Humphreys again with a view to having the Marquess bound over to keep the peace. Nothing came of this because the theatre staff refused to provide the necessary evidence. The solicitor commented prophetically, '... the only consolation we can offer to you now is that such a persistent persecutor as Lord Queensberry will probably give you another opportunity sooner or later of seeking the protection of the Law...' Sure enough, four days after the theatre incident, Queensberry left his card at the Albemarle. The porter put it in an envelope and ten days later when he next saw Wilde handed it to him. It read, 'To Oscar Wilde posing Somdomite [*sic*]'. (Queensberry later revealed that the words were intended to be, 'To Oscar Wilde posing *as a Sodomite*'.)

a criminal prosecution if its publication was likely to disturb the community or provoke a breach of the peace. (Today, the crime is even wider in scope.)
30   Wilde was known to wear such a flower, but in a letter to the *Pall Mall Gazette* denied that it stood for anything.
31   14 February 1895.

This cryptic and barely legible epistle was to be the precipitating factor in Wilde's downfall.

As Queensberry had hoped, Wilde had been pushed to the limit and he consulted Humphreys again, but this time over the possibility of prosecuting the Marquess for libel. Asked if there was any truth in the libel, Wilde assured his solicitor that there was not. Humphreys – who, unlike Lewis, had little experience in cases of this nature – advised his client with a lawyer's care, 'If you are innocent you should succeed.'[32] Douglas pressed Wilde to bring a prosecution and offered his near penniless lover the full resources of himself and his brother to pay the costs of the case. It was enough to persuade him to swear out a warrant for Queensberry's arrest. The proceedings before the lower court were mostly formal and on 9 March the Marquess was committed on bail to stand his trial; it was exactly the outcome he had wished for.

Queensberry's position was considerably aided by the wording of his card; he did not have to prove that Wilde was a sodomite, merely that he posed as one. He immediately engaged private detectives to obtain evidence to prove his charge against Wilde. They were fortunate in coming across Charles Brookfield, an actor who had appeared in Wilde's plays but who as a result of a careless remark had formed an antipathy towards the dramatist. He led them to the former lodgings of Alfred Taylor at which they discovered the names and addresses of many of Wilde's catamites. Some of them were traced and cajoled into giving witness statements. (They could not be offered immunity in exchange for giving evidence because this was a private prosecution, but they would almost certainly have been made aware of the threat of exposure if they failed to cooperate.) Queensberry had already entered a plea of justification to the libel, that is a plea that the words complained of were true and had been published for the public benefit. Now he was able to add flesh to the bone by specifying that Wilde had sought to persuade various named young men to commit acts of sodomy and gross indecency with him at specific times and places.

---

32   Charles Humphreys, lacking experience in cases of this nature, counselled a course which, though legally justifiable, was practically disastrous.

Sodomy had been a crime since the days of Henry VIII; the offence of 'gross indecency' had been newly minted by an Act of 1885 in what was known as the Labouchere Amendment after the MP who proposed it. Though not further defined in the Act, 'gross indecency' was interpreted to mean any sexual act short of anal penetration, and the offence was criminal whether committed in public or in private.

Queensberry's defence had another string to its bow; it alleged that Wilde had published, or caused to be published, two immoral and indecent works, namely *The Picture of Dorian Gray* and *The Chameleon. Dorian Gray* was the story of a debauched young man whose physical beauty was preserved at the expense of a portrait of him which aged in his stead. *The Chameleon* was an Oxford University literary journal which contained in its issue of December 1894 a homoerotic story, *The Priest and the Acolyte*, as well as a number of epigrams by Wilde.

Just before the trial began Frank Harris tried to knock common sense into his friend. 'You paid blackmail to Wood for letters you had written to Douglas ... and you will not be able to explain that fact to the satisfaction of a jury. I am told that it is possible that witnesses will be called against you. Take it from me, Oscar, you have not a ghost of a chance.'[33] Next day the two men lunched together at the Café Royal, along with another Dubliner, George Bernard Shaw, who told Wilde that he agreed that the prosecution was doomed to failure. Recollections differed as to what took place after Douglas joined them at the table. Harris remembered the younger man crying out, 'Such advice shows you are no friend of Oscar's' and Wilde weakly assenting, while Shaw remembered Wilde displaying 'a mixture of infatuate haughtiness'.[34] Whatever the truth of the matter, the last hope of stopping Wilde's act of self-immolation ended with this lunch.

33   Frank Harris, *The Life and Confessions of Oscar Wilde* (New York, Duffield, 1914), p.115.
34   *Ibid.*, p. 338.

QUEENSBERRY IN THE DOCK

The prosecution of the Marquess of Queensberry was to involve two of the ablest advocates of their day. Leading the prosecution team was Sir Edward Clarke QC, MP, a former Solicitor General. Clarke looked, in the words of the lawyer and writer Montgomery Hyde, more like an old-fashioned parson than a successful Queen's Counsel. The tall, saturnine and lantern-jawed Sir Edward Carson QC, MP led for Queensberry. (Learning that he would be cross-examined by his boyhood friend and college contemporary Wilde remarked, 'No doubt he will perform his task with all the added bitterness of an old friend'.) Before accepting the brief, Clarke, like Humphreys, had taken the precaution of saying, 'I can only accept this brief, Mr. Wilde, if you assure me on your honour as an English gentleman that there is not and never has been any foundation for the charges that are made against you.' Wilde assured him that the charges were 'absolutely false and groundless.' Clarke then asked Wilde if he was a homosexual. He replied, 'It is not true that I was expelled from the Savoy Hotel at any time. Neither is it true that I took rooms in Piccadilly for Lord Queensberry's son.' Faced with this evasive reply, Clarke put his question another way, 'Is there any truth in any of these accusations?', to which Wilde replied, 'There is no truth whatever in any one of them.' And the die was cast.

Queensberry's trial began at the Old Bailey on 3 April 1895 before Mr. Justice Henn Collins sitting with a jury. The *Sun* described His Lordship as looking 'old, thin and dry' and Wilde as 'big, loose and picturesque.' The Marquess, a diminutive figure with red mutton-chop whiskers and pendulous lip, was dressed in a hunting stock instead of a collar and tie. Wilde assumed a frock coat, but without the customary flower in his buttonhole. The public gallery was crowded. Clarke opened for the prosecution with a fighting speech which tackled the defence of justification head-on. After outlining his client's history, his relationship with Douglas and the attempts which were made to blackmail him Clarke went straight to the Hyacinth Letter, which he read out in full:

My Own Boy,

Your sonnet is quite lovely, and it is a marvel that those red-roseleaf lips of yours should be made no less for the madness of music and

song than for the madness of kissing. Your slim gilt soul walks between passion and poetry. I know Hyacinthus, whom Apollo loved
so madly, was you in Greek days. Why are you alone in London, and
when do you go to Salisbury? Do go there to cool your hands in the
grey twilight of Gothic things, and come here whenever you like. It is
a lovely place and lacks only you; but go to Salisbury first.

Always, with undying love,

Yours, Oscar

While the language might appear extravagant to those accustomed
to commercial correspondence, Clarke began until stopped by courtroom laughter. The author, he went on, was a poet and the language
no more than that of a prose sonnet. It was a fair point: the letter,
rendered into French verse, had in fact been published in 1893. Turning to Wilde's written work, Clarke said that as soon as his client had
seen *The Priest and the Acolyte,* he had protested to the editor of the
Chameleon in which it had appeared. As for *Dorian Gray,* he said,
the book could be bought in any bookstall in London; he defied the
defence to point to any immoral passage in it.

After formal evidence of the presentation of Queensberry's card
at the Albemarle, Clarke called his client into the witness box where
he dealt deftly, even wittily with the history of the case. When Carson
rose to cross-examine, the *Daily Chronicle* recorded that 'Mr. Wilde
folded his arms across the rail of the witness box, his gloves drooped
gracefully from his graceful hand and faced Lord Queensberry's counsel with a smile.' Determined to dent the prosecutor's image, Carson
began with a detail, but it was a detail in which the witness had to
admit error. The forty year old playwright had erroneously given his
age as thirty-nine. Challenged on this petty vanity, Wilde said airily,
'I have no wish to pose as being young. I am 39 or 40.' Carson then
turned to Wilde's literary works, starting with the epigrams. One of
these was, 'Wickedness is a myth invented by good people to account
for the curious attractiveness of others.' Asked whether he thought
that this was true, Wilde replied, 'I rarely think that anything I write is
true.' Asked whether *The Priest and the Acolyte* was immoral, Wilde
said, 'It was worse; it was badly written.' Despite reading out large
chunks of *Dorian Gray*, Carson was unable to shake Wilde's refusal
to acknowledge that the novel reflected any impropriety upon himself.

Instead, the writer reaffirmed his statement in the preface to the book that, 'There is no such thing as a moral or an immoral book. Books are well written, or badly written', adding, 'No work of art ever puts forward views. Views belong to people who are not artists.' When it was put to him that he had promoted the admiration of young men, Wilde replied, 'The whole idea was borrowed from Shakespeare, I regret to say — yes, from Shakespeare's sonnets.'

Carson had got nowhere with this line of questioning, although he did manage to elicit a degree of intellectual arrogance when Wilde said that a 'majority of persons would come under [his] definition of Philistines and illiterates.' They were not, said Wilde, cultivated enough. These were hardly answers calculated to endear the witness to any jury. Carson then read out another letter from Wilde to Douglas dated March 1893:

> Dearest of all Boys,
>
> Your letter was delightful, red and yellow wine to me; but I am sad and out of sorts. Bosie, you must not make scenes with me. They kill me, they wreck the loveliness of life. I cannot see you, so Greek and gracious, distorted with passion. I cannot listen to your curved lips saying hideous things to me. I would sooner be blackmailed by every renter [A 'renter' is a male prostitute] in London than to have you bitter, unjust, hating ... I must see you soon. You are the divine thing I want, the thing of grace and beauty; but I don't know how to do it. Shall I come to Salisbury? My bill here, is £49 for a week. I have also got a new sitting-room over the Thames. Why are you not here, my dear, my wonderful boy? I fear I must leave – no money, no credit, and a heart of lead.
>
> Your own Oscar

Asked if this was an ordinary letter, Wilde replied, 'Everything I write is extraordinary.' The letter was 'a tender expression of my great admiration for Lord Alfred Douglas.' So far, Wilde had had the better part of the exchange, shrugging off each of his outrageous remarks as 'an amusing paradox, a play on words'. But everything was to change when the questioning moved on to Wilde's sex life, for which he seemed quite unprepared.

Carson jumped in at the deep end by asking the playwright about the nature of his relationship with the young man, Wood. Wilde replied that he had entertained him and given him £2 'out of pure kindness' and because Douglas had asked him to be nice to the lad. Asked about Alfred Taylor, Wilde admitted having been to his lodgings seven or eight times, but denied having seen anything sinister take place there. Taylor, he said, was 'a man of great taste and intelligence', 'extremely intellectual and clever' who had introduced him to five young men whom he had later wined and dined, usually in private rooms. Among them were Charles Parker, an unemployed gentleman's valet, and his older brother, William, an unemployed groom. Carson bitingly asked, 'What enjoyment was it to entertain grooms and coachmen?', to which Wilde replied, 'The pleasure to me was being with those who are young, bright, happy, careless and free. I do not like the sensible and I do not like the old.' Pressed on the social divide between himself and the young men, Wilde insisted that he 'recognize[d] no social distinctions at all of any kind.' But he was visibly shaken when Carson took him through the details of his relationships with the various rent boys.

His most damaging remark was to come in answer to the question of whether he had ever kissed the sixteen year old, Walter Grainger: 'Oh dear no. He was a peculiarly plain boy. He was unfortunately extremely ugly.' The courtroom was still. When Carson asked why he had mentioned the boy's ugliness, Wilde became uncharacteristically incoherent. 'Here the witness began several answers almost inarticulately, and none of them he finished. His efforts to collect his ideas were not aided by Mr. Carson's sharp staccato repetition: 'Why? Why? Why did you add that?' At last the witness answered: 'You sting me and insult me and try to unnerve; and at times one says things flippantly when one ought to speak more seriously. I admit it.' But the harm had been done. Reading the exchanges, it is possible to see how a man who delighted in verbal wit, incongruous juxtapositions and scandalizing his listeners responded as Wilde did. His reply was probably intended to be flippant, but that was not the way it must have appeared to the jury. What Wilde saw as light banter was completely out of place in the witness box.

In view of the way the cross-examination had gone, Clarke felt with reluctance that he had to read out a number of letters from Queensberry threatening to disown his son. (The purpose, of course, was to demonstrate the Marquess' motives in making his allegation against Wilde.) Queensberry, who was present in court, was distressed, but the real sensation lay in the references in the correspondence to Rosebery, who by now had become Prime Minister. When the court adjourned Wilde asked Clarke whether, if he went back in the witness box, Carson would be able to question him on any subject and not merely on what had gone before. Told that he could with the judge's permission, Wilde confessed to Clarke for the first time that there had been an incident when he had been turned out of the Albemarle in the middle of the night and that a boy had been with him. In fact, this event never came up in re-examination, but counsel was badly shaken by the disclosure.

Clarke closed the case for the prosecution without calling Alfred Douglas and Carson opened for the defence. Lord Queensberry's pursuit of Wilde, he claimed, had been solely for the purpose of protecting his son from what would nowadays be called a predatory homosexual. He starkly exposed Wilde's inconsistencies:

> Let us contrast the position which Mr. Wilde took up in cross-examination as to his books, which are for the select and not for the ordinary individual, with the position he assumed as to the young men to whom he was introduced and those he picked up for himself. His books were written by an artist for artists; his words were not for Philistines or illiterates. Contrast that with the way in which Mr. Wilde chose his companions! He took up with Charles Parker, a gentleman's servant, whose brother was a gentleman's servant; with young Alphonse Conway, who sold papers on the pier at Worthing; and with Scarfe, also a gentleman's servant. Then his excuse was no longer that he was dwelling in regions of art but that he had such a noble, such a democratic soul, that he drew no social distinctions, and that it was quite as much pleasure to have the sweeping boy from the streets to lunch or dine with him as the greatest littérateur or artist.

Finally, he revealed to a startled courtroom that Charles Parker and Alfred Wood were available in court and prepared to give evidence on Queensberry's behalf. When the court rose that day Clarke warned Wilde in the plainest terms of the peril he would be in if he continued with the prosecution. He gave this warning 'hoping and expecting' that Wilde would leave the country: he did not. Next morning, on 5 April while Carson was concluding his opening speech, Clarke and his client were conferring anxiously in another room. The lawyer returned to the courtroom to interrupt his opponent and announce that, since it was likely that the defence would be able to substantiate the charge of Wilde 'posing' as a sodomite, he was prepared to submit to a verdict of 'Not Guilty', but only with reference to the publication of *The Picture of Dorian Gray* and *The Chameleon.* It was a gallant try, but the judge ruled that the verdict could only be one of 'Guilty' or 'Not Guilty' overall. He went on to direct that the libel was true in fact and in substance, after which the jury decided that it had been published for the public benefit. The inevitable verdict of Not Guilty was followed by prolonged cheering in court which, Frank Harris noted with despair, the judge did nothing to stop.

Immediately after the verdict Queensberry wrote to Wilde, 'If the country allows you to leave all the better for the country! But if you take my son with you, I will follow you wherever you go and shoot you.' Wilde went at once to the now available Sir George Lewis who could only say, 'What is the good of consulting me now?' Queensberry instructed his solicitors to send a copy of all the witness statements they had gathered to the Director of Public Prosecutions, together with a shorthand note of the trial. The Director decided to prosecute and instructed the police to apply for a warrant for Wilde's arrest. In his chambers the Bow Street magistrate, Mr. (later Sir) John Bridge, asked his clerk when the last train left for the continent and deferred issue of the warrant of arrest until that time had passed. However, Wilde, who was lunching in the Cadogan Hotel along with Douglas, his brother Percy and Ross, remained in a state of indecision (and, it seems, mild inebriation from Hock and Seltzer) until the police arrived and arrested him. Later he was to tell Douglas that, 'I decided that it was nobler and more beautiful to stay ... I did not want to be called a coward or a deserter. A false name, a disguise, a hunted life, all that is not for me ...'

After spending the night in a cell Wilde was brought before the magistrate next morning. There was never any question of bail and he was committed in custody to Holloway Prison where he remained until his trial. Having been ordered to pay Queensberry's costs in the first trial as well as his own, he was now insolvent and his effects were sold at his Tite Street home by order of the Sheriff only two days before he was due to stand trial. When Sir Edward Clarke generously offered to act on his behalf without fee Wilde gratefully accepted.

Opinion in the clubs and the press was united against Wilde. His books were withdrawn from sale, the production of *An Ideal Husband* was cancelled at the Haymarket theatre; even his children had to be withdrawn from school. Ross and some of his more louche friends did what Wilde had been expected to do and ran off to the Continent for their own safety;[35] most of those who remained deserted him. Frank Harris described the prevailing mood as 'an orgy of Philistine rancour', but it was more likely a fit of homophobia aggravated by middle-class disgust at the 'unnaturally' close relations between the classes which had been revealed in Queensberry's trial, coupled with the delight of the mob at the downfall of the great and famous.

WILDE'S FIRST TRIAL

Wilde appeared in the dock at the Old Bailey for the first time on 26 April looking haggard and worn with his long hair dishevelled. He was standing beside Alfred Taylor, who had bravely declined to turn Queen's evidence against him. Mr. Justice (Sir Arthur) Charles was on the bench and Charles Gill (another Trinity College man) replaced Carson as leader for the prosecution. Otherwise, the cast of the drama and its plot looked remarkably like those in which he had so recently taken part.

Both defendants were charged with gross indecency and conspiracy to commit gross indecency with Wood, Charles Parker and Shelley during the years 1892 and 1893. Wilde was not accused of sodomy, but Taylor was charged with acting as a procurer for Wilde and with attempting to commit sodomy with both the Parker brothers. This joinder of charges gave rise to a procedural difficulty of some importance. At common law, the prisoner had never been allowed to give sworn evidence in his own defence.[36] Offences of gross indecency had been made an exception to this rule and Sir Edward Clarke un-

35   Hesketh Pearson wrote that the trains and steamers for the Continent enjoyed a sort of holiday rush out of season.
36   It is thought that this was because lying on oath would put his immortal soul at risk. This archaic rule was finally abolished by an Act of 1898.

derstandably objected to an indictment which lumped both classes of offence together. The judge, while acknowledging the inconvenience, ruled against him.

The first and perhaps most damaging witness for the prosecution was Charles Parker, now aged about twenty-one and a soldier. (He had, he said, joined up after having witnessed a 'disgusting orgy' at Taylor's lodgings.) He gave evidence of a champagne dinner at which he had been introduced by Taylor to Wilde as 'a man who was good for plenty of money'. Wilde had remarked, 'This is the boy for me' and taken him to his rooms at the Savoy where he was sodomized and given £2. Parker also claimed to have masturbated Wilde at his request, but to have refused to fellate him. The pair had also had sex at Wilde's Tite Street home, at rooms which Wilde had taken at St James's Place, at the Savoy and elsewhere. Wilde, he said, had asked him to 'act as a woman'. In his cross-examination Clarke did his best to discredit Parker as a blackmailer and an accomplice of blackmailers and got him to concede that his activities with Wilde had often been conducted 'openly' in unlocked rooms and public places. It did little to dispel the impression that his earlier testimony had given. Charles was followed in the witness box by his brother William, who added little beyond the titivating detail that Wilde sometimes fed his lovers from his fork and spoon.

Wood was then called to tell the court that Wilde had entertained him at dinner at the Florence restaurant in Rupert Street where he had fondled him intimately under the table. Afterwards, at his Tite Street home Wilde had made him 'nearly drunk' with Hock and Seltzer, after which the witness claimed he allowed Wilde 'to actually do the act of indecency'. (It is curious how counsel on both sides were so delicate about going into details over answers like this.) So far, it was going well for the prosecution, but the next two witnesses were to be a disaster.

Frederick Atkins, formerly a bookmaker's clerk and comedian but now unemployed, took the stand to describe how Wilde had kissed a waiter at dinner at the Florence and how he himself had been taken by Wilde to Paris. One night, coming back to their hotel late, he had found Wilde in bed with Schwabe. Later in the proceedings the witness was dramatically exposed as a liar for having denied that he had tried to blackmail Douglas, and was reported for perjury. This totally devalued any credibility he might have had for the prosecution. The next witness, Sidney Mavor, proved to be equally disappointing when he went back on his witness statement and denied that anything improper had taken place between Wilde and himself in bed. (Years later, Douglas admitted having got to the witness before the trial and reminded him of his duty 'as a public schoolboy'.) The result was that Mavor's evidence too proved to be useless to the prosecution.

The twenty-one year old and visibly unbalanced Edward Shelley then gave evidence of having gone to the Albemarle Hotel with Wilde, whom he said he regarded as a 'philanthropist'. Wilde had taken the lad to his bedroom and kissed him; he had felt 'insulted' and 'degraded', but had nevertheless stayed the night and shared Wilde's bed.

The third day of the trial was concerned with what proved to be the controversial events at the Savoy between 6 and 20 March 1893. 'Professor' Antonio Migge, the resident masseur, gave evidence of seeing someone in Wilde's bed one morning whom he took at first to be a lady but later realized was a young man. Wilde, who had been at the washstand at the time, had said that he had no need for the witness's services and Migge had left the room. A chambermaid, Jane Cotter, said that she had seen a boy of sixteen with close cropped hair and a sallow complexion in the same bed. She had drawn the housekeeper's attention to the bed sheets which had been 'stained in a peculiar way'. The (now former) housekeeper confirmed this and put the stains down to excrement, Vaseline and semen.

On the fourth day of the trial, after all the prosecution evidence had been called, counsel withdrew the charges of conspiracy for lack of evidence. (One effect of this was to remove the difficulties over the accused giving evidence on their own behalf.) In his opening speech for the defence Clarke said that it was not fair to judge a man by his books, or in the case of *The Chameleon,* by the contribution of others. The fact that Wilde had brought the prosecution against Queensberry was evidence of his innocence and the young men who had been called by the prosecution were not independent witnesses. He then called Wilde into the witness box. After confirming that the evidence he had given at the libel trial was 'entirely true' Wilde was tendered to the prosecution for cross-examination. Gill began by reading out two of Douglas' poems. One of them entitled, *Two Loves,* ended with the line, 'I am the Love that dare not speak its name' Asked what that meant, Wilde replied eloquently:

'The Love that dare not speak its name' in this century is such a great affection of an elder for a younger man as there was between David and Jonathan, such as Plato made the very basis of his philosophy, and such as you find in the sonnets of Michelangelo and Shakespeare. It is that deep, spiritual affection that is as pure as it is perfect. It dictates and pervades great works of art like those of Shakespeare and Michelangelo, and those two letters of mine, such as they are. It is in this century misunderstood, so much misunderstood that it may be described as the 'Love that dare not speak its name', and on account of it I am placed where I am now. It is beautiful, it is fine, it is the noblest form of affection. There is nothing unnatural about it. It is intellectual, and it repeatedly exists between an elder and a younger man, when the elder man has intellect, and the younger man has all the joy, hope and glamour of life before him. That it should be so the world does not understand. The world mocks at it and sometimes puts one in the pillory for it.

It was met with loud applause mingled with hisses. Gill then asked Wilde whether an ordinarily constituted being would address to a younger man expressions such as he had used in his letters. Wilde could not resist replying, 'I am not, happily I think, an ordinarily constituted being.' Apart from this remark he mostly refrained from the light bantering tone that he had so disastrously adopted at the libel trial. Gill turned next to the incident of 'the boy in the bed'. Asked whether he was prepared to contradict the evidence of the hotel servants, Wilde replied, 'It is entirely untrue. Can I answer for what hotel servants say years after I have left the hotel?' Asked whether there was a woman with him in the room, he replied, 'Certainly not.' Concerning the rent boys he commented, 'Their evidence as to my association with them, as to the dinners taking place and the small presents I gave them is mostly true. But there is not a particle of truth in that part of the evidence which alleged improper behaviour.' He admitted frequenting Taylor's rooms, but only for the purpose of 'music, singing, chatting, and nonsense of that kind, to while an hour away.'

Clarke closed Wilde's case with an impassioned and wholly justifiable plea to the jury to consider the evidence against the two defendants separately. Wilde had been open throughout, an attitude which he contrasted with that of the shameless young men upon whose evidence the Crown relied; they were blackmailers who had admitted willing participation in shocking practices; and Atkins was an admitted perjurer. It was a fine speech and as Clarke sat down a tearful Wilde passed him a short note of thanks.

Closing for the Crown, Gill reminded the jury that Queensberry had succeeded in proving his defence of justification at the earlier trial. He dealt neatly with the young men's character; they were in his words, 'accusing themselves, in accusing another of a shameful and infamous act, and this they would hardly do if it were not the truth.' The admitted gifts and the dinners were corroboration of their story, and the gifts, he reminded the jury, were only given after Wilde had been alone with them.

Before summing up, the judge directed that, since Mavor had denied all impropriety with the prisoner, he would direct that the counts concerning him be struck out. Turning to the jury, he said that it was a wise rule of practice that no one may be convicted on the uncorroborated evidence of an accomplice. Corroboration existed, he ruled, in this case in 'the acquaintance of the defendants with the witnesses and as to many particulars of the narrative they gave'. Nevertheless, the jury should also bear in mind their bad character. As to Wilde's literary work, he strongly discouraged the jury from placing any unfavourable opinion on Wilde's authorship of *Dorian Gray*. He took a similar line with the letters which Wilde had written to Douglas: 'I question if Mr. Carson was right in regarding [them] as of a horrible or indecent character'. He even expressed doubt as to the Savoy incident. 'To my mind it seems strange that, if what the hotel servants alleged is true, there was so little attempt at concealment'. The defence could not have wished for a better summing up. The jury retired at 1.30 p.m. to consider their verdict and returned to court at 5.15 p.m. to announce that they found the charges concerning Atkins not proved. Despite their best endeavours, however, they were unable to agree on a verdict on the other charges, and there was no prospect of their doing so even if given more time. The judge discharged the jury and ordered a retrial of the remaining charges.

Wilde managed to secure bail from a judge in chambers in the sum of £2,500 with two sureties of £1,250 each. One of them was Douglas' brother Percy, and the other a sympathetic clergyman unknown to the accused.[37] After they had entered into their recognizances Wilde was released from custody on 7 May. He went first to the Midland Hotel, but thugs employed by Queensberry forced the management to turn him out. His younger brother gave him refuge in his house with their mother, but pressures proved too much and Wilde found shelter in the home of a friendly couple. The question arose once more, should he flee the country, or should he stay? His romantically inclined mother had no doubt where his duty lay. 'If you go to prison, you will always be my son. It will make no difference to my affection. But if you go, I will never speak to you again.' The more practical Constance, who despite their separation was still on good terms with her husband, urged him to flee and well-wishers placed a yacht and a large sum of money at his disposal. In the end he refused to go.

To bring to trial a second time someone who has been discharged because a jury could not agree on his guilt is always a risky business. Prosecute and fail and you will be accused of persecution. Fail to prosecute and you will be accused of having brought the first prosecution recklessly. In this case there was a further complication; the Prime Minister's name had been mentioned in a scandalous context and not to prosecute would inevitably be seen as covering up the sins of the mighty. That proved to be the deciding factor; when asked by an Irish politician not to bring Wilde to court a second time, the Solicitor General replied, 'I would not, but for the abominable rumours against Rosebery.'[38] Carson too asked the Solicitor General to 'let up on the fellow', but got a similar reply.[39]

---

37   Incensed at Percy for having stood bail for Wilde, Queensberry blew a raspberry at him in Bond Street; a scuffle ensued and father and son were arrested and bound over to keep the peace. In revenge, Queensberry disinherited Percy. Douglas later revealed in his autobiography that the clergyman's surety had in fact been underwritten by Percy.
38   Ellmann, *Oscar Wilde*, p. 447. *The Dictionary of National Biography* comments, '[T]he danger of collateral damage from any exposure of the Douglas family's sexual adventures was considerable'.
39   Hyde, *Oscar Wilde: A Biography*, p. 224.

WILDE'S LAST TRIAL

Wilde's last trial began at the Old Bailey on 21 May before the seventy year old Mr. Justice (Sir Alfred) Wills sitting with a different jury. To signify the importance of the case the prosecution was undertaken by the Solicitor General himself, Sir Frank Lockwood. (No one seems to have been disturbed by the fact that one of Wilde's bed mates, Maurice Schwabe, was Lockwood's nephew by marriage.) This time Clarke succeeded in persuading the judge to have Wilde tried separately from Taylor, but Lockwood, who was known as a fighting advocate, had by virtue of his office the right to decide which defendant should be tried first and he was not going to give it up. Clarke was unable to upset this decision and, after a brief trial, Taylor was found 'Guilty' on the charges concerning the Parker brothers and 'Not Guilty' of procuring Wood. The jury were discharged on the remaining charges and sentencing was postponed until the conclusion of Wilde's trial. Queensberry telegraphed his daughter-in-law: 'Must congratulate on verdict. Cannot on Peter's appearance. Looked like a dug up corpse. Fear too much madness of kissing.[40] Taylor guilty. Wilde's turn tomorrow.'

The prosecution witnesses gave much the same evidence as in the previous trial, except that Charles Parker was forced to admit under cross-examination that he had also blackmailed another man. When the chambermaid Jane Cotter entered the witness box, Clarke's first question to her was a *coup de théâtre*: 'Why do you wear glasses?' 'Because my sight is bad,' she replied. Asked whether she used them at work, she answered, 'Oh dear, no.' 'Why do you wear them today?' brought the damning answer, 'Because I thought I might have to identify someone.' Under further questioning she admitted that she had not been wearing glasses on the day when she had seen a boy in Wilde's bed. When Mr. Migge was called to the stand he could not recollect whether the boy he saw was fair or dark. Armed with these concessions Clarke naturally made a submission to the judge that there was insufficient evidence to put the Savoy incident to the jury, particularly since Parker had sworn that he had left the hotel at midnight on both occasions he was there. Somewhat surprisingly, this plea was rejected

40   A phrase which echoes the terms of the Hyacinth Letter.

by the judge who said, 'The very fact that a man in such a position in life as the prisoner is found with a boy in his bedroom seems to me so utterly unusual that very little additional evidence would make the case go to the jury.' He agreed that the evidence concerning the 'boy in the bedroom' was borderline, but considered that the wiser and safer course would be to allow the count to go to the jury.[41] The judge took a different view of the evidence of the boy, Shelley. Since he was on his own admission an accomplice his evidence required corroboration. In the judge's view no such corroboration existed and he accordingly withdrew the charge relating to him from the jury's consideration.[42] The unbalanced Shelley later had a breakdown and discovered religion.

By now, Wilde was so weakened that he had to give his evidence seated. After briefly denying the charges against him and dismissing his letters to Douglas as of no importance he was offered for cross-examination to the Solicitor General. Lockwood went immediately to the issue of the letters. Asked why he had referred to Douglas as 'My own Boy', Wilde described it in a hollow voice as 'a fantastic, extravagant way of writing to a young man ... It was like a sonnet of Shakespeare ... a prose poem.' It was an accurate simile, but the more literary among the jurymen would have been aware that a number of Shakespeare's sonnets were believed to represent the illicit love of an older for a younger man. Asked about Taylor's habit of sleeping with boys, Wilde replied with astounding naivety, 'I don't think it is necessary to conclude that there was anything criminal. It was unusual.' It was an answer which on the most generous interpretation must have raised doubts in the jury's mind about Wilde's judgement. Asked, 'What pleasure could you find in the society of boys much beneath you in social position?' Wilde replied that he made no social distinctions. Finally, when the events at the Savoy were put to him he denied that anyone had been in the room with him. 'There was no one there, man or woman.' As for the linen, he had not examined it: 'I am

41   Judges are seldom criticized for leaving issues to the jury so this course was safer for the judge also.
42   Sir Travers Humphreys QC, Charles's son and a junior counsel for Wilde in the libel trial, has pointed out that then, as now, a judge did not have this power, but no one seems to have objected.

not a housemaid,'. And if the stains were there, 'they were not caused by the way the prosecution has most filthily suggested.'

In his concluding address to the jury Sir Edward Clarke suggested that, 'This trial seems to be operating as an act of indemnity for all the blackmailers in London. Wood and Parker, in giving evidence, have established for themselves a sort of statute of limitations. In testifying on behalf of the Crown they have secured immunity for past rogueries and indecencies. It is on the evidence of Parker and Wood that you are asked to condemn Mr. Wilde. ... The positions should really be changed. It is these men who ought to be the accused, not the accusers.' As for the incriminating stains on the bed linen, there was a perfectly innocent explanation; his client had merely been suffering from diarrhoea.

The Solicitor General rose to pour scorn on the idea of the 'prose poem'. 'If that letter had been seen by any right-minded man,' he said, 'it would have been looked upon as evidence of a guilty passion.' The transaction with regard to the letters was capable of one construction only. 'Mr. Wilde knew they were letters which he must recover; he bought them and tore them to pieces.' As to not relying on the evidence of blackmailers, 'The genesis of the blackmailer is the man who has committed these acts of indecency with him. And the genesis of the man who commits these foul acts is the man who is willing to pay for their commission.' 'It is no conclusive answer,' he went on, 'to say that Mr. Wilde did everything openly. If crime were always cautious it would always go unpunished, and it is in moments of carelessness that crime is detected. Why,' he asked, 'was Lord Alfred Douglas, who slept in the next room [at the Savoy], not called to deny the statements of the chambermaid? I maintain that she and the other witnesses from the Savoy Hotel could have no possible object in patching up a bogus case.' Finally, he said of Wilde, 'He is a man of culture and literary tastes, and I submit that his associates ought to have been his equals and not those illiterate boys whom you have heard in the witness box.'

Concluding his address the following morning Lockwood said that Wilde had brought the prosecution against Queensberry because he could rely on the evidence of 'his intimate friend, Taylor.' This was too much for Clarke who rose to object to 'what has never been proved in evidence.' Lockwood responded by pointing to the fact that the two men called each other by their Christian names and that Wilde had said of Taylor, 'Bring your friends; they are my friends. I will not enquire whether they come from the stable or the kitchen'. Lockwood had got the better of the exchange, but it was an unedifying spat between counsel which the judge deplored. When one of their remarks provoked laughter in court he protested, 'To have to try a case of this kind, to keep the scales even, and do one's duty is hard enough; but to be pestered with the applause or expressions of feeling of senseless people who have no business to be here at all except for the gratification of morbid curiosity is too much.' Lockwood went on to deal skilfully with the weight to be placed on the evidence of blackmailers, 'Were it not that there are men willing to purchase vice in the most hideous and detestable form, there would be no market for such crime and no opening for these blackmailers to ply their calling.' It was a most capable speech.

Mr. Justice Wills' summing up was far less favourable to Wilde than that of Mr. Justice Charles, but by no means entirely adverse. He said that he would prefer to have seen Wilde tried before Taylor, but that he did not believe that the accused had suffered thereby. As to Wilde's letters, he took a different view from that of Mr. Justice Charles and 'very much doubted' that they were harmless and trivial. On the incident of the 'boy in the bed', he deplored the lack of medical evidence concerning the bed sheets and commented, 'If a servant noticed anything wrong and said nothing about if for two years, I would not consider that as evidence on which I would hang a dog'. The evidence of Migge the masseur he described as 'remarkable' and that of the chambermaid as 'no less extraordinary', both terms being used in a critical sense.

The jury took two hours to arrive at a verdict of 'Guilty' on all the outstanding charges. The judge refused a defence application for sentence to be deferred and pronounced:

Oscar Wilde and Alfred Taylor, the crime of which you have been convicted is so bad that one has to put stern restraint upon one's self to prevent one's self from describing, in language which I would rather not use, the sentiments which must rise in the breast of every man of honour who has heard the details of these two horrible trials … It is no use for me to address you. People who can do these things must be dead to all sense of shame, and one cannot hope to produce any effect upon them. It is the worst case I have ever tried. That you, Taylor, kept a kind of male brothel it is impossible to doubt. And that you, Wilde, have been the centre of a circle of extensive corruption of the worst kind among young men, it is equally impossible to doubt. I shall, under the circumstances, be expected to pass the severest sentence that the law allows. In my judgment it is totally inadequate for a case such as this. The sentence of the Court is that each of you be imprisoned and kept to hard labour for two years.

'And I?', said Wilde piteously. 'May I say nothing, My Lord?' The plea was ignored and a broken Wilde swayed in the dock before being taken down to the cells on the arms of two warders. That night Brookfield entertained Queensberry to a celebratory dinner, while Constance took the children to her brother, Otho Holland Lloyd, in Switzerland; they were never to see their father again.

'A SOUL IN PAIN'

Wilde was taken first to Holloway Prison and then to Pentonville, where he was expected to serve his time. Certified as fit for 'hard labour' by the prison doctor, he was required to spend six hours a day on the treadmill during the first month of imprisonment. In fact, he spent only four days under this regime before succumbing to 'mental prostration and melancholy' aggravated by diarrhoea, and was taken to the infirmary. Six weeks later he was transferred to Wandsworth Prison, where his health continued to deteriorate. No longer on potassium bromide,[43] the prison chaplain reported that he was resorting to 'perverse sexual practices' in his cell, in other words compulsive masturbation, a practice which in those days was seen as a sign of mental imbalance.[44]

In order to recover the costs of his defence in the libel trial Queensberry made Wilde bankrupt. In November the poet was brought from prison twice for a public examination at the court in Carey Street.

---

43 'Bromide' was then supposed to suppress the sexual impulse.
44 *The Ballad of Reading Gaol* (1898) spoke of his cell where 'all but Lust is turned to dust.'

Ross managed to attend the proceedings and tip his hat to his friend, a gesture that meant much to the older man.[45]

Wilde had now lost some two stone in weight and the authorities were so concerned for his health that it was decided to transfer him to somewhere more congenial. In November he was taken to Reading Gaol; the journey was a bitter experience:

> From two o'clock till half-past two on that day I had to stand on the centre platform of Clapham Junction in convict dress, and handcuffed, for the world to look at. ... Of all possible objects I was the most grotesque. When people saw me they laughed. Each train as it came up swelled the audience. Nothing could exceed their amusement. That was, of course, before they knew who I was. As soon as they had been informed they laughed still more. For half an hour I stood there in the grey November rain surrounded by a jeering mob.

In fact, Reading Gaol under its brutal governor, Lieutenant-Colonel Henry Bevan Isaacson, proved to be the opposite to the rest cure the authorities had hoped for. Isaacs announced his intention of 'knocking the nonsense out of Wilde' and the prisoner found himself 'caught up in a cycle of substantial punishments for small offences such as not sweeping his cell clean, or uttering a word or two with another prisoner.'[46] A middle ear infection which he had suffered as a result of a fainting fit in the chapel of Holloway Prison was now playing up. Fearing that Wilde could not survive the experience, Frank Harris approached the chairman of the Prison Commission and was allowed to visit his friend in private. Shortly afterwards, Wilde petitioned the Home Secretary for release on medical grounds. He accepted that he had been 'rightly found guilty' of indecency, but urged that he should be treated not as a criminal but as a victim of 'sexual madness'. He went on, 'For more than thirteen dreadful months, the petitioner has been subject to the fearful system of solitary cellular confinement: without human intercourse of any kind; without writing materials whose use might help to distract the mind: without suitable or sufficient books, so essential to any literary man, so vital for the preservation of mental balance: condemned to absolute silence: cut off from

45   Before his release from gaol, Wilde appointed Ross his literary executor; but it was not until 1905 that he was able to pay Wilde's creditors.
46   Ellmann, *Oscar Wilde*, p. 474.

knowledge of the external world and the movements of life: leading an existence composed of bitter degradations and terrible hardships, hideous in its recurring monotony of dreary task and sickening privation.' The petition was refused on the advice of the prison medical officer, Dr Maurice JP, who in Wilde's eyes was even more vindictive than Isaacson.[47]

Three months after Wilde had been transferred to Reading, his mother fell seriously ill with bronchitis. Her request to see her son was refused and her last words were, 'May the prison help him.' Her death, Wilde wrote in *De Profundis* that her death:

> was terrible to me; but I, once a lord of language, have no words in which to express my anguish and my shame. She and my father had bequeathed me a name they had made noble and honoured, not merely in literature, art, archaeology, and science, but in the public history of my own country, in its evolution as a nation. I had disgraced that name eternally. I had made it a low by-word among low people. I had dragged it through the very mire. I had given it to brutes that they might make it brutal, and to fools that they might turn it into a synonym for folly. What I suffered then, and still suffer, is not for pen to write or paper to record.

Constance had visited Wilde in prison in September 1895. She found the experience shattering and withdrew the divorce proceedings she had begun. She saw him again in February 1896, when she travelled from Switzerland to break the news of his mother's death. They agreed on the income which he should receive after his release and he suggested that, if the bringing up of their children should be too onerous, an additional guardian should be appointed for them. Relations between the couple took a turn for the worse, however, when the person looking after Oscar's affairs outbid her for his life interest in the marriage settlement.[48] When she next visited the gaol in February 1897 to get the papers signed, Constance asked to see her husband through the peep hole in the door without his being aware that she was there. It was to be her last sight of him.

---

47 *The Ballad of Reading Gaol* refers to the 'coarse mouthed doctor'.
48 As a bankrupt, Wilde's interest in the allowance was a saleable property.

DE PROFUNDIS

In July 1896 Isaacson had been replaced as prison governor by Major J.O. Nelson, whom Wilde was to describe – with the understandable exaggeration of the grateful – as 'the most Christlike man' he had ever met. The regime became far more relaxed and Wilde was allowed writing materials. He promptly used them to write an extended letter to Douglas which was later published under the title, *De Profundis*. ('Out of the depths' – The title was given to the work by Ross when it was published in 1905.) As well as a bitter condemnation of the prison system, *De Profundis* was also a diatribe against Bosie whom he believed to have abandoned him. In this he was misled. Douglas had been strongly advised by Clarke to leave the country and had been reluctantly persuaded not to return. He had sought and been refused permission to write to his friend, but this had not stopped him writing to the papers on Wilde's behalf. In June 1895 he addressed a petition to Queen Victoria seeking clemency for his friend who, he wrote, had been punished 'a thousand times more cruelly than he deserves.' It was summarily rejected by the Home Secretary.

Although he blamed himself desperately for his fate, Wilde reserved his strongest criticism for Bosie. Their friendship, he claimed, had been 'intellectually degrading'. He compared Douglas' undeveloped brain and dead imagination unfavourably to those of his other lovers. Douglas had brought him to 'to utter and discreditable financial ruin.' He referred to the young man's 'insistence on a life of reckless profusion' and complained of his incessant demands for money. 'You demanded without grace and received without thanks.' He condemned Douglas for his 'incessant scenes' and for his 'mania for writing revolting and loathsome letters.' Wilde was bored to death by the young man's passion for music halls and his absurd extravagance in eating and drinking. 'But most of all,' he wrote, 'I blame myself for the entire ethical degradation I allowed you to bring on me.' This letter, which was signed 'Your affectionate friend', is a curious mixture of self-awareness, shrewd character judgement and bitter recriminations which cannot be read without distress.

Bernard Shaw dismissed *De Profundis* as 'nothing worse than any record of the squabbles of two idlers',[49] but the description of 'our ill-fated and most lamentable friendship' was devastating to Douglas when he read the fuller version which was published in 1908 after Wilde's death. (The comments critical of Douglas had been omitted in first publication.) It was to destroy what remained of his regard for Wilde, and in a letter to Harris he described *De Profundis* as a 'dreadful piece of cold-blooded, malignant malice, hypocrisy and lying.'[50]

'CLEFTS IN THE ROCK'

After serving the full term of his sentence Wilde was released from prison on 18 May 1897 in conditions of great secrecy and, along with Ross, left for France the same night under the pseudonym, Sebastian Melmoth. The name had been carefully chosen; the Christian martyr Saint Sebastian was a handsome youth who, after being tied to a post and shot with arrows, had become a homoerotic icon. *Melmoth The Wanderer* was a Gothic novel written by Lady Wilde's maternal great-uncle. It was the story of a man who sold his soul to the Devil for a few extra years of life, but who spent those years seeking someone who would take over his burden. In France, Wilde settled in a villa at Berneval, a quiet village near Dieppe. André Gide described him there as 'no longer the sensualist puffed out with pride and good living', but 'the sweet Wilde of the days before 1891.' Friends reported that he was looking in better health and that his mind was turning toward higher things.

And so it was. Wilde's experience in prison had moved him deeply; on one occasion, he remembered, a warder had been dismissed for the crime of giving sweets to a hungry child. One of the poet's first acts after leaving prison had been to write a long letter to the *Daily Chronicle* pleading for the better treatment of convicted children. An even more traumatic experience had been the hanging in prison of a young trooper of the Royal Horse Guards for slitting the throat of his unfaithful wife. It was the inspiration for Wilde's greatest poem, *The*

49 Harris, *Life and Confessions of Oscar Wilde*, p. 342.
50 Lord Alfred Douglas, *The Autobiography of Lord Alfred Douglas* (London, Martin Secker, 1929), p. 40.

Ballad of Reading Gaol, written after he left prison and published in February 1898 over the signature, C.C.3, Wilde's prison number.[51] It remains to this day one of the most moving condemnations of a harsh penal system:

> The vilest deeds like poison weeds,
> Bloom well in prison-air;
> It is only what is good in Man
> That wastes and withers there:
> Pale Anguish keeps the heavy gate,
> And the Warder is Despair.

Wilde's attempt at a reconciliation with Constance having failed, he found in the arms of Ross the consolation he longed for. Inevitably, Oscar became bored with village life and, despite everything that he had written in *De Profundis,* turned yet once more to Bosie (who had as yet not seen the full text of that curious document). After a tempestuous correspondence the two were reunited in a hotel in Rouen, despite a warning from his solicitor that to do so would be in breach of his undertaking in the deed of separation. A week later the couple eloped to a villa outside Naples.

Constance duly stopped Wilde's allowance[52] and Lady Queensberry stopped her son's. Despite the fact that none of the English colony in Naples left calling cards, the two lovers were happy and began writing again; it was not to last. Wilde complained that Bosie had offered him a home and an income, but had not delivered on either. Bosie left for Paris in December,[53] and Oscar followed him early the following year. It was the day that *The Ballad of Reading Gaol* was published and Oscar sent Constance an unsigned copy of the poem, for which she was touched. His response to her letter of thanks was to reply demanding a restoration of his allowance, which she naturally refused. Constance died on 7 April that year of the effects of a spinal injury and was buried in the Protestant cemetery in Genoa.[54]

---

51 Frank Harris suggested that its form was modelled on that used by A.E. Houseman in *A Shropshire Lad.*
52 McKenna believes that it was a bitter Robbie who tipped off the solicitor.
53 McKenna suggests that it was a ploy to regain the allowances.
54 When Oscar visited the grave he found that the inscription bore no reference to him. His name has since been added to the stone.

In the end, neither penal reform, penury nor remorse could hold a candle to the attractions of the cosmopolitan life and no sooner was he in Paris than Wilde resumed his pursuit of young men with undiminished vigour. All he thought about and dreamed about, wrote Douglas, who saw him from time to time, was the gratification of his vice and getting money by any means. Douglas claimed that it was Ross who had revived the poet's interest in young men, but Wilde's letters give the lie to this.[55] Douglas also professed to have left his philandering days behind, but this was far from true. (He was, according to Wilde, particularly devoted to a fourteen year old street urchin.) At the end of 1898 after Bosie had returned to England Wilde travelled to Monte Carlo and Nice as a guest of Frank Harris. The following February he enjoyed the hospitality of another friend on Lake Geneva. Despite being a social pariah to many, the generosity of others was extraordinary. When he returned to Paris penniless, Oscar was taken in by the kindly proprietor of the Hotel d'Alsace on the Left Bank where he was permitted to run up a large bill which he could not afford to pay. In January 1900 Douglas inherited a large sum of money on the death of his father. It only led to more recriminations from Wilde who was convinced that 'the Queensberry family' were indebted to him.[56] He went on to spend a few days in Palermo with another friend – where he managed to pick up a fifteen year old boy – and a few in Rome as the guest of Ross. ('Do you observe that I have fallen in love with you again?'). His was never an exclusive passion.

Now 'shabby and down at heel', Wilde lived on an allowance from the trustees of his late wife's estate[57] and the generosity of friends like Ross; Douglas contributed little. In October his old ear problem reemerged and had to be operated on. When food and champagne were sent in to his room Wilde quipped with a resurgence of his old wit, 'I am dying beyond my means.' Later, confined to his room, he said, 'My wallpaper and I are fighting a duel to the death. One or other of us has got to go.' Now in great pain and on morphine, he wrote to Ross that his throat was a lime kiln, his brain a furnace and his nerves a coil of angry vipers. When a painful abscess formed in the ear he

---

55   Hyde, *Oscar Wilde: A Biography*, p. 347.
56   Douglas claimed that he gave Wilde £1,000 during this period.
57   Constance had provided for this in a codicil in her will.

lapsed into a fever; Ross was called urgently from London, arriving the day before Wilde died. It was 30 November 1900 and he was forty-six.[58]

At his funeral there was an undedifying squabble in which Douglas nearly fell into the grave in his attempts to maintain his role as principal mourner.[59] In his last hours, though unable to speak, Wilde had been received into the Catholic church. Nine years later his body found its final resting place in the great Père Lachaise cemetery in Paris beneath a modernist tomb which Ross had commissioned from the sculptor Epstein whom the poet had admired.

AFTERWARDS

Queensberry frittered away his fortune and developed an obsession that he was being persecuted by 'the Oscar Wilders'. He died before Wilde. Almost his last act was to spit on his son Percy when he hurried to his bedside seeking a reconciliation.

Douglas married in 1902 and had a son. The couple separated ten years later, but remained on speaking terms. He went on to write over twenty volumes of poetry and prose, which were praised in his time but little remembered today. In 1911 he converted to Roman Catholicism, but it did nothing to restrain his tempestuous nature. In 1913 he was charged with libelling his former father-in-law and in 1915 with libelling Ross as 'an habitual debaucher and corrupter of young boys'. The jury could not agree on a verdict and he was discharged. But Douglas could not control his mouth[60] and in 1923 he was sentenced to six months hard labour for libelling Winston Churchill. [61]

Douglas had defended Wilde's memory at first, but *De Profundis* changed his attitude. In his book, *Oscar Wilde and Myself*, he claimed that he had been 'born in this world chiefly to be the instrument,

58 Death was put down to cerebral meningitis.
59 Douglas paid for *un enterrement de 6ieme classe.*
60 In his autobiography Douglas wrote that he had lost count of the number of libel actions he had been involved in.
61 He alleged that Churchill had taken part in a Jewish-financed conspiracy to have Kitchener murdered.

whether I would or not, of exposing and smashing Wilde's cult and the Wilde myth.' But perhaps the greatest betrayal was in 1918 when in the course of legal proceedings to which, for once, Douglas was not a party, he described his old friend and lover as '... the greatest force for evil that has appeared in Europe in the past 350 years ...'[62] Douglas died of a heart attack in 1945. It is difficult to make a balanced judgement on his elusive character and his on and off relationship with Oscar Wilde. There are those who have argued that, for all his deficiencies, he was a devoted lover[63] and others who see him as vindictive, petty and disloyal. Perhaps the most important fact about Douglas is that Wilde loved him before any other man.

Compared with the unattractive Douglas, it is tempting to paint Ross as sweet and saintly, but this would be far from the truth. He was as promiscuous as Wilde, shared his fascination with 'rough trade' and was a pederast to boot, weaknesses that are viewed with distaste even today. Unlike Douglas, however, Ross was comfortable with his homosexuality and offered Wilde a friendship that lasted, with only a few bumpy passages, throughout the poet's life – and beyond. After Wilde's death he paid off his creditors and regained the poet's copyrights for his sons. He became a gallery owner and art critic and converted to Roman Catholicism. After his death in 1918 his ashes were placed inside Wilde's tomb, as he had intended.

Little is known of the minor characters in this drama except that Brookfield fittingly became joint censor of plays in the Lord Chamberlain's office. And one day in 1923, when Douglas was staying at a hotel in Chicago, he rang for the wine waiter and Taylor appeared.

WHY DID WILDE BRING ABOUT HIS OWN DOWNFALL?

Whatever myths may have since built up, Oscar Wilde never saw himself as a martyr to what would nowadays be called gay rights. Though

62 A right-wing MP was accused of implying that an actress friend of Ross was a lesbian. Douglas was, for once, merely a witness in the case and not a principal.
63 See Douglas Murray, *Bosie: A Biography of Lord Alfred Douglas* (London, Hodder & Stoughton, 2000).

perfectly content to adopt a homosexual image, he would never admit to homosexual practices. And, apart from a brief interest in a secret society founded to promote 'the cause',[64] Wilde was never a campaigner for law reform in this area. The real reason he brought legal proceedings against Queensberry was to satisfy Bosie's hatred of his father.

In *Autobiography* Douglas blamed Ross for persuading Wilde to prosecute Queensberry, but this was the opposite of the truth. Determined to bring his father down by any means, Douglas pressed relentlessly for a prosecution, which he was confident would succeed if only his advice were to be followed. In a confusing passage in *Autobiography* Douglas claimed, 'Sir Edward Clarke was pledged to fight the case according to my ideas and to put me into the witness box immediately after his opening speech.'[65] Clarke protested vigorously that there was 'not a fragment of truth' in this assertion, not least because Douglas' argument was specious in law: Queensberry's motives for libelling Wilde were simply not relevant to the prosecution. But why did Wilde give way to Douglas' urgings?

Hesketh Pearson suggested that, corrupted by applause and success, Wilde saw himself in the role of Christ with Calvary yet to come.[66] But this probably over-dramatizes the dramatic. Wilde enjoyed risk; as he wrote to Douglas later of flirting with evil, 'it was like feasting with panthers; the danger was half the excitement.' It seems more likely that in deciding to bring the prosecution Wilde, comforted by the belief that the worst that Queensberry could throw at him were his literary works and his way of life, decided that he could cope with both. It was only when Queensberry put in his amended plea of justification, spelling out the names and dates of his relations with the rent boys, that he realized with horror the dangers that awaited him. Even then he could have backed out and withdrawn his action; we can only assume that it was pride that compelled him to continue with it. As Mr. Justice Wills said, 'This was a message which left the defendant no alternative but to prosecute, or else be branded publicly as a man who could not deny a foul charge.'

64 The Order of Chaeronea.
65 Douglas, *Autobiography*, pp. 90-91.
66 Pearson, *Oscar Wilde, His Life and Wit*, p. 252.

Having decided to bring this foolish prosecution Wilde made the worst of it by lying. He lied on oath in court, as he himself later admitted, and that is bad enough; worse, however, he lied to his lawyers, not lightly but solemnly, and not once, but frequently. In a letter to Douglas he reminded him of how 'in the ghastly glare of a bleak room you and I would sit with serious faces telling serious lies to a bald man [Humphreys] till I really groaned and yawned with ennui …'

WHY WASN'T DOUGLAS CHARGED ALONG WITH WILDE?

At one point in Wilde's second trial the foreman of the jury pertinently asked the judge, 'In view of the intimacy between Lord Alfred Douglas and Wilde was a warrant ever issued for the arrest of Lord Alfred Douglas?' Mr. Justice Wills had to reply that there might be a thousand considerations that prevented Douglas' appearance in the witness box; which was true, but we now know exactly why the authorities took the decision they did.

In a letter to the Director of Public Prosecutions before Wilde's first trial Charles Gill, senior Treasury counsel and subsequent prosecutor, advised that there was, 'little room for doubt that immoral relations existed between [Wilde and Douglas], yet if an attempt were to be made to prove anything definite, it would be found, I think, that the evidence available only disclosed a case of grave suspicion.' There was, he wrote, no corroborating evidence against Douglas such as would be required by law. 'Comments', he added prophetically, 'will no doubt be made as to Douglas not being prosecuted, but these comments are made by people who do not understand or appreciate the difficulties of proving such a case.' And the Director agreed with him.

Gill's advice was correct as far as it went; a trial is all about what can be proved. But that is never the case with an investigation. Surely it would have been prudent for the police to have at least interviewed Douglas, who was widely rumoured to have been Wilde's lover, and to have sought evidence from hotels other than the Savoy? The failure to do so could only have been down to Gill's further advice that because of the age gap between Wilde and Douglas, the younger man 'may fairly be regarded as a victim.' It was far from the truth. As Douglas himself was to write to the journalist, W.T. Stead, 'So far from [Wilde's] leading me astray it was I that (unwittingly) pushed him over the precipice.'[67]

WAS JUSTICE DONE?

In *De Profundis* Wilde wrote cryptically:

> The sins of another were being placed to my account. Had I so chosen, I could on either trial have saved myself at his expense, not from shame indeed, but from imprisonment. Had I cared to show that the Crown witnesses – the three most important – had been carefully coached by your father and his solicitors, not in reticence merely, but in assertions, in the absolute transference, deliberate, plotted, and rehearsed, of the actions and doings of someone else on to me, I could have had each one of them dismissed from the box, by the judge more summarily than even wretched, perjured Atkins was... To have secured my acquittal by such means would have been a lifelong torture to me.

What he seems to be suggesting in this passage is that he had refrained from exposing what actually went on at the Savoy, and thus from securing his freedom, solely out of his love for Douglas. There is support for this interpretation in a conversation Frank Harris reported as having had with him. It went:

> 'The chambermaid's evidence is wrong,' Oscar declared. 'They are mistaken, Frank. It was not me they spoke about at the Savoy Hotel. It was ... [presumably Douglas]. I was never bold enough. I went to see [Douglas] in the morning in his room.'

> 'Thank God,' [Harris] said, 'but why didn't Sir Edward Clarke bring that out?'

> 'He wanted to; but I would not let him. I told him he must not. I must be true to my friend. I could not let him.'

---

67   Quoted in Merlin Holland, *Irish Peacock and Scarlet Marquess: the Real Trial of Oscar Wilde* (London and New York, Fourth Estate, 2005), p. 325.

If this conversation took place (and Harris is not always a trust-worthy witness), and if Wilde spoke truly, and if these facts had been brought out at Wilde's trial, the outcome might have been dramatically different. The evidence against Wilde consisted of four elements: his literary works, his letters to Bosie, the evidence of the rent boys and the incident at the Savoy. The judges at both trials rightly discounted the literary works as evidence against him. Mr. Justice Charles (though not Mr. Justice Wills) thought that Wilde's letters added little to the case against him. Charles ruled that the corroboration required by law could be provided by the surrounding circumstances, but it is difficult to know what circumstances he was referring to other than those to which the rent boys themselves attested. That left the evidence of the Savoy staff. Clarke made a good fist of weakening their testimony and both judges expressed serious misgivings about it. If Wilde could have shown that the boy had been in Douglas' bed rather than his own that day it would have completely destroyed the force of the incident. And if that had been removed the prosecution case would have been greatly weakened.

Is it possible that it was Wilde's gallant attempt to protect the reputation of his lover that consigned him to two year's misery, disgrace and, eventually, death?

WAS HE JUSTLY PUNISHED?

Even if he was correctly convicted, a strong case can be made for thinking that Oscar Wilde was punished too severely for his crimes.

For a start, it is difficult to know how Mr. Justice Wills could have described the case of Taylor and Wilde as the worst he had ever tried. As Douglas pointed out in *Autobiography*, it did not involve any of the usual aggravating features, such as the abuse of authority, the corruption of the innocent or the use of force, which are normally used to justify a maximum sentence. Could it be that the judge was affronted, less by the homosexuality (which though officially disapproved of was known to go on widely), as by the fact that it had taken place between two ex-public schoolboys on the one hand and young men from the lower social classes on the other? Certainly, many of the comments of prosecuting counsel suggest that this might have been the case.[68]

Although the prosecution at Wilde's trial were not alleging the crime of buggery, merely that of gross indecency, it seems that the constant references to and insinuations of it in the evidence may have influenced the judge. Only one witness, Charles Parker, actually accused Wilde of sodomy, and it was an assertion that he had failed to mention in his written statement to Queensberry's solicitors. Montgomery Hyde wondered whether Parker might have been ignorant of the meaning of the word, 'sodomy'.[69] We shall never know since the point was not further explored at the trial, no doubt because it was sufficient for the prosecution to prove any form of gross indecency. Did the judge's reference to 'corruption of the worst kind' indicate his belief that Wilde had engaged in the 'worst kind' of homosexual practice when this had in fact neither been alleged or proved?

It is also hard to credit Wills' description of Wilde as 'the centre of a circle of extensive corruption of the worst kind'. The only accusations of gross indecency involving men with even the slightest claim to a good reputation (Shelley and Mavor) had been struck out and the other lads whom Wilde was accused of indecency with were rent boys, already well corrupted.

It was widely considered among lawyers at the time that if Wilde had been convicted at his first trial Mr. Justice Charles would have imposed a sentence not longer than six months, and that, surely, is the sentence which should have been passed, according to the sentencing practice of the day.

'THE SPENDTHRIFT OF MY OWN GENIUS'

The harshest and most insightful condemnation of Wilde came from himself in *De Profundis*:

> The gods had given me almost everything. But I let myself be lured into long spells of senseless and sensual ease. I amused myself with

68   Wilde himself was hypocritical over the matter of class; while frankly contemptuous of the uncultured, he was always happy to share their beds.
69   Hyde, *Oscar Wilde: A Biography*, p.187.

being a FLANEUR, a dandy, a man of fashion. I surrounded myself with the smaller natures and the meaner minds. I became the spend-thrift of my own genius, and to waste an eternal youth gave me a curious joy. Tired of being on the heights, I deliberately went to the depths in the search for new sensation. What the paradox was to me in the sphere of thought, perversity became to me in the sphere of passion. Desire, at the end, was a malady, or a madness, or both. I grew careless of the lives of others. I took pleasure where it pleased me, and passed on. I forgot that every little action of the common day makes or unmakes character, and that therefore what one has done in the secret chamber one has some day to cry aloud on the housetop. I ceased to be lord over myself. I was no longer the captain of my soul, and did not know it. I allowed pleasure to dominate me. I ended in horrible disgrace.

From a longer perspective we are able to balance Wilde's enor-mous moral frailties and stupidities against his gigantic talents, his wit and his compassion, to which justice cannot possibly be done in a book of this nature. Fittingly, it was Douglas more than any other who captured all that was best in Wilde with his sonnet, *The Dead Poet*:

I dreamed of him last night, I saw his face
All radiant and unshadowed of distress,
And as of old, in music measureless,
I heard his golden voice and marked him trace
Under the common thing the hidden grace,
And conjure wonder out of emptiness,
Till mean things put on beauty like a dress
And all the world was an enchanted place.

And then methought outside a fast locked gate
I mourned the loss of unrecorded words,
Forgotten tales and mysteries half said,
Wonders that might have been articulate,
And voiceless thoughts like murdered singing birds.
And so I woke and knew that he was dead.

REVOLT AT HARPERS FERRY
THE TRIAL OF JOHN BROWN, 1859

It was 8 p.m. when the little band of armed men moved off in pairs into the cold drizzling rain; their mission, to seize an armoury and provoke a slave revolt.

The Southern States of America, fearful of Northern proposals to curtail the institution of slavery, were preparing to secede from the Union. Its President, Abraham Lincoln, was determined to do whatever was necessary to prevent this and civil war was only a few months away. Critical to the military power of the Union was the Federal armoury at Harpers Ferry, Virginia.[1] It was a large complex of buildings containing some 100,000 muskets and rifles, together with a rifle works capable of manufacturing more weapons than anywhere else in the South. It was located on a peninsula surrounded by towering cliffs at the confluence of the Shenandoah and Potomac Rivers. So strategically important was the armoury that the town was to change hands thirteen times during the coming civil war. But on Sunday, 16 October 1859, it was threatened by a small group intent on seizing it for their own purposes.

The group was led by 'Captain' John Brown, a 'striking figure with whitening hair, burning eyes and a great white beard which hardly hid the pendulous lips of Olympian Jove.' He was suffering from fever and 'difficulties in [his] head and ear.'[2] Apart from Brown, the raiding party consisted of three of his sons: 'Captain' Owen Brown (35), 'Captain' Watson Brown (25) and Oliver Brown (20), as well as his son-in-law, 'Captain' Dauphin Thompson, and Dauphin's brother, William. There were in addition at least ten other

---

1 Now West Virginia.
2 W.E. Burghardt Du Bois, *John Brown, a Biography, a New Edition with Primary Documents and Introduction by John David Smith* (New York, Armonk, 1997, M. E. Sharpe), p. 144.

John Brown, abolitionist (Topfoto)

whites and six blacks, though exactly how many and who they were remains a mystery since the survivors were later reluctant to disclose the part they had played.

For over three months the raiding party had been hiding out in what was known as the Kennedy Farmhouse in nearby Maryland, some five miles north of Harpers Ferry. The farm, which stood 300 yards back from the road from which it was partially hidden by shrubbery, had been rented by Brown under the name, 'Isaac Smith'. As well as his followers, Brown had brought along his two young daughters, Ann and Martha, to act as cook and lookout respectively, though they were sent home some days before the attack. For reasons of security the men were kept indoors during the day and allowed out only at night. They studied military tactics and assembled spears from heads and shafts that had been sent there separately. With characteristic secrecy, Brown waited until the last moment to let his band in on his plans; they were met with consternation, one of the party even leaving the building for three days to calm down. Eventually their leader's strength of character won through and he obtained a written undertaking from everyone to follow him. On the day of the attack after a short Bible service Brown assigned tasks to each of his followers. The main party would attack the armoury, while four men were to remain behind to guard the farmhouse.

At first everything went well. They entered the town of Harpers Ferry by the covered road and rail bridge over the Potomac, where they came across the bridge watchman, William Williams, and took him prisoner. It was the first anyone knew of the raid and he thought that it was all a joke. Two of the raiders, a one-time law student, John E. Cook, and Charles Plummer Tidd, went off to cut the telegraph wires, while Watson Brown and Stewart Taylor (the only Canadian in the party) remained guarding the bridge. The rest ran to the armoury. When the watchman refused to hand over the key of the gate they forced the door with a crowbar. Brown cried out exultantly, 'I have possession of the States' armoury, and if the citizens interfere with me I must only burn the town and have blood'.

Oliver Brown and William Thompson then secured the other bridge, the one over the Shenandoah, while others went out and seized anyone they could find on the street. They put their prisoners in a single-storey building near the gate. It was a combined guard house and fire engine store and was to become the scene of the band's last stand.[3] Meanwhile, John Brown led a small party to take Hall's rifle works half a mile away. After overwhelming an elderly guard, Brown returned to the armoury, leaving John Henry Kagi, sometimes described as Brown's second-in-command, and an educated black, John Anthony Copeland Jr., to secure the rifle works.

Brown now sent out six men, three white and three black, under Aaron D. Stevens, a cashiered soldier, to undertake at least locally the principal objectives of the raid, namely the liberation of the slaves and the arrest of their masters.[4] The first to be taken was Lewis W. Washington, the much respected great-grandnephew of the founder of the Republic. Colonel Washington was wakened from his bed at about 1 a.m. and brought captive to the Ferry by wagon, along with his family and four of his servants. Brown told him that he had been seized 'for the moral effect it would give our cause having one of your name as a prisoner'. He was ordered to hand over the pistols which he had received from General Lafayette[5] and a sword which had been presented to him by Frederick the Great. At about 3 a.m. a local farmer, his son and six of his slaves received similar treatment. When daylight came some thirty to forty people had been abducted by Brown as 'hostages'.

A small party was sent with some of the liberated slaves to bring the raiders' weapons, which had been stored at the farm, to a schoolhouse near the town on the Maryland side. Brown now sat back and waited for the black slaves and white abolitionists to flock to his cause; he was to be bitterly disappointed.

The first the townsfolk knew of the attack on the armoury was when Patrick Higgins arrived at the bridge to relieve Williams the watchman. Told to halt, Higgins promptly punched his captor and fled into the nearby saloon, receiving a grazing bullet wound to the skull for his pains. He later commented, 'I didn't know what 'Halt' mint

3   For this reason it is now known as Brown's Fort.
4   Stephen Vincent Benet described Aaron D. Stevens in his poem *John Brown's Body* as 'a singing giant, gunpowder-tempered and rash'.
5   A Frenchman who served as a major-general in Washington's rebel army.

[*sic*] then any more than a hog knows about a holiday'.[6] When the barman went out to investigate Higgins' improbable story he in turn was arrested by the raiders. At 1.25 a.m., the wounded Higgins heard the eastbound express approaching the Ferry and ran to warn the conductor ('guard' in UK English). The engineer and another employee got off the train and walked down the track to investigate, but when they came under fire from the raiders they got back in the train and steamed rapidly away. Shortly after this, the first tragedy occurred.

Hayward Shephard, a free black who acted as baggage master at the station, walked onto the bridge; he was told to stop by Oliver Brown and Taylor. Instead of complying, he turned on his tracks and started walking back to the railroad office, but the raiders shot him in the back before he could get there. Despite the efforts of a doctor, Shephard died in agony the following day, the first casualty of Brown's struggle against the enslavement of his race. At 3 a.m. for reasons which even now are not clear, Brown's men allowed the train to continue on its way, though fears of armed men on the bridge delayed its departure for four hours. When it finally reached the next station a wire was sent to Baltimore warning that '150 abolitionists' had taken Harpers Ferry, killed the porter and were intent on freeing the slaves. It was met with disbelief.

When the liberated slaves arrived at the armoury they were astonished to be handed pikes and told to guard their masters. No doubt aware of the likely consequences for them if found in possession of weapons when the raid was over, they accepted the pikes only reluctantly, if at all. Some even fled. (Colonel Washington's coachman was an exception: he is said to have 'fought [for the raiders] like a tiger' until killed.) While slave rebellions were by no means unknown, this unexpected nocturnal intervention by a fierce-looking white man was not the best circumstance to inspire feelings of rebellion, no matter how resentful the slaves might have been of their bondage.

News of the attack spread swiftly. The bell of the Lutheran church was rung in warning and the doctor, who had tended Hayward, rode to the town of Charlestown, some eight miles away to raise the alarm.

6   Robert Penn Warren, *John Brown, the Making of a Martyr* (New York, Payson & Clarke Ltd, 1929), p. 356.

When the townspeople woke on the Monday morning and realized what was happening many of them, armed with nothing more lethal than squirrel guns and fowling pieces, surrounded the armoury and the rifle works and began firing sporadically at the raiders. Others went to the railway track to halt any trains before they reached town. During a lull in the firing Brown exchanged one of his prisoners for breakfast for his men and his hostages, though he and others refused to touch the food for fear of poison. The next unnecessary death occurred, seemingly without any provocation, when one of the raiders, a freed slave called Dangerfield Newby, shot and killed Thomas Boerly, an unarmed grocer walking peacefully to work.

Just before 10 a.m. Brown assured his prisoners that he intended them no harm; his object, he said, was to 'place the United States' arms in the hands of the black men, and he proposed to free all the slaves in the vicinity'. Cook, Tidd and some of the liberated slaves were then sent to guard the schoolhouse where the raiders' weapons were stored. The townsfolk had now discovered better weapons in the armoury workshop and the exchange of gunfire became continuous. At about noon two militia companies arrived from Charlestown and made short work of evicting Oliver and his companions from the bridge. When they came to attack the armoury, however, they were repelled with casualties. A makeshift projectile fired by a sniper had severed Dangerfield Newby's throat from ear to ear and his bloody corpse was mutilated by the gleeful crowd. Six-foot two and the son of a Scotsman, Newby's one ambition had been to free his enslaved wife and seven children.

Brown's plans were beginning to go seriously awry: the slaves were showing no disposition to throw off their chains, the townspeople had offered spirited resistance and his only means of escape were cut off, but things were going to get worse. Realizing the hopelessness of his position, the rebel leader sent Will Thompson and one of the hostages out under a white flag in an attempt to exchange the hostages for his freedom. Thompson was promptly made prisoner, the hostage was freed and the offer to negotiate ignored.

Brown now retreated with eleven of what he considered to be his most important hostages to the engine house, whose brick walls and stout oak doors seemed to offer the best hope of holding out. The windows were barred, firing holes were made in the walls and the fire engines, which the building contained, were dragged behind the doors. Brown made another attempt at negotiation, sending his son Watson, Aaron Stevens and the armoury clerk out under a flag of truce. They were met with a fusillade of bullets. Both raiders were badly wounded. Joseph Brua (or Brewer), one of the hostages, bravely ventured out to drag the wounded Stevens to the railroad station; astonishingly, he went back to resume his role as a hostage. Watson managed to crawl back into the engine house. One of the youngest raiders, the twenty year old and now desperate Will Leeman, got permission from Brown to attempt an escape, but was wounded while trying to cross the river. One of the townsmen waded out and shot him at point-blank range as he lay on a rock. Thereafter, his body was used for target practice by the crowd until it floated off downstream. Two more raiders, Hazlitt and Anderson, who had been left behind in the unguarded armoury, escaped during the night. The rearguard party at the farm under Owen Brown, now realizing they were unable to do anything to assist their comrades at the Ferry, snatched up some provisions and made off over the hills.

At about 2 p.m. yet another townsman died. George W. Turner was shot in the neck while walking down the high street; he had gone into town in an attempt to rescue a neighbour. An hour later Kagi and his companions were forced out of the rifle works. They desperately attempted to wade the Shenandoah, but were caught in crossfire. Some made a stand on a rock midstream where they were picked off until only one of them, a mulatto called Copeland, was left alive. He surrendered when his weapon failed to fire and it took the intervention of a doctor to prevent him from being lynched. One of the released slaves was caught at the rifle works with a pike in his hand and was only saved from a similar fate by the actions of a clergyman.

The railroad agent and Mayor of Harpers Ferry, Fontaine Beckham, was the last non-combatant to die. At 4 p.m., while trying to see how the battle at the engine house was going, he was shot in the heart by one of the raiders. Beckham was much admired in town and had provided in his will for the liberation of his slaves. It was the signal for Will Thompson to meet his end. After being captured he had been held prisoner at the hotel, but it was not enough to save him. He was

225

dragged out of bed and shot by Beckham's nephew and best friend. Afterwards, his dead body was thrown into the river where the towns-folk took pot-shots at it from time to time.

In the late afternoon another militia company arrived from a neigh-bouring town. They helped free the bulk of the hostages from the un-guarded watch house and drove the remaining raiders into the engine house. Brown's situation was now desperate and he sent out a signed offer to release his hostages in exchange for his freedom. The offer was refused, but the true identity of the raiders' leader was now out of the bag: 'Isaac Smith' signed his name as 'Osawatomie Brown', the infamous anti-slavery activist. John Brown's son, Oliver, was the next of the raiders to meet his fate when he received a bullet in the belly on attempting to fire out of the part-opened doors. That night he begged his father to end his suffering and was told, 'If you must die, die like a man'. The lad did his best, but he endured agony for nearly twelve hours.

Despite his parlous situation (he had only four unwounded men and was encumbered with eleven prisoners), Brown refused to con-sider surrender. When one of his party asked whether what they were doing was treason Brown replied, 'Certainly'. Hearing this, two of his men, Anderson and Dauphin Thompson, played no further part in the battle, but it was not enough to save them. By late morning on the Monday, news of the raid had reached Washington DC. Ninety horse marines were swiftly rounded up from the navy yard and sent to Harpers Ferry under the command of brevet Colonel Robert E. Lee.[7] The raiders, who had been some forty hours without sleep and only slightly less than that without food, had to listen to the shouts of the angry crowd outside, many of them now well affected by drink. Arriv-ing at 11 p.m., Lee's first action was to close the town's saloons. After reviewing the situation he decided against a night assault in view of the presence of hostages in the engine house.

At 7 a.m. the next morning Lee sent a young First Lieutenant, J.E.B Stuart, under a white flag to ask the defenders of the engine

7   Lee was to be offered command of the Northern armies in the Civil War, but turned it down to serve his home state of Virginia. His leadership of the Southern armies in the field only narrowly failed to save their cause.

house.[8] 'Are you ready to surrender, and trust to the mercy of the government?' Brown sought at first to negotiate better terms but in the end replied, 'No, I prefer to die here.' Stuart waved his hat; it was the signal for an all-out assault by a dozen marines under the command of a Lieutenant Green. Their sledgehammers proved to be ineffective because the ropes, which were securing the doors, gave when hit. Realizing this, Green decided to use a heavy ladder as a battering ram. When the doors burst open he rushed in with his men. One of them was immediately shot dead; another fell with a wound to his face. In order to prevent injury to the hostages the attackers had decided to rely on their bayonets, one of which pinned Anderson to the wall. Dauphin Thompson suffered a similar fate as he tried to crawl beneath a fire engine. Both men, who only hours before had declared that they would not fight, were to die later of their wounds. The hostage, Colonel Washington, indicated to Lieutenant Green which of the raiders was their leader and Green made an upward thrust with his sword at Brown. The force of the blow lifted him off the floor, but in his haste Green had not thought to change his dress sword for a service model and it bent on contact with Brown's belt, preventing serious injury. The officer promptly reversed the weapon and beat Brown over the head with its hilt until he lost consciousness. The raid on Harpers Ferry was over.

Eleven hungry hostages were released at once and the freed slaves returned to their masters. The wounded were taken outside the engine house and laid on the grass. Watson was to die of his wounds the next morning. Aaron Stevens was riddled with bullets to the head, breast and arm and could breath only with difficulty. Brown was bleeding freely, but his wounds were not life threatening. That afternoon in the paymaster's office of the armoury the two survivors were questioned by Senator James M. Mason, as well as the Governor of Virginia, Henry A. Wise, and Representative Clement Vallandigham, an Ohio Democrat. Several reporters and townspeople were also present.

Asked about the funding of his raid, Brown said that he had paid for most of it himself and refused to implicate others. Questioned about its purpose, he replied, 'We came to free the slaves and only

8 'Jeb' Stuart went on to become Lee's brilliant cavalry general and was mortally wounded at the Battle of Yellow Tavern (1864).

227

that'. He denied that he had expected a general rising of the slaves, but made clear his bitter disappointment at the failure of anyone to come to his support. His was a religious movement, he claimed, and his raid 'the greatest service man can render to God'. He went on, 'I pity the poor in bondage that have none to help them: that is why I am here; not to gratify any personal animosity, revenge, or vindictive spirit. It is my sympathy with the oppressed and the wronged that are as good as you and as precious in the sight of God'. In answer to a bystander, Brown answered, 'I killed no man except in fair fight' (a claim which, as we shall see, was far from the truth.). If any innocent civilian had been killed, he added, it was not with his knowledge.

Asked by Governor Wise whether, as a criminal, he should not be preparing himself for the afterlife, Brown replied:

> Governor, I have, from all appearances, not more than fifteen or twenty years the start of you in the journey to that eternity of which you kindly warn me; and whether my tenure here shall be fifteen months, or fifteen days, or fifteen hours, I am equally prepared to go. There is an eternity behind and an eternity before, and the little speck in the centre, however long, is but comparatively a minute. The difference between your tenure and mine is trifling and I want to therefore tell you to be prepared; I am prepared.

Addressing all present, Brown concluded with chilling foresight:

> ...you had better – all you people of the South – prepare yourselves for a settlement of this question, that must come up ... sooner than you are prepared for it. ...You may dispose of me very easily – I am nearly disposed of now; but this question is still to be settled – this negro question I mean; the end of that is not yet...

Of Brown's bravery in the face of adversity there can be no doubt. A reporter commented that, 'with the gallows staring him in the face, he lay on the floor, and in reply to every question, gave answers that betokened the spirit that animated him.' Governor Wise declared, 'He is the gamest man I ever saw'.[9]

9   David S. Reynolds, *John Brown, Abolitionist* (New York, Alfred K. Knopf, 2005), p. 332.

THE TRIAL AT CHARLESTOWN

The raid caused fear and consternation all over the nation, all the more frightening because of ignorance of what was behind it and what might follow. Soon after order had been restored, Brown and Stevens were taken by train under heavy guard to the county gaol in Charlestown some eight miles away, where on 25 October they were brought in the first instance before a bench of magistrates. Cannon were placed in front of the Court House, and an armed guard patrolled around it. While Stevens' terrible wounds meant that he had to be supported, Brown walked erect from his cell across the road into the court under the gaze of a silent crowd.

The prosecution was undertaken by Charles Harding. Unfortunately, he suffered from a drink problem, and he had to be helped by his assistant, Andrew Hunter. He began by inviting the court to assign counsel to the prisoners. Brown, convinced that he was about to go before a kangaroo court, protested:

> The Governor of the State of Virginia tendered me his assurance that I should have a fair trial; and, under no circumstances whatever, will I be able to have a fair trial. If you seek my blood, you can have it at any moment, without this mockery of a trial. I have had no counsel. I have not been able to advise with any one. I know nothing about the feelings of my fellow-prisoners, and am utterly unable to attend in any way to my own defence. My memory don't serve me. My health is insufficient, although improving. There are mitigating circumstances that I would urge in our favor, if a fair trial is to be allowed us.'

Brown eventually agreed that, until the counsel he had sent for arrived, he would be represented by two court-appointed lawyers. One of these later withdrew, leaving Brown represented by Lawson Botts, a prominent attorney, and his assistant, Thomas C. Green. After evidence was called of the incriminating maps and weapons found at the Kennedy Farmhouse, the prisoners were remanded to a grand jury the following day; the jury returned a true bill on each of the accused. There were four counts in the indictment, all framed in the archaic language of the day. The first alleged that the accused, 'not having the fear of God before their eyes, but being moved and seduced by the false and malignant counsel of other evil and traitorous persons and the instigations of the devil', did 'Traitorously make rebellion and levy war against the said Commonwealth of Virginia'. The second count alleged conspiracy to induce certain named slaves 'to rebel and make insurrection against their masters and owners, and against the Government and the Constitution and laws of the Commonwealth of Virginia'. The third and fourth counts alleged assault by 'Sharpe's [*sic*] rifles, and other deadly weapons to the Jurors unknown' which had been used to wound and kill certain named townsfolk. A fresh jury were then sworn in to try the case.

The trial proper began on Thursday, 27 October, before Judge Richard Parker in a courtroom packed with five to six hundred observers. Everyone present conducted themselves according to the casual Southern fashion of the times, eating peanuts, puffing cigars and spitting tobacco juice on the floor. Reynolds describes how the judge, though a capable lawyer, 'contributed to the casualness of the scene. His table on an elevated platform, was a chaos of law books, papers and inkstands. Holding a tremendous book open on his lap, he tilted back on his chair with his legs on the table. Many others present assumed a similar position.'[10] Because of their injuries the prisoners were allowed to lie on a mattress on the floor. Stevens was described as having the appearance of a dying man, breathing with great difficulty.

Lawson Botts began the proceedings unexpectedly by raising the issue of his client's sanity. He produced a telegram from one of the defendant's Ohio neighbours claiming that insanity was hereditary in his family. 'His mother's sister died with it, and a daughter of that sister has been two years in a lunatic asylum. A son and daughter of his mother's brother have also been confined in the lunatic asylum, and another son of that brother is now insane and under close restraint.'[11] Brown reacted with indignation to this defence made by his court-appointed lawyer, calling it 'a miserable artifice and pretext'. He told the judge that he was content for the trial to go ahead, but wished to wait until his preferred counsel could attend. After both prisoners had pleaded not guilty to all charges the prosecution elected to have Brown tried first and Stevens was returned to gaol to be tried

10   *Ibid.*, p. 350.
11   Had he known of it, he might also have mentioned the mental state of Brown's son, John Jr. See below.

later. Brown then sought 'a very short delay' so as to recover from his wounds and temporary deafness. Judge Parker ruled against it on the ground of 'the nervous condition of the country'.

Harding opened the case for the prosecution with an address which painted the Harpers Ferry raid as part of a wider conspiracy to free the slaves by means of a civil war. Green intervened to object that the court had no jurisdiction to try Brown, but the point was not upheld. The rest of the day was taken up with evidence from the train conductor, and others about what had taken place during the raid.

Brown's own counsel, the young George H. Hoyt of Boston, arrived the following day, Friday.[12] Because he had had insufficient time to prepare his case Botts and Green offered to continue to represent Brown, which they did with the aid of a list of tasks which had been drawn up by their client. ('We gave to numerous prisoners perfect liberty. *Prove that.* We allowed numerous other prisoners to visit their families, to quiet their fears. *Get all their names.'* And so on.)[13] Recalled for cross-examination by the defence, Colonel Washington accepted that he had heard Brown give frequent orders not to fire on innocent citizens. Armstead Ball, master machinist at the armoury, told the court that, when he was taken prisoner, Brown had said to him that 'his object was to free the slaves, and not the making of war on the people; that my person and private property would be safe; that his war was against the accursed system of slavery; that he had power to do it and would carry it out'. In fact, all the hostages agreed that they had been treated with consideration by their captors, but that was probably no more than the natural relief of a captive who has not been mistreated. Hostages tend to overlook the fact that the point of their being held prisoner is to protect with their lives the security of their captors. Only once did Brown evince any emotion; it was when evidence was given of the distressing death of his son-in-law's brother, William Thompson.

The prisoner now rose to his feet to complain that he had no confidence in either Botts or Green. It was a harsh judgement which left

---

12   His expenses were being met by a northern sympathizer.
13   Oswald Garrison Villard, *John Brown 1800-1859: A Biography Fifty Years After* (Gloucester, Mass., Peter Smith, 1965), p. 490.

them with no alternative but to retire from the case. Botts neverthe-less lent Hoyt his office and stayed up all night to assist him in his preparation. Hoyt renewed the application for an adjournment on the ground that further counsel were coming from Ohio to represent Brown and that he himself had had insufficient time to prepare. Judge Parker agreed to adjourn the hearing, but only until the following day. Fortunately, the additional counsel, Samuel Chilton of Washington and Hiram Griswold of Cleveland, arrived in time for the Saturday hearing, which was put back a few hours for their convenience. In the afternoon the defence made an unsuccessful attempt to get Brown tried on only one charge at a time. It was refused. The prosecution then closed their case.

Griswold began Brown's defence on the following Monday by making it clear that he had 'no sympathy whatever' with any man guilty of the offences with which his client was charged. As to the insurrection charge, he demanded to know, possibly to his client's discomfort, where the evidence was that Brown had induced any sin-gle slave to rise in rebellion. Griswold attacked the charge of levying war on Virginia by saying that his client's intention was to establish a government in opposition to the Government of the United States, and not to subvert the Commonwealth of Virginia. His defence to the charge of treason was that, since Brown was not a citizen of Virginia, he could not be guilty of treason to that State. Finally, Griswold ad-dressed the charge of murder, claiming that his client was justified in returning the fire directed at him. It was, he suggested weakly, 'a sort of self-defence'.

Hunter responded by pointing out that the crime of insurrection was complete even without a single slave having risen in revolt. As to the argument that there was no proof that Brown had killed anyone deliberately, he replied that 'the law was, that if the party perpetrating a felony, undesignedly takes life, it is a conclusive proof of malice. If Brown was only intending to steal negroes, and in doing so took life, it was murder.' Lastly, he said of the charge of treason that it could, by virtue of the constitution, be committed by people who were not citizens of the Commonwealth. In any event, by coming to Harpers Ferry and showing an intention to reside there permanently Brown fell within the definition of 'citizen' in the State Code:

The prisoner had attempted to break down the existing Government of the Commonwealth, and establish on its ruins a new Government: he had usurped the office of Commander-in-Chief of this new government, and, together with his whole band, professed allegiance and fidelity to it; he represented not only the civil authorities of state, but our own military; he is doubly, trebly and quadruply guilty of treason.

The following Monday, after closing speeches from counsel of both sides, the jury retired. They were out for only three quarters of an hour before returning to deliver a verdict of 'Guilty' on all three counts. The decision was heard in silence in the crowded courtroom. 'Old Brown himself said not even a word, but, as on any previous day, turned to adjust his pallet, and then composedly stretched himself upon it.' When the court resumed two days later the defence made a final desperate bid in the form of a submission in arrest of judgment; the points they made were not new and Judge Parker ruled against them. Brown was now asked the customary question, whether he had anything to say before sentence was passed. He drew himself to his feet and declared in words that have been widely quoted:

I have, may it please the Court, a few words to say. In the first place, I deny everything but what I have all along admitted, of a design on my part to free slaves. I intended certainly to have made a clean thing of that matter, as I did last winter when I went into Missouri, and there took slaves without the snapping of a gun on either side, moving them through the country, and finally leaving them in Canada. I designed to have done the same thing again on a larger scale. That was all I intended to do. I never did intend murder or treason, or the destruction of property, or to excite or incite the slaves to rebellion, or to make insurrection.

I have another objection, and that is that it is unjust that I should suffer such a penalty. Had I interfered in the manner which I admit, and which I admit has been fairly proved – for I admire the truthfulness and candor of the greater portion of the witnesses who have testified in this case – had I so interfered in behalf of the rich, the powerful, the intelligent, the so-called great, or in behalf of any of their friends, either father, mother, brother, sister, wife, or children, or any of that class, and suffered and sacrificed what I have in this interference, it would have been all right, and every man in this Court would have deemed it an act worthy of reward rather than punishment. This Court acknowledges, too, as I suppose, the validity of the law of God. I see a book kissed, which I suppose to be the Bible, or at least the New Testament, which teaches me that all things whatsoever I would that men should do to me, I should do even so to them. It teaches me further to remember them that are in bonds as bound with them. I endeavored to act up to that instruction.

I am yet too young to understand that God is any respecter of persons. I believe that to have interfered as I have done, as I have always freely admitted I have done in behalf of His despised poor, is no wrong, but right. Now, if it is deemed necessary that I should forfeit my life for the furtherance of the ends of justice, and mingle my blood farther with the blood of my children and with the blood of millions in this slave country whose rights are disregarded by wicked, cruel, and unjust enactments, I say let it be done.

Let me say one word further. I feel entirely satisfied with the treatment I have received on my trial. Considering all the circumstances, it has been more generous than I expected. But I feel no consciousness of guilt. I have stated from the first what was my intention, and what was not. I never had any design against the liberty of any person, nor any disposition to commit treason or excite slaves to rebel or make any general insurrection. I never encouraged any man to do so, but always discouraged any idea of that kind. Let me say also in regard to the statements made by some of those who were connected with me, I fear it has been stated by some of them that I have induced them to join me, but the contrary is true. I do not say this to injure them, but as regretting their weakness. Not one but joined me of his own accord, and the greater part at their own expense. A number of them I never saw, and never had a word of conversation with till the day they came to me, and that was for the purpose I have stated. Now I am done.

Judge Parker then passed the inevitable sentence of death and appointed 2 December as the date of execution. The courtroom was silent except for the sound of one man clapping; it was swiftly suppressed.

The state of fear gripping the South now intensified to such an extent that the army had to be alerted. Slave owners, fearing a slave revolt, called for revenge. Hayricks were burned around Charlestown, a shot was fired one night under a judge's window and there was talk of armed parties being ready to rescue Brown. (In fact, the only plot foundered in face of the accused's adamant refusal to condone it.)

234

Against this background it is not surprising that Governor Wise rejected all the 'petitions, prayers, threats from almost every free State in the Union' urging him to exercise clemency. In a letter of 4 November he wrote that, had he been able to do so at the time of the raid, he would have killed Brown and all his party. Since that did not happen he welcomed the fact that they had received a fair trial, but could see no ground for clemency for what in his view was a crime 'of the deepest and darkest kind which can be committed against our people'.[14]

It is not known why execution of sentence was deferred for so long a period, but Brown used it to the full. The day after he left court he wrote the first of a number of moving letters to his wife and children. After commending them all to God, he exhorted them to, 'Never forget the poor nor think anything you bestow on them to be lost to you even though they may be black as Ebedmelch the Ethiopian eunuch who cared for Jeremiah in the pit of the dungeon or as black as the one to whom Phillip preached Christ'. And in another letter to a relative he denied feeling 'mortified, degraded, nor in the least ashamed of my imprisonment, my chain, or my near prospect of death by hanging'. He rejected an offer of prayers from a clergyman on learning that he was a believer in slavery.

The night before the execution Mrs. Brown was permitted to see her husband in private for the last time. Both were stoical in the face of death, though Brown protested indignantly when his wife was refused permission to keep vigil with him overnight. Next day he made his will and presented a book to each of his guards and his silver watch to the gaoler. As he left the cell he handed over a short note to one of them which read: 'I, John Brown am now quite certain that the crimes of this guilty land will never be purged away; but with blood. I had, as I now think, vainly flattered myself that without very much bloodshed it might be done.'

On 2 December, wearing slippers and a broad-brimmed hat and seated on his coffin, Brown was taken by wagon to the execution field outside Charlestown under the Blue Ridge mountains.[15] Looking

14   *Ibid.*, p. 503.
15   Among the 1,500 cavalry and militia guarding the scene were an eccentric military instructor who was to become the famous General 'Stonewall' Jack-

around, he proclaimed, 'This is a beautiful country. I never had the pleasure of seeing it before'. He asked the executioner not to keep him waiting, but organisational delays led to his standing on the gallows some ten minutes before being cast off. Death is said to have been instantaneous. Six days later his body was buried in the presence of his wife at their North Elba farmhouse, where it lies 'a'mouldering' to this day.

The trials went on for another three months. Edwin Coppoc, Shields Green, John Cook and John Copeland were all convicted and sentenced to death. They were hanged a fortnight after their leader on 16 December.[16] Albert Hazlett was captured in Pennsylvania in October and hanged on 16 March the following year, along with the badly wounded Stevens.

Some of the raiders had managed to escape from the debacle at Harpers Ferry. Edwin Coppoc's brother, Barclay, was one of them, only to be killed in a train accident in 1861 while serving as a First Lieutenant in the Kansas Infantry. Tidd also made his escape, but died of a fever in 1862 while serving as a sergeant in the 21st Massachusetts Volunteers. Meriam escaped to fight and be wounded under Grant in the Civil War. He died naturally in 1865. Anderson fought as a non-commissioned officer in the Civil War and died of natural causes in 1872. John Brown's son, Owen, the man who failed to burn the incriminating papers at the Kennedy Farmhouse, was the only survivor not to serve in the Union army. He died in 1891.

DID HE HAVE A FAIR TRIAL?

It is difficult to fault the conduct of Brown's trial, but that has not prevented many from attempting to do so. The abolitionist, Frederick Douglass, for example, described it as a 'nominal trial... [Virginia] had not given Captain Brown the benefit of a reasonable doubt, but

---

son, and a twenty-one year old actor, John Wilkes Booth, who had joined the Richmond Greys especially to witness the execution. Booth went on to assassinate Abraham Lincoln, the only man who could have bound up the wounds of America's dreadful civil war.

16   Green and Copeland managed to escape from their cell, but were detected climbing the wall and returned to custody.

hurried him to the scaffold in panic-stricken haste.'[17] This is far from the case. Judge Parker's decision to refuse to sever the various charges seems perfectly supportable on the facts of the case. The judge had certainly refused an adjournment to the defence more than once, but they were decisions which seem well justified by the need for an early conclusion to the proceedings. Before taking his decision to continue with the case Judge Parker satisfied himself by careful inquiries of the doctor and the gaoler that Brown was in fact capable of playing a full part in the proceedings. And that, indeed, was how it proved to be. The record shows that Brown was capably represented in court, both by the court-appointed attorneys and, later, by his own choice of counsel, albeit that the latter were forced to act at short notice. On the third day of the trial Brown complained that the witnesses he had asked to be called had not been subpoenaed, but in this he was mistaken, although it is true that some of his witnesses who had been subpoenaed had not in fact turned up at court.

There was ample evidence before the jury to support the charge of insurrection; the charge of treason is more debatable. The common law rule is that a citizen owes fealty only to a state of which he is a member or, at least of which he enjoys the privileges of citizenship on a fixed basis. Brown had spent a few weeks in Virginia in 1840, but had never been a resident or taxpayer of that state. Rejecting this argument, Judge Parker ruled that:

> The Constitution of the United States provides that citizens of each State shall be entitled to all the immunities of citizens of the several States. Brown came here with the immunities given by the Constitution. ... Again, our Code defines who are citizens of Virginia, as all those white persons born in any other State of this Union who may become residents here. The evidence in this case shows, without a shadow of a question, that when this man came to Virginia and planted his feet on Harper's Ferry [sic],[18] he came there to reside and hold the place permanently.[19]

---

17   Frederick Douglass, *The Life and Times of Frederick Douglass, Written by Himself* (Hartford, Conn., Park Publishing Co, 1881).
18   Harpers Ferry was originally spelled with an inverted comma which it lost some time before the raid.
19   See, for example, Daniel C. Draper, 'Legal Phases of the Trial of John Brown,' *West Virginia History*, vol. 1, no. 2, (January 1940).

It was a moot point.

More than once during the trial the defence raised the issue of the court's jurisdiction, that is to say, its right to hear the case. The point must have seemed academic to the jurors when the man standing before them was the acknowledged leader of a gang which had violently seized a Federal armoury in the course of which several people had met their deaths. However, jurisdiction is more than academically important; a good analogy would be a house purchaser who challenges the vendor's right to the title of the property he is selling. The defence argued that the Federal government had exclusive jurisdiction over the armoury where the events charged had occurred. They quoted the State's Attorney General to the effect that residents of the armoury could not even be taxed by the state of Virginia. The prosecution dismissed the Attorney General's views as contrary to established law: Virginia had never ceded jurisdiction over the armoury to the Federal government. Even if that were not the case, they argued, it did not matter since none of Brown's victims had died within the boundary of the armoury. And that was how Judge Parker approached the question.

All these points have been discussed extensively since the trial.[20] At the time, however, the Virginia Supreme Court of Appeals expressed its agreement with all Judge Parker's rulings when it rejected Brown's petition for what is called a writ of *supersedeas*.[21] More significantly, Brown himself never complained of not having received justice: quite the contrary. In his concluding remarks he said, 'I feel entirely satisfied with the treatment I have received on my trial. Considering all the circumstances, it has been more generous than I expected.' His death would serve a higher purpose. In the last letter to his brother Jeremiah he declared himself as 'fully persuaded that I am worth inconceivably more to *hang* than for any other purpose' (emphasis in original).[22] It

20　See, for example, Daniel C. Draper, 'Legal Phases of the Trial of John Brown,' *West Virginia History*, vol. 1, no. 2, (January 1940).
21　The writ of *supersedeas* is somewhat similar to the English order of *certiorari*; that is an order that the case be brought before a higher court for review. Unfortunately, the court failed to give the reasons for its rejection of Brown's petition.
22　Villard, *John Brown 1800-1859*, p. 496.

took a special sort of man to make this stand. Who was John Brown and what fashioned his remarkable character?

THE MAKING OF A REBEL

John Brown was born at Torrington, Connecticut, on 9 May 1800, the second son of Ruth and Owen Brown. Both parents were strict Congregational Calvinists who believed that life on earth was simply a trial for the hereafter. When John was aged five his father moved his family by oxcart to the frontier town of Hudson, Ohio, where he set up a tannery.

John's mother died in childbirth when he was eight years old and his father remarried; it was to be the grown-up John's impression that the new union did not enjoy the intimacy of the first.[23] John received little in the way of formal education and was later to regret that, as a child, he had been 'excessively fond of the hardest and roughest kind of play'. The experience left him accustomed to being obeyed, a state of mind which never seems to have left him.[24] His home town Hudson was a centre of abolitionist activity and from his earliest days John Brown was brought up to fear God and honour His commandments. Writing in the third person, he was to leave this account of an incident that made its mark on him:

> [D]uring the war with England[25] a circumstance occurred that in the end made him a most determined Abolitionist: & led him to declare, or Swear: Eternal war with Slavery. He was staying for a short time with a very gentlemanly landlord since a United States Marshall who held a slave boy near his own age very active, intelligent and good feeling; & to whom John was under considerable obligation for numerous little acts of kindness. The master made a great pet of John: brought him to table with his first company; & friends; called their attention to every little smart thing he said or did: & to the fact of his being more than a hundred miles from home with a company of cattle along; while the negro boy (who was fully if not more than his equal)

23 Letter to H.L. Stearns dated 15 July 1857. Quoted in Villard, *John Brown 1800-1859*, p. 3.
24 Letter to H.L. Stearns dated 15 July 1857. Quoted in Villard, *John Brown 1800-1859*, p. 6.
25 That is, the war of 1812.

was badly clothed, poorly fed; & lodged in cold weather, & beaten before his eyes with Iron Shovels or any other thing that came first to hand. This brought John to reflect on the wretched, hopeless condition, of Fatherless & Motherless slave children: for such children have neither Fathers or Mothers to protect, & provide for them. He sometimes would raise the question is God their Father?[26]

At the age of sixteen Brown felt a calling to the ministry, but an eye problem and lack of funds dashed his hopes, and he and his adopted brother opened a tannery of their own. On 21 June 1820 John married his housekeeper's daughter, Dianthe Lusk, describing her later as a 'neat, industrious and economical girl; of excellent character; earnest piety; and good practical common sense', albeit 'remarkably plain'. Dianthe became pregnant and John Jr. was born thirteen months later; he was to be the first among seven from this union. Brown proved to be a stern father who drew up a tariff of physical punishments for his children. In this they were probably treated no more harshly than others of the same background. More worrying is his son's account of how John Sr. once asked to be whipped until he bled. In 1825 Brown took his family to New Richmond, Pennsylvania where he bought and cleared land to build a cabin and a tannery of his own. The business prospered, but one of his sons died and an illness left him deeply in debt. Dianthe, who by then had become insane, died in childbirth the following year. Within months Brown had married Mary Anne Day, a sixteen year old who was only four years older than his oldest child. The union was no sinecure; she was to bear thirteen more of Brown's children.

Throughout his life the horrors of slavery were never far from Brown's mind and he did what he could to assist runaway slaves by constructing a concealed room in the hayloft of his barn in which they could hide. It was his first venture into what was to become known as the 'underground railroad', a name given to various arrangements to spirit slaves from the South to the North by such means as wagons with false bottoms and what would nowadays be called safe houses. (Arrangements like these had been in existence in one form or another since the late eighteenth century.) But it was not enough, and in his

26   Letter to H.L. Stearns dated 15 July 1857. Quoted in Villard, *John Brown 1800-1859*, p. 4.

thirty-fifth year Brown resolved to 'do something in a practical way for my poor fellow men who are in bondage'. It was his intention, he wrote to his brother, Frederick, to give 'at least one negro boy a good and religious education'. He thought that this would be helped by the fact that townships were permitted to levy a tax for the support of such education, but seemed naively unaware of the strong resistance such proposals would meet with in practice.

Thereafter, Brown's business life took many forms, including horse breeder, sheep-herder, timber trader and land speculator. However, except for a ten-year stint as a large scale sheep farmer, most of his enterprises folded rapidly; some for understandable reasons, such as when he was caught up in the financial panic of 1837, but most through simple lack of commercial ability. For all his energy, Brown was never any great shakes as a businessman.[27] His attitude to business reflected his fiery temperament; at one point he was arrested by the Sheriff, along with two of his sons, on suspicion of threatening to shoot someone claiming land from him. He was eventually declared bankrupt on 28 September, 1842 and lost most of his worldly possessions. But nature was to hit him harder. The following year he lost four of his children to dysentery within a week. A man with an unshakable belief in divine providence and a strong sense of personal guilt, Brown must have been deeply affected by their loss. During this period he moved his family from Pennsylvania to Ohio, from Virginia to Massachusetts, from New York State to Ohio and back again.

Long before this an event had occurred which was to harden Brown's hatred of slavery; in 1837 Elijah P. Lovejoy, a prominent Presbyterian minister and anti-slavery newspaper editor, had been shot dead in Illinois by a mob from Missouri. A memorial service was held for him in Brown's home town of Hudson, as it was in many abolitionist communities. From his seat at the back of the church, Brown had stood up, raised his right hand and said, 'Here, before God, in the presence of these witnesses, I consecrate my life to the destruction of slavery.' His father made a similar declaration. The following year he scandalized the deacons of his church when he brought some of the blacks, who normally sat by the door, to the Brown family pew. An

27 Reynolds describes him as a 'bumbling capitalist'. *John Brown, Abolitionist*, p. 45.

excuse was found to expel him from the church and the incident seems to have put him off churchgoing thereafter. In 1839 Brown took the most decisive step in his life by asking his family to make common cause with him 'to break the jaws of the wicked and pluck the spoil out of his teeth'. His anger at their plight even led him to criticize negroes for 'tamely submitting to every species of indignity, contempt and wrong, instead of ... resisting their brutal aggressions from principle and taking my place as a man and assuming the responsibilities of a man ....'[28] It was an augury of things to come.

THE ROAD TO HARPERS FERRY

One of the enduring enigmas of the Harpers Ferry raid is exactly when the plan finally matured in John Brown's mind. Given his fiercely secretive nature we shall probably never know. The first clear reference to it seems to have been in 1847, when he was visited at his home in Springfield, Ohio by one of the most significant figures in the fight against slavery. At the age of thirty, the ex-slave Frederick Douglass was a tall, imposing and powerful public speaker.[29] At that time Brown's plan, in Douglass's words, was to 'destroy the money value of slave property' by taking 'at first twenty-five picked men, and, beginning on a small scale, supply them arms and ammunition, post them in squads of fives on a line of twenty-five miles, the most persuasive and judicious of whom shall go down into the fields from time to time as opportunity offers, and induce the slaves to join them, seeking and selecting the most restless and daring.' They would then run off into the Alleghenies and be taken north by the underground railroad.[30] 'An insurrection, [Brown] thought, would only defeat the object, but his plan did contemplate the creating of an armed force which should act in the very heart of the south.' After this meeting,

28   In an article he wrote for a black newspaper in 1848 entitled, '*Sambo's Mistakes*'.
29   Douglass, formerly 'Frederick Augustus Washington Bailey', had been born into slavery in Maryland the son of a black mother and a white father. After an abortive attempt to escape which saw him thrown into prison, he finally escaped in 1838 via the underground railroad and discarded his slave name.
30   A photograph taken at about this time shows Brown holding a flag bearing the letters 'SPW', which is presumed to stand for 'Subterranean Pass Way'.

Douglass, who had hitherto been opposed to violence as a means of freeing the slaves, confessed that he would be pleased to hear that slaves in the South had revolted and 'were spreading death and destruction.' That such sentiments could proceed from the mouth of a professed humanitarian speaks volumes for the barbarity of the 'peculiar institution', as slavery was then known, and the reactions to which it gave rise in decent men.

Two years later Brown moved with his family to North Elba in the Adirondack mountains of New York State, or Timbuctoo as it was known, to rent a cabin on land set aside for free blacks by the wealthy philanthropist, Gerrit Smith. Brown preached to the blacks and helped them to settle in the new territory, even though they were not always welcome. A neighbour described Brown at this time as a 'thin, sinewy, hard favored, clear-headed, honest-minded man, who had spent all his days as a frontier farmer. On conversing with him we found him well informed on most subjects, especially the natural sciences. He had books and evidently made a diligent use of them'.[31]

But secretly Brown was planning violence. In 1850 on a business trip to Europe he 'visited forts, studied plans and ordnance, carefully looked at soldiers and their equipments'.[32] In January of the following year, Brown, now living in Springfield, formed a small black militia to resist slave catchers. He called it the United States League of Gileadites.[33] His instructions to his followers were, 'Do not delay one moment after you are ready; you will lose all resolution if you do. Let the first blow be the signal for all to engage; and when engaged do not do your work by halves, but make clean work with your enemies – and be sure you meddle not with any others'.[34]

The first known mention by Brown of a proposed attack on the arsenal at Harpers Ferry appears to have been in late 1854 or early 1855

---

31   Villard, *John Brown 1800-1859*, p. 74.
32   Richard J. Hinton, *John Brown and His Men* (New York: Funk & Wagnalls, 1894); Reprint New York: The Arno Press, 1968, p. 35.
33   Judges 12, 1-15 recounts how the Gileadites beat the Ephriamites in a great battle and set up a blockade to capture their fleeing enemies. They were identified by their inability to pronounce the 'sh' sound in the word, 'shibboleth'.
34   Quoted in Villard, *John Brown 1800-1859*, p. 51. The League's membership never exceeded forty-four and the organization was not copied elsewhere.

in a conversation with a Colonel Woodruff. Its objects, the Colonel was later to recall, would be to frighten Virginia and detach it from the Southern slave interest, to capture the rifles, to destroy the arsenal so that its equipment could not be used against him, and to arm the slaves.[35] John Brown Jr. insisted that the prime aim was to induce the North to 'whip the South back into the Union without slavery'. Brown's daughter, Sarah, would later remember her father planning around this time to build a fort at Harpers Ferry; so powerful was the memory that she later shivered and her heart raced in dread at any mention of the name. Brown's eldest sons shared their father's hatred of slavery in full measure and were determined to do something about it. The obvious place was Kansas.

BLEEDING KANSAS

Kansas in the 1850s was in dire straits. Tensions had long been growing between the slave owning South and the nascent industrial economy of the North. It centred on the question of whether the vast tracts of land acquired from the French in the Louisiana purchase should become slave owning or 'free' States of the Union. The so-called Missouri compromise agreement of 1820 was shattered when Congress decided to open Kansas up to settlement. Inspired by the notion of 'popular sovereignty', an Act of 1854 allowed the new Territories to decide for themselves whether they wanted slavery or not.[36] The abolitionists, described as Free Staters, or Free Soilers, were horrified. With the help of an anti-slavery organization called the Emigrant Aid Company, settlers from New England and elsewhere poured into Kansas Territory determined to resist a decision in favour of slavery. They came prepared with the very latest in personal weapons, the Sharps rifle.[37] This influx provoked a counter-immigration from the West. When the first election for a delegate to Congress was held in November, hundreds of heavily armed men from the neighbouring (slave) state of Missouri descended on the Territory and camped around the

35 Quoted in Villard, *John Brown 1800-1859*, p. 54.
36 A territory was an area administered by an appointed or elected governor and an elected legislature while awaiting statehood.
37 Fast-firing cavalry rifles known as 'Beecher's Bibles' after the abolitionist minister, Henry Ward Beecher, who raised money to provide them.

polling stations. (Free Staters called the rag tag army of Missourian pro-slavers 'border ruffians'; they in turn were called 'Jayhawkers' by the Missourians after the mythical bird that survives by stealing from other birds.) With intimidation and voter fraud on a massive scale the pro-slavery candidate won easily.

A further election in March 1855 resulted in yet another victory for the pro-slavery faction. When a lawyer protested against the vote rigging he was tarred and feathered and run out of town. The new government moved the State capital from the abolitionist town of Lawrence to the town of Lecompton near the Missouri border. The Free Staters retaliated by calling a constitutional convention of their own, which declared, unsurprisingly, in favour of a Free State. In retaliation, the territorial legislature refused to recognize the Free State delegates and moved its base to the Shawnee Mission near the Missouri border where it adopted the draconian Missouri slave code, disqualified abolitionists from holding public office and imposed a sentence of ten-years hard labour for the crime of assisting fugitive slaves. The Northerners responded by setting up their own Free State legislature at Topeka. There were now two separate governments in the territory, one slave and one free. 'Bleeding Kansas' had been born.[38]

It was into this ferment that the Brown boys and their families travelled in 1854, in those days almost an epic journey. They settled and made claims in what became known as Brown's Station, Osawatomie.[39] John Brown Jr. wrote to his father that they had answered a call to 'all lovers of freedom who desired homes in a new region to go (to Kansas) as settlers, and by their votes save Kansas from the curse of slavery.' His worst fears were confirmed by what he found at the end of their long journey. As he told his father, the pro-slavery forces were 'armed to the teeth with revolvers, Bowie knives, rifles and cannon' and were terrorizing the rest of the people. '[T]he remedy we propose is, that the anti-slavery portion of the inhabitants should immediately, thoroughly arm and organize themselves in military companies'.[40] He asked his father to borrow money from someone

38   The term was coined by Horace Greely writing in the *New York Tribune*.
39   Osawatomie was named after two Indian tribes, the Osage and the Pottawatomie. The settlement was also known as Brownsville and Fairfield.
40   Villard *John Brown 1800-1859*, p. 83.

like Gerrit Smith to buy rifles, to which bayonets could be fitted. 'The Minnie rifle,' he wrote, 'has a killing range almost equal to cannon and of course is more easily handled, perhaps enough so as to make up the difference'.[41]

The boys pleaded with their father to join them and, after some initial reluctance, John Brown gave in and left for Kansas, leaving his youngest son Watson to look after his wife and younger children. (His willingness to move may have been due in part to the fact that he was once again on the point of bankruptcy.) In any event, the move was a turning point. The historian Villard describes how at this time;

> ... the shackles of business life dropped from him. He was now bowed and rapidly turning gray; to everyone's lips the adjective, 'old' now leaped as they saw him. But his was not the age of senility, nor of weariness with life, nor were the lines of care due solely to family and business anxieties, or the hard labor of the fields. They were rather the marks of the fires consuming within; of the indomitable purpose that was the mainspring of every action; of a life devoted, of a spirit inspired. Emancipation from the counter and the harrow came joyfully to him at the time of life when most men begin to long for rest and the repose of a quiet, well-ordered home. Thenceforth, he was free to move where he pleased, to devote every thought to his battle with the slave power, which then knew nothing of his existence.[42]

As he left to take up his burden, Brown turned to his family and said, 'If it is so painful for us to part with the hope of meeting again, how of poor slaves?' He had discovered his life's work.

THE SACKING OF LAWRENCE

John Brown arrived in Osawatomie on 6 October 1855 determined to defeat slavery. He formed a company of 'Liberty Guards' and was elected Captain. He did not have to wait long for an excuse to act.

After a Free Stater was murdered in a land dispute, a pro-slaver arrested for the crime was freed by a group of sympathizers from the nearby town of Lawrence. In response, the local pro-slavery Sheriff, Samuel J. Jones, called for assistance from (slave-owning) Missouri.

41   The Minnie rifle was the latest French design.
42   Villard, *John Brown 1800-1859*, p. 77.

The response was overwhelming and a week-long siege of the town ensued. Eventually, the Governor managed to broker a peace.[43] 'Captain' Brown arrived only after the negotiations had begun; it was his first venture onto the stage of history.[44] Later, when an armed band of pro-slavers arrived from Georgia and camped by the Marais des Cygnes River[45] which ran through Osawatomie, Brown, who had taught himself surveying as a youngster, and his sons went among them posing as surveyors and noting down their strengths and dispositions. It was a subterfuge he was to employ again later.

The Governor's 'treaty' did not last long. When Sheriff Jones made a second attempt to arrest the men who had rescued his prisoner he was shot while sitting in his tent, and left partially paralyzed for life. The pro-slavery faction called for revenge and a grand jury indicted eight men on a charge of treason. US marshal I.B. Donaldson issued a proclamation commanding all law-abiding citizens 'to be and appear at Lecompton as soon as practicable, and in numbers sufficient for the proper execution of the law'. It was the opportunity the pro-slavers had been waiting for. Sheriff Jones brought up some seven hundred and fifty 'border ruffians' to block all roads leading out of Lawrence and trained guns on the town. Realizing their parlous position, the townspeople declared that they would not resist the execution of the law and surrendered their arms. It did them no good; when the pro-slaver forces entered the town they gutted two printing houses and demolished the hotel. During the course of the action two men were killed. Before leaving, the mob burned down the house of an ex-Governor who had been indicted by the grand jury.

As the news from Lawrence came in – slowly and not always accurately – the Free Staters were alarmed, angered and confused in equal measure. Brown assembled a band of fifty men, but it was too late. Before they could get to Lawrence the town had already been

---

43 This near tragic incident later became known as the Wakarusa War after the tributary of the Kansas River where the invaders had camped.
44 The Liberty Guards were first mustered on 27 November 1855. They grandly declared themselves to be part of the 5th Regiment, 1st Brigade of Kansas Volunteers, although consisting only of Brown, four of his sons and fifteen other men.
45 The marsh of the swans.

sacked without a finger raised in its defence. News now arrived of a fresh atrocity which raised the temperature yet further. An abolitionist Senator, Charles Sumner, had been beaten senseless at his desk in the Senate by his father's cousin, Congressman Preston Brooks. The attack was so violent that Brooks' gold-topped cane broke in two. Brown is said to have gone crazy hearing of the assault.[46] Hard on the heels of this came the news that Brown's beloved father Owen had died.

THE SHARPENING OF THE SWORDS

Always a man of strong passions, Brown seems finally to have cracked. He declared, 'We have got to defend our families and our neighbours as best we can. Something is going to be done now. We must show by actual work that there are two sides to this thing and that they cannot go on with impunity.'[47] John Brown Jr. later related how 'it was now and here resolved that they, their aiders and abettors who sought to kill our suffering people, should themselves be killed, and in such manner as would be likely to cause restraining fear'.[48] The names of those who were to be 'picked off' were enthusiastically written down. Urged by his sons and others to be cautious, John Brown said he was tired of hearing that word and ignored their counsel: it was the parting of the ways. As the bulk of the men left camp with John Jr. his father put together a handful of men to carry out his plans. They were his son-in-law, Henry Thompson, four of his sons – Frederick, Owen, Salmon and Oliver – and an Austrian, Theodore Weiner. They armed themselves with rifles, revolvers, knives and short, heavy two-edged swords which they ground to a sharp edge. Originally made as artillery broadswords, these fearsome weapons had been adapted by an eccentric society, whose aim was to invade Canada, and were later donated to Brown by one of its former members.

---

46   Salmon Brown, as quoted in Villard, *John Brown 1800-1859*, p. 154. Brown later visited the wounded Sumner and inspected his blood-stained coat.
47   Statement of Jason Brown dated 13 December 1908, quoted in Villard, *John Brown 1800-1859*, p. 151.
48   Quoted in Villard, *John Brown 1800-1859*, p. 152. The attack occurred after the Senator had made a two day speech in the US Senate in which he accused a South Carolina Senator of taking the 'harlot, Slavery' as his mistress.

At about noon on Friday, 23 May, Brown's party left Osawatomie on a lumber wagon belonging to a neighbour, James Townsley. Some-one who met them on their way described Brown as looking 'wild and frenzied'.[49] The group spent that night and most of the following day in a ravine a mile north of what was known as Dutch Henry's crossing on the Pottawatomie. (The anti-abolitionist Dutch Henry was one of their foremost targets.) It was here that Brown revealed to his companions his plan to 'sweep the Pottawatomie of all pro-slavery men living on it'. It was, he said, 'better that a score of bad men should die than that one man who came here to make Kansas a Free State should be driven out'.[50] It was necessary to 'strike terror' into the hearts of the pro-slavery people. Not everyone liked what they heard and it took all Brown's formidable powers of persuasion to bring them round to his point of view. Townsley, now realizing the enormity of what was intended, asked to be allowed to go home. Brown's reaction was to take out his revolver and say, 'Shut up;! You are trying to discourage my boys. Dead men tell no tales'.

The group's first attempt at 'terror' was ingloriously unsuccessful. At about 10 p.m. on Saturday, 24 May, they knocked at the door of a settler's cabin. A carbine was poked out and the aspiring assassins ran off. Their next stop proved to be more deadly; it was the home of James Doyle, his wife and their six children. Doyle's two bulldogs reacted violently when they heard the men approach; Townsley dis-patched one of them with his sword and the other ran off. One of the group knocked at the door asking the way to Wilkinson's cabin. When James Doyle opened the door, Brown and four others forced their way in, saying that they were from the Northern army and that he and the boys must surrender.[51] Resistance was useless in the face of the weapons confronting the family; Mr Doyle and his two eldest sons, William and Drury were taken outside. The youngest were spared fol-lowing pleas from a tearful Mrs Doyle. One of the surviving boys later described how, when he ventured out later, he had found one of his

---

49   Stephen B. Oates, *To Purge This Land with Blood* (New York, Harper Torchbooks, 1970), p. 132.
50   *Ibid.*, p. 133.
51   Townsley (who was not always to be trusted) claimed that they first threw lighted rolls of hay into the cabin mixed with gunpowder.

brothers 'lying dead on the ground, about 150 yards from the house, in the grass near a ravine; his fingers were cut off, and his arms were cut off; his head was cut open, and a hole was in his jaw, as though it was made with a knife, and a hole was also in his side. My father was shot in the forehead and stabbed in the breast.' Either the men had put up a fight (which could be one explanation for the severed fingers) or their bodies had been deliberately mutilated after death.

Salmon and Owen appear to have done the butcher's work while John Brown looked on. Townsley was later to claim that Brown had shot the father dead before his sons were murdered. Much later Brown told an audience in Cleveland that 'he had never killed anybody, although on some occasion he had shown the young men how some things might be done as well as others, and they had done the business'.[52] There is nothing apart from Townsley's report to contradict him on this and it is possible that Browns' carefully chosen words were meant to conceal the fact that he had fired the bullet into Doyle's forehead as some sort of *coup de grâce* after he had been butchered; we will probably never know.

Before daybreak on what was now the Sabbath morning John Brown and four of his companions moved on to the home of another settler, Allen Wilkinson. One of them knocked on the door and asked the way to Dutch Henry's place. The owner appeared and was asked whether he supported the Free Staters. When he answered 'No', he was told that he must surrender. Despite his wife's pleading that she was sick with the measles and needed him, Wilkinson was ordered to put his clothes on but not his shoes and go with the intruders. With them they took his gun and powder flask, returning later to steal two saddles. Next morning, Wilkinson was found in the brush some 150 yards from his house with a gash in his head and another in his side and his throat cut in two places. This time the butchery was down to Thompson and Weiner. Mrs Wilkinson later described the gang's commander as an old man wearing soiled clothes with a straw hat pulled down over his face.

The murderers then made their way to the next cabin where Brown woke James Harris and his wife at sword-point while others kept guard

---

52   Hinton, *John Brown and His Men*, p. 235.

outside. Staying in the house with the Harris's were William Sherman (Dutch Henry's brother), John S. Whiteman and Jerome Glanville, who had come to buy a cow. The intruders announced themselves as 'the Northern army' and ordered everyone to surrender. After ransacking the cabin and seizing two rifles and a Bowie knife, the intruders took Glanville and Harris outside for questioning. Asked where Henry Sherman was, Glanville said he was out looking for strayed cattle. Harris reports his interrogation:

> They asked if I had ever taken any hand in aiding pro-slavery men in coming to the Territory of Kansas, or had ever taken any hand in the last troubles at Lawrence, and asked me whether I had ever done the free State party any harm or ever intended to do that party any harm; they asked me what made me live at such a place. I then answered that I could get higher wages there than anywhere else.

This explanation was enough to save his life and Brown ordered Sherman to go outside in his place. Later that morning Sherman's body was found in the creek. A large hole had been cut in his breast and his left hand had been almost entirely hacked off. His skull had been split open in two places and some of his brain had washed away. Weiner and Thompson appear to have carried out the murder, while their leader Brown stood by. Afterwards, the two butchers cleaned their swords in the creek.

The killing party now made their way back to camp where news of the massacre had already arrived. Almost by tacit consent, it seems, their bloody work was over. Despite the fact that their plans had been known to their comrades beforehand, a horrified Jason asked his father, 'Did you have anything to do with the killing of these men on the Pottawatomie?' 'I did not', Brown replied, 'but I approved of it'. A tearful Frederick protested, 'When I came to see what manner of work it was I could not do it'. Jason condemned it as 'an uncalled-for, wicked act'. After this confrontation his father resigned his leadership of the company and another was elected in his place.

Although none of Brown's victims had been involved in the sack of Lawrence, all were known for their pro-slavery views. Brown's apologists have gone further and painted them as 'among the worst of their kind',[53] but this is a misreading. People like the victims had neither the desire nor the funds to own slaves. Doyle may have been a pro-slavery bigot, but the murdered men were for the most part settlers fearful of the threat to white jobs which slaves were seen as representing.

The victims' names had not been drawn from a hat. Earlier, on 21 April, there had been a confrontation between pro-slavery and abolitionist factions in court. Fearing that the new pro-slavery laws would be enforced against them, the Brown family had determined to do what they could to resist it. John Brown Jr. and his private militia, the 'Pottawatomie Rifles', went to the court of the pro-slavery Judge Cato sitting in Dutch Henry's tavern to present it with a resolution condemning the 'bogus' laws. The acting prosecutor was the attorney, Allen Wilkinson, who was also the local postmaster and a member of the Kansas territorial legislature. Among the jury were James Harris, who lived in the cabin of his employer, Henry Sherman, and James P. Doyle.[54] Doyle's eldest son was the court bailiff.[55] It is difficult to resist the conclusion that it was this confrontation which was to prove to be their death warrant.

THE HUNTED MEN

As soon as news of the Pottawatomie massacre got out – some of it grossly exaggerated – fear and rage gripped the Territory. Armed bands roamed the countryside arresting and ejecting prominent Free Staters. On 28 May Judge Cato reacted by issuing warrants for the arrest of John Brown and others.[56] Brown went into hiding, but his house was burned and a dozen men killed. John Brown Jr. and his brother Jason managed to find sanctuary in the home of a clergyman. The events at Osawatomie had greatly upset young John and he suf-

53   See, for example, Du Bois, *John Brown*, p. 75.
54   It is thought that the owner of the cabin first visited by Brown was another juror.
55   Reynolds speculates that the subject of the first unsuccessful attempt at murder had been a juror on Cato's court.
56   Townsley was the only member of the gang to be tried for the Pottawatomie murders, but the prosecution had to be dropped for lack of evidence.

fered what we would now call a nervous breakdown. Next morning, while attempting to leave, the two brothers were caught by a company of Shannon's Sharp-shooters under a journalist, 'Captain' Henry Clay Pate, and subjected to a mock hanging.[57] Later, the pair were seized by an even more brutal group and forced to march twenty miles a day tied with ropes or chains. John Jr, was treated particularly brutally, to such an extent that Jason described him as having 'not a glimmer of reason'. It was a condition from which he was never fully to recover.

Brown was determined to free his sons and when on 2 June he learned that Pate was camped in Black Jack Creek on the Santa Fé Trail near the town of Palmyra he stationed his party of seventeen where they could ambush the pro-slavers the following morning. The battle lasted some three hours and only ended when Brown began shooting Pate's horses.[58] The slaver agreed to exchange his freedom and that of another of his officers for the release of Brown's sons. It nevertheless took until September for the brothers to be released. By this time Jason's house had been burned and his cattle driven off. Four of Pate's men had been killed in what came to be called the Battle of Black Jack. From then on a virtual state of war existed in Kansas.

In the summer of 1856 militia bands, both for and against slavery, roamed Kansas with impunity. On 5 August the Lawrence companies under John Brown, broke up a pro-slavery settlement at New Georgia on the Marais des Cygnes. They burned a blockhouse and stole the settlers' property. But a greater threat now appeared. A force of between 150 and 300 Missourians under 'Major-General' John W. Reid, a prominent lawyer, had crossed into Kansas. As it approached Osawatomie on 30 August the advance guard came across Frederick Brown and a companion and shot them both dead.[59] John Brown and some forty men barely had time to quit the town and take up position in the woods on the south side of the Marais des Cygnes. After an exchange of fire Brown realized that his position was untenable

---

57   Twenty-four year old Pate was a captain in the Missouri militia, a deputy US marshal and a newspaper correspondent. He was to prove a capable cavalryman and died at the Battle of Yellow Tavern (1864).
58   He was later to claim that he had been tricked and captured while under a flag of truce.
59   The exact circumstances are not clear.

and retired. The Missourians spent their rage on looting the town and burning its houses. Three of Brown's men were killed in the action and four captured, one of whom was to be murdered later; Brown himself was bruised by passing shot. The engagement was far from a success, but it gained the abolitionist the title, 'Brown of Osawatomie'. As a result of this notoriety he was forced to adopt various aliases when on his travels.

Eventually, the new territorial governor, John W. Geary, managed to cool the 'border war' with the aid of Federal troops, although violence continued on a smaller scale into 1861. In all, fifty-six people are thought to have died in 'Bleeding Kansas'.[60]

'THE SECRET SIX'

But Kansas was for Brown never more than a diversion from his main purpose, the instigation of a slave uprising in Virginia. To achieve this he would need substantial funds, and in early 1857 he went to Boston to find them. His name had gone before him and many in that part of the world saw him as a new Oliver Cromwell, the English regicide then undergoing a popular rehabilitation. The writer David S. Reynolds observed that 'the hunted criminal was transformed into a venerated warrior, the frontier pariah into an urban celebrity courted by a small but influential cluster of business people and intellectuals'.[61] Brown finally hit paydirt when he met the enthusiastic young journalist, Franklin Sanborn, secretary of the Massachusetts State Kansas Committee (for the abolition of slavery). Sanborn introduced his new friend to five other enthusiastic abolitionists who were to become his principal backers.

Known collectively as 'the Secret Six', they were, in addition to Sanborn, the Boston physician, Dr. Samuel Gridley Howe, husband of Julia Ward Howe, writer of the *Battle Hymn of the Republic*, the Unitarian minister and amateur boxer, Thomas Wentworth Higginson (the most radical of the six), the distinguished theologian and social

60 Estimate of Dale E. Watts, 'How Bloody was Bleeding Kansas? Political Killings in Kansas Territory 1854-1861,' *Kansas History: A Journal of the Central Plains,* vol. 18, no. 2 (Summer 1995), 116–129.
61 Reynolds, *John Brown, Abolitionist*, p. 206.

reformer, Theodore Parker, the eccentric millionaire, President of the Massachusetts State Kansas Committee and financial backer of the Emigrant Aid societies, Gerrit Smith, and the millionaire factory owner, George Luther Stearns. Another notable contributor (but not one of the Six) was the wealthy textile merchant, Amos Adams Lawrence. Most were in varying degrees associated with what was called the transcendentalist movement.[62] Great play is sometimes made of the financial contributions of the Secret Six, which were certainly substantial. However, a Senate Select Committee later charged with looking into the Harpers Ferry raid was to comment that 'these contributions were made occasionally in large sums paid directly to Brown, but more usually by collections made in the villages and towns throughout the country by itinerant lecturers'.

Well aware of the unpopularity which would be caused by revealing his real plans Brown sought funds 'for the defence of abolitionists'. The subterfuge was characteristic of his secretive character. In January 1857 the Massachusetts State Kansas Committee voted to give Brown 200 Sharps rifles and ammunition 'for the defence of Kansas'. Later that month the committee voted him a grant of $5,000, but refused to hand over the rifles after he stubbornly declined to disclose his plans ('I will not be interrogated'). Brown's greatest coup – potentially at least – was when Sanborn managed to arrange for him to address the Massachusetts Joint Committee on Federal Relations; the event proved to be a disappointment, Brown was offered kind words, but little more. In desperation, he placed an advertisement in the press soliciting funds for 'Liberty in Kansas' (a deliberately misleading title). At the same time he launched himself on a fund-raising lecture tour across New England in the course of which he stayed with both Henry David Thoreau and Ralph Waldo Emerson, both towering figures in the transcendentalist movement.

It was in March 1857 in New York that Brown met an English adventurer, Hugh Forbes, who was to play a significant part in his plans. Impressed by his knowledge of military matters (he was said to have fought with Garibaldi in Italy) Brown employed the Englishman at $150 a month to train his troops and to translate a French military

62 Transcendentalism was a literary, philosophical and political movement that emerged in New England in the early nineteenth century.

pamphlet. Later that year, with a US Marshal hard on his heels, Brown thought it prudent to hide for a week in the house of an abolitionist judge. At the end of the year he and Forbes fell out over strategy. Their differences are instructive. Forbes wanted to stimulate a series of 'slave stampedes' resulting in large numbers of fugitive slaves being helped to get to Canada. Brown on the other hand was more ambitious. Slave resentment was so great, he believed, that a small company of men, black and white, could 'beat up a slave quarter in Virginia' giving rise to a general rebellion all over the South. Despite this fundamental disagreement the two men claimed to have arrived at a compromise, a 'well matured plan' as they called it, to defeat slavery. Forbes set about creating a military school and Brown threw himself into a study of guerilla tactics.

By the time he returned to Kansas, Brown's north-eastern tour had raised $23,000 in cash and promises, but much of the promised money failed to materialise. Brown was a disappointed man, an outlook made all the worse by an attack of the ague (or fever), the effects of which he seems never to have fully shaken off. Things did not get better when the disgruntled Forbes, who had not been paid for six months, started writing letters to Brown's Boston backers demanding payment of his back-pay under threat of publishing their plans; he even approached a Massachusetts Senator on the floor of the Senate to air his grievances. Brown's backers were rattled, some wanting to bring the action forward, while others urged caution. Since most of the money came from the cautious their counsel carried the day and the raid was deferred. In future, the Secret Six would live up to their name by communicating with Brown only under conditions of the greatest security.

Brown now set about the task of putting together a raiding party. According to the so-called 'confession' which John Cook was to make while awaiting trial, Brown asked him to 'organize a company for the purpose of putting a stop to the aggression of the pro-slavery man' in Kansas. It was only after they had set out that they discovered that their ultimate destination was in fact Virginia. Not everyone was pleased with the news and 'some warm words passed between (Brown and Cook)'. Nevertheless, after collecting weapons and supplies, the group embarked on the long journey to Springfield, Iowa, where Brown decided to over-winter. Here, while their weapons and supplies were being shipped out to the Kennedy farm, Brown's small force studied war with the help of a pamphlet written by Forbes entitled, *Duties of a Soldier*.

With warrants out for his arrest, Brown felt compelled to move constantly. (Villard records 35 moves in 1858 alone). At one point he hid out for nearly a month in the home of Frederick Douglass in Rochester, New York. Apparently, he now felt able to share his plans with his friend. 'Once in a while', Douglass was to write later in his *Life and Times*, 'he would say he could, with a few resolute men, capture Harper's Ferry [sic], and supply himself with arms belonging to the government at that place, but he never announced his intention to do so. It was however, very evidently passing in his mind as a thing he might do.' The following month Brown approached Higginson for money for 'the most important undertaking of my whole life'. Asked to explain, Brown replied untruthfully that it was 'the railroad business on a somewhat extended scale'. (By 'railroad' he meant the underground railroad by which escaped slaves were helped to freedom.) To a later request, Higginson replied that 'I am always ready to invest in treason, but at present have none to invest'. A similar letter to Stearns sought funds 'for secret service and no questions asked'. Stearns warned Brown that the arms that had been supplied to him were 'to be used for the defense of Kansas', and 'not to use them for any other purpose'.[63] Brown ignored this condition.

In February 1858 Brown went to Gerrit Smith's home, where he finally laid out his plan to invade 'northern Virginia near the Alleghenies'. (Harpers Ferry was not mentioned by name.) His backers were sceptical of success given the limited means available to the enterprise. Nevertheless, they resolved to do what they could to raise funds. Realizing that a campaign to free the slaves would look odd without any black participation, Brown convened a secret anti-slavery convention in a black church in Chatham, Ontario on 9 May. It was a bold stroke, but hardly successful. About a third of Chatham's population were fugitive slaves, but only thirty-four of them attended the convention, along with twelve whites. Brown proposed a new government for a territory he intended to found in the South and produced a

---

63   Letter of 15 May 1858, quoted in the report of the Senate Select Committee.

'Provisional Constitution and Ordinances for the People of the United States', which he had drafted while staying with Douglass. The constitution's preamble revealed his thinking:

> ... slavery, throughout its entire existence in the United States is none other than a most barbarous, unprovoked and unjustifiable War of one portion of its citizens upon another portion; the only conditions of which are perpetual imprisonment and hopeless servitude or absolute extermination; in utter disregard and violation of those eternal and self-evident truths set forth in our Declaration of Independence.

The implication was that any black would be justified in defending himself in such a war and any abolitionist justified in coming to his aid. Brown was elected commander-in-chief of the proposed administration and John Kagi, Secretary of War. Blacks were appointed to the posts of Secretary of State and acting president, but few of them were enthusiastic enough to sign up. (Even fewer were to turn up when the call came.) Once again, Brown was less than frank about his intentions. One of the convention organizers, Delany, recollects him declaring that his aim was no more than to improve what he described as the 'subterranean passway' for the escape of slaves to Kansas, rather then Canada. He divulged nothing of his real intentions.

During the convention Brown learned for the first time of Forbes' threats to disclose his planned insurrection and decided to defer the attack, sending one of his men to retrieve his incriminating letters to the Englishman. While the convention was going on, an atrocity occurred which would lend further bitterness to the struggle. A pro-slavery band crossed into Kansas and seized eleven Free Staters, lined them up in a ravine near the Marais des Cygnes and opened fire on them. Five died and most of the rest were wounded. Brown returned to Kansas in the autumn under the alias, 'Shubel Morgan' and sporting a large, white beard. One of his first acts was to build a fort near the ravine so that the massacre could not happen again. Along with the Jayhawker, James Montgomery, he took part in a series of guerrilla raids across the border into Missouri. In December, his group forcibly liberated twelve slaves from Venona County, Missouri, capturing two white men and stealing horses, wagons and provisions. In the course of the raid one of the farmers resisted the attackers and was shot dead by Aaron Stevens. Brown then took the liberated slaves on an arduous eighty-two day winter journey from Missouri to Detroit and then on to Canada and liberty. During the journey the 'Osawatomie Brown' myth was given added allure when he saw off a party of Federal troops which outnumbered his small force by four to one.

In June 1858 Brown sent Cook to reconnoitre the Harpers Ferry area to discover how many slaves could be freed. Hearing of this, a worried Gerrit Smith wrote to Sanborn, 'I do not wish to know Captain Brown's plans; I hope that he will keep them to himself'. Irked that he still had to live in hiding, Brown wrote letters to the press in January 1859, indignantly pointing out that, while posses were being organized to find him, nothing was being done to prosecute the perpetrator of the Marais des Cygnes atrocity.[64] He failed to mention that he himself had gone unpunished for the Pottawatomie massacre and the murder of the Venona farmer.

Eventually feeling safe from exposure, Brown returned to New England, where on 9 May 1859 he gave a lecture in Concord, Massachusetts attended by Emerson and Thoreau. In June he visited his family in North Elba for the last time. Once again he seems to have felt the need for black participation and asked Douglass to meet him secretly in an abandoned quarry at Chambersburg, Pennsylvania. According to Douglass, '[Brown] had completely renounced his old plan, and thought that the capture of Harper's Ferry [sic] would serve as notice to the slaves that their friends had come, and as a trumpet to rally them to his standard.' Douglass thought the plan was doomed; Brown 'was going into a perfect steel-trap, and that once in he would never get out alive; that he would be surrounded at once and escape would be impossible'. To Brown's disgust, Douglass rejected an offer to accompany the expedition.[65] It saved his life; just over two months later Brown and most of his party were either captured or dead. The world saw it as the deaths of martyrs.

---

64 The letters became known as 'the Parallels' because of the comparisons they made.
65 Douglass, *The Life and Times of Frederick Douglass*, pp. 350-354.

'THE ANGEL OF LIGHT'

On the day before Brown was sentenced to death Thoreau wrote a eulogy to him entitled, *A Plea for Captain John Brown:* 'Some eighteen hundred years ago, Christ was crucified; this morning, perchance, Captain Brown was hung. These are the two ends of a chain which is not without its links. He is not Old Brown any longer; he is an angel of light.' Emerson pushed the Christ analogy even further. Five days after the trial he gave a lecture in the Boston Music Hall, describing Brown as 'the new saint awaiting his martyrdom, and who, if he shall suffer, will make the gallows glorious like the cross.' And the poet John Greenleaf Whittier penned a panegyric, *Brown of Osawatomie* (Ironically, it included the line, 'Perish with him the folly that seeks through evil good!' It could not have been written by anyone who knew the truth about Pottawatomie.)[66] Before Brown was even in his grave, the abolitionist lawyer Wendell Phillips delivered a lecture from the pulpit of Henry Ward Beecher's Church in Brooklyn in which he claimed that 'John Brown has twice as much right to hang Governor Wise, as Governor Wise has to hang him.' In Boston the formerly peaceful, William Lloyd Garrison told a crowd that he was now prepared to say, 'Success to every slave insurrection at the South, and in every slave country'. After Brown's death, church bells rang out in the North, and in Albany, New York a 100-gun salute was fired in his honour. A fortnight later a play was produced in New York entitled, *Osawatomie Brown or the Insurrection*.

The Kansas correspondent of the *New York Tribune*, James Redpath, wrote a hagiographic biography, *The Public Life of Captain Brown*. Throughout the civil war which followed the Harpers Ferry raid Northern soldiers marched to Julia Ward Howe's 'Battle Hymn of the Republic', sung to the tune of 'John Brown's Body'.[67] And when at the height of the war Lincoln declared the emancipation of the slaves[68] Stearns unveiled a marble bust to 'the martyr'.

But not everyone rejoiced in this apotheosis.

66 This poem popularized a newspaper story that was the source of the baseless legend of Brown kissing a little negro girl on the way to the scaffold.
67 The words of the latter were composed by soldiers for an entirely different John Brown and only later appropriated to the abolitionist.
68 Albeit only in the rebel States.

'A TERRIBLE REMEDY'

Brown had been remarkably successful in enrolling among his supporters so many of the rich and famous. The renowned mystic and advocate of passive resistance Henry David Thoreau defended Brown even after his involvement in Pottawatomie had become public knowledge. Another supporter was his friend Ralph Waldo Emerson who stood head and shoulders above all other intellectuals of his day. A one-time candidate for the Unitarian ministry and supporter of the American Peace Party, Emerson nevertheless nodded his approval when Brown visited him to declare that it was 'better that a whole generation of men, women and children should pass away by a violent death than that a word of either (the Bible or the Declaration of Independence) should be violated in this country'. They were strange views for the country's foremost humanitarian.

The fame of Thoreau and Emerson was such that they could ride the whirlwind thrown up by Harpers Ferry, but this was not true of all of Brown's backers. None was more frightened than Frederick Douglass. He fled to Canada and thence to England, from where he denied any part in the raid. But nothing would quell his admiration of Old Osawatomie. Writing many years later of his hero, Douglass commented, 'The horrors wrought by his iron hand cannot be contemplated without a shudder, but it is the shudder which one feels at the execution of a murderer. The amputation of a limb is a severe trial to feeling, but necessity is a full justification of it to reason. To call out a murderer at midnight, and without note or warning, judge or jury, run him through with a sword, was a terrible remedy for a terrible malady.'[69] But the Pottawatomie victims were anything but murderers and it would take a long stretch of the imagination to describe their horrifying deaths as a 'remedy'.

Among the documents seized at the Kennedy Farmhouse was an incriminating bundle of letters between Gerrit Smith and Brown. When they appeared in the press, Smith was so overcome with fear and guilt that he had to be committed temporarily to an asylum. Of the other members of the Secret Six, Frank Sanborn, Samuel Howe and

---

69 *The Life and Times of Frederick Douglass, Written by Himself.* (Park Publishing, Hartford, Conn. 1881).

George Stearns also found it convenient to visit Canada. The report of a Senate Select Committee later commented on Stearns' 'feeble, and, as it resulted, abortive effort ... to prevent a murderous use of these arms by Brown'. It was faint condemnation for men who had encouraged and supported one of the most murderous assaults in American history. Howe for his part issued a blatantly untruthful disclaimer of any knowledge of the raid. Only Higginson (who declared himself 'always ready to invest in treason') and the now dying Parker attempted to defend it. Reynolds points out that, although they denied it to the Senate committee, they must all have been aware from the outset of Brown's leading part in the Pottawatomie massacre, which had been on public record since 1856.[70] Perhaps the most balanced judgement on the Secret Six was to come from Villard when he wrote, 'its members were plainly unaware that to support a forcible attack upon a system, no matter how iniquitous, in a country founded upon a principle that differences of opinion must be settled by the ballot, carries with it both heavy responsibilities and grave personal danger.'[71]

But the main responsibility for the Harpers Ferry raid lay with one man only. What did he expect would come of it?

THE UNANSWERED QUESTION OF HARPERS FERRY

Whatever he may have told Judge Parker's court, it is clear that Brown's real intention was to incite a slave insurrection. His small party of twenty-one, while perfectly adequate for taking a relatively unguarded armoury, was a long way from the numbers that would be needed for a general insurrection.[72] Everything turned on the assault being followed by a mass uprising of whites and slaves, and this was exactly what Brown had contemplated. When the Kennedy farm was searched after the raid it was found to contain, in the words of the Senate Committee, '200 Sharp's rifled carbines, and 200 revolver pistols, packed in the boxes of the manufacturers, with 900 or 1,000 pikes, carefully and strongly made, the blade of steel being securely riveted

70   Reynolds, *John Brown, Abolitionist*, pp. 221-222.
71   Villard, *John Brown 1800-1859*, p. 528.
72   In custody, he refused to answer the question, 'What in the world did you suppose you could do here in Virginia with [so few] men?'

to a handle about five feet in length; many thousand percussion caps in boxes, and ample stores of fixed ammunition, besides a large supply of powder in kegs, and a chest that contained hospital and other military stores, beside a quantity of extra clothing for troops.'[73] Altogether, Brown had sufficient weapons for an army of 1,500. What did he intend to use it for, except for a general insurrection?

After the trial, Governor Wise taxed Brown on his declared motives. He replied:

> I deny everything but what I have all along admitted, of a design on my part to free slaves. I intended certainly to have made a clean thing of that matter, as I did last winter when I went into Missouri, and there took slaves without the snapping of a gun on either side, moving them through the country, and finally leaving them in Canada. I designed to have done the same thing again on a larger scale.'[74]

Brown spoke only of his intention to arm the negroes to permit them to defend themselves. If he was serious it was a daydream. The slaves knew that insurrection was their owners' worst nightmare – it had happened more than once before and their reaction had been immediate and violent to the point of sadism. The idea that slaves could be helped to defend themselves with pikes simply does not stand up, as Brown must have known. Either he was trying to cover up his real intention or he was working on a plan that was doomed to failure. The Senate Select Committee were probably right when they concluded that, 'There can be no doubt that Brown's plan was to commence servile war on the border of Virginia, which he expected to extend ... throughout the entire South'.

Whichever way you look at it, the raid was misconceived, ill-planned and badly executed. Harpers Ferry was a curious place to start a slave revolt. In the year 1859 the town's population of about 2,500

---

73   The Committee observed that 'these arms, which had been refused to Brown by the national committee, for the very satisfactory reason that he gave evasive answers to their inquiry how they were to be used, were proffered to him, and without request on his part, by the Massachusetts committee...'

74   Seeking to explain these in a letter to Andrew Hunter, Brown was to write that, 'I intended to convey this idea, that it was my object to place the slaves in a condition to defend their liberties, if they would, without any bloodshed, but not that I intended to run them out of the slave States'.

included 1,251 free blacks but only 88 slaves. Nothing had been done to prepare them for an uprising; Brown had certainly not consulted them. As he had been sensibly advised by Forbes beforehand, 'no preparatory notice having been given to the slaves... the invitation to rise might, unless they were already in a state of agitation, meet with no response or a feeble one'. Militarily, it was a disaster. For all his study of tactics, Brown had chosen a site where he was separated from his source of supplies by a river, and he had made no plans for retreat. The errors continued during the raid. The mail train, once it had been stopped, was permitted to continue to the next station, from which it must have been obvious that a call for help would immediately be sent out. Even before Brown had finally been surrounded in his 'fort' he ignored increasingly frantic pleas from Kagi to quit the town. He was later to claim that he had delayed his departure out of a desire to negotiate with the locals who had frustrated him by their deliberate prevarication. He told the Governor, 'I had thirty odd prisoners, whose wives and daughters were in tears for their safety, and I felt for them. Besides, I wanted to allay the fears of those who believed that we came here to burn and kill.' (He offered the same explanation for allowing the train to proceed.) This was an odd explanation from the author of a raid which had resulted in seventeen deaths and it seems more likely that his reaction was due to his being stunned by the vigour of the townsmen's resistance and downcast at the lack of any response from those he sought to free. Faced with such setbacks, the fierce old man had become indecisive, and it was to be his downfall.

BROWN THE MAN

Brown seems, almost uniquely among abolitionists, to have been entirely free from any taint of racism. At a time when even Abraham Lincoln could not conceive the races ever being able to live together in harmony, Brown was convinced that the black man was equal in intelligence and bravery to the white. And there can be no question of his bravery, or of his determination to do what he believed to be right in furtherance of a noble but unpopular cause. Stephen Vincent Benet's poem, *John Brown's Body* (1926), summed it up in the lines, 'He was a stone/A stone eroded to a cutting edge/By obstinacy, failure and cold prayers'. But there is a fine line between determination and obduracy. As the widowed Mrs Doyle told the Charlestown court, 'He said that if a man stood between him and what he considered right, he would take his life as coolly as he would eat his breakfast.' It was a fact she could confirm from bitter personal experience. Brown's thoughts never seemed far from violence. Only weeks before Pottawatomie he had declared at a public meeting that that he would rather see the Union dissolved and the country 'drenched with blood' than to pay taxes to a government that had recognized the pro-slavery legislature.[75]

As befitted a man with a direct line to God, Brown had no time for the advice of others. It is true that there were, in the dangerous days in which he lived, plenty of reasons for a man to keep his own counsel, but even among his friends Brown was notorious for his secretiveness. He fooled both his backers and his own supporters by consistently dissimulating. He was capable of deceit, sometimes even of himself. When he addressed the Charlestown court for the last time Brown described his Missouri raid as having happened 'without the snapping of a gun'; he must have known that this was untruthful. In the course of the raid Aaron Stevens had shot and killed the settler David Cruise. His statement to the court that tried him for the Harpers Ferry raid that he was 'sorry men had been killed; it was not by his orders or with his approbation' was at best the most egregious self-deception.

While Brown was awaiting execution, his attorney Hoyt made energetic but unsuccessful efforts to establish his insanity. Nevertheless, the idea that he was mentally unbalanced persists to this day, aided in part by an unfortunate photograph (the so-called 'mad photograph') which shows him with his mouth and eyes distorted in a manner familiar to every amateur photographer. Writing in 1875, a Captain Walker described Brown as having been 'insane', but the only facts he gave in support of this (the discharge by Brown of a firearm when awakened from sleep after the Pottawatomie massacre) are equally consistent with the actions of a frightened man on the run.[76] Some

75 Reynolds, *John Brown, Abolitionist*, p. 152. It is interesting to compare this with Lincoln's, 'If there be those who would not save the Union, unless they could at the same time save slavery, I do not agree with them. If there be those who would not save the Union unless they could at the same time destroy slavery, I do not agree with them.' (Letter to Horace Greeley, 22 August 1862.)
76 Quoted in Villard, *John Brown 1800-1859*, p. 228.

have suggested that Brown suffered from monomania, or obsession with a single idea, but Thoreau was probably right when he wrote that the word was 'a mere trope with most who persist in using it'.

Brown's greatest achievement was to recognize slavery for the abomination that it was. Unlike others who were prepared to speak and spend, but not to act, Brown was in the end willing to lay down his life in this noblest of causes. But did it achieve anything? History is divided as to the effects of the Harpers Ferry raid on the bloodletting that was to engulf America so soon after its author's demise. 'More than any other man,' said the radical lawyer Clarence Darrow, 'his mad raid broke the bondsman's chains.'[77] Others take a different view: the raid only convinced the South that Northern force had to be met with force, thus escalating the descent into civil war. This is not the place to attempt judgement. What is clear, however, are Brown's motives for his other act of supreme violence.

THE STAIN OF POTTAWATOMIE

No judgement of Brown is complete which fails to face up to the fact of Pottawatomie. It cannot be stressed too strongly that there was no military justification for the massacre.[78] Even the usually sympathetic Villard had to concede that 'not a single person had been killed in the region around Osawatomie, either by the lawless characters or by armed representatives of the pro-slavery cause'.[79] It is true that much about Pottawatomie rests on conflicting reports, many from people who had reason to misrepresent the facts, but that the massacre took place and that Brown was its author and director there can be no doubt.[80]

Immediately after the massacre Brown disclaimed all responsibility for it. He told his son, Jason, that he 'did not do it', adding, 'but I approved of it'. He flatly denied to James Redpath that either he or

77 Lecture to the Radical Club Forum, San Francisco, 12 December 1912.
78 James C. Malin, *John Brown and the Legend of Fifty Six* (Philadelphia, The American Philosophical Society, 1942), p. 561.
79 Villard's *John Brown 1800-1859*, p. 170.
80 For a useful account of alternative scenarios, see Oates, *To Purge This Land with Blood*, p. 384.

his family had any part in the massacre.[81] Brown continued with this denial, even to his wife.[82] He also gave various justifications for Pottawatomie, none of which stand up to examination. 'God is my judge', he said on one occasion, 'we were justified under the circumstances' – whatever that means. Later, he was to tell a friend that his victims deserved to die because 'they had committed murder in their hearts already',[83] a curious reason for multiple butchery.

It has been suggested that Brown's object in carrying out the massacre was to terrorise the pro-slavers out of Kansas, as he himself once told his companions. A more convincing explanation, however, was the growing tide of indignation that had been welling up in his breast following the successive blows of Shawnee, Lawrence and Sumner. The motive for Pottawatomie in other words was Brown's vindictive fury, fury at the wrongs which blacks had for so long suffered, fury at the indignities that Senator Sumner and other opponents of slavery were suffering, and the more fundamental fury of a self-willed man on being frustrated. The news of his father's death may have been the last straw. In any other person such feelings might have given rise to nothing more than anger. For a man who knew his crusade to be just and God-given they gave permission for acts of the utmost brutality.

Whatever view you take of the consequences of Harpers Ferry, and for all that it was a botched job which resulted in the unnecessary deaths of innocents, it had at least the merit of having been undertaken for the noblest of motives. The same cannot be said for the sadistic butchery that was Pottawatomie. It served no useful purpose other than to vent an old man's rage, and Brown is the smaller for it. As John Greenleaf Whittier wrote:

Perish with him the folly that seeks through evil good!
Long live the generous purpose unstained with human blood!
Not the raid of midnight terror, but the thought which underlies;
Not the borderer's pride of daring, but the Christian's sacrifice.[84]

81   Reynolds, *John Brown, Abolitionist*, p. 183.
82   Du Bois, *John Brown*, p. 205.
83   Oates, *To Purge This Land with Blood*, p. 147.
84   *John Brown of Ossawatomie* (1859).

George-Jacques Danton (Topfoto)

THE END OF A REVOLUTIONARY
THE TRIAL OF GEORGES-JACQUES DANTON, 1794

One day, after borrowing money for the journey from his friends, a sixteen year old boy played truant from school and walked the seventy miles to Rheims where, as had happened so often in the past, a new King of France was to be crowned. His most lasting memory of that ceremony was the release inside the cathedral of a flock of birds. 'Pretty freedom, that', he told his school friends, 'to flutter between four walls without a crumb to eat or a straw for a nest.' Nineteen years later Georges-Jacques Danton was to vote for the death of the King whose coronation he had witnessed as a child.

There is a remarkable statue in the Boulevard St Germain in Paris. It is of a young man pugnaciously pointing the way forward to two young soldiers. But look more closely and it is possible to imagine conflicting emotions in the face. George-Jacques Danton was at one and the same time an idealist and a freeloader, a humanitarian and a tolerator of violence, a passionate lover and a rabble-rouser. Like Oliver Cromwell before him, Danton was to seek the overthrow of a king but for a long time shied away from the logic of his ambition. With the death of Louis XVI he might have been pardoned for thinking that the revolutionary struggle he had played so prominent a part in was over; it was not. The forces that he and his young companions had unleashed had fallen into the hands of others more extreme than themselves. The hero of the early days of revolution found himself desperately trying to moderate the excesses of the terror state they had unleashed. Hauled before the very tribunal that he had created, the accuser became the accused and, after one of the most blatant show trials in European history, Danton's head was to follow that of the King's into the basket of the guillotine. How had all this come about?

France in the middle of the eighteenth century was still a semi-feudal society in which wealth and power resided almost exclusively in the monarch, the nobility and the church. In wondrous palaces like Versailles, the King and his Austrian Queen, Marie Antoinette, enjoyed a life of luxury unimaginable to the mass of the population. But behind the extravagancies of his court, Louis had inherited a kingdom in crisis. 'Farming', the archaic system of collecting taxes, was widely abused and the country's financial situation had been made worse by the cost of its seemingly endless wars with Britain. The twin burdens of taxation and inflation fell most heavily on the poor. The cost of bread accounted for over half a peasant's income, yet in many parts of the country most of them were out of work. But it was not only the peasants who were unhappy. The literary and professional classes, imbued with the ideas of the Enlightenment, of Voltaire, Rousseau and Descartes, were no longer prepared to accept the state of their world as God-given and unalterable. In May 1789 popular discontent forced the King to restore the Estates General, the nearest semblance to a Parliament France had ever enjoyed; it was to be his undoing. The new assembly gave scant support to the King's faltering attempts at financial reform, while at the same time offering the malcontents a platform from which to address the nation. Perhaps the most articulate among them was the young attorney, Georges-Jacques Danton.

ARCIS-SUR-AUBE

Danton was born on 26 October 1759 to comfortably off parents in the village of Arcis-Sur-Aube in the Champagne region of France. His father, who died when he was two and a half years old, was *procureur,* an office not unlike that of the Scottish Procurator Fiscal, his mother, the daughter of a local builder. Sent to a local seminary with the intention of becoming a priest, the young Danton left at the age of sixteen in order to read law. At the age of twenty-one he was articled to a solicitor in Paris, qualifying five years later. Along with other young intellectuals, he frequented the *Café du Parnasse*, eventually marrying the owner's daughter, Antoinette-Gabrielle Charpentier. With the aid of her dowry he purchased the office of *avocat aux Conseils du Roi,* practising from a law office on the north bank of the Seine.[1] There was

---

1 The *avocats aux Conseils du Roi* had monopoly rights to practise before Royal councils and commissions.

even talk of his having been offered the post of secretary to the Minister of Justice. At this stage the upwardly mobile Georges-Jacques was signing his name as 'd'Anton', a style that he continued to favour until 1792 when such *ancien régime* names fell out of favour. How did this young man, with his feet firmly planted on the ladder of professional advancement, find his way into revolutionary politics? The answer, like so many things about the man, is not entirely clear, but the circle of friends he acquired at this stage of his life must have had a great deal to do with it.

Some months after his marriage, Danton and his wife moved into a large first-floor apartment on the corner of the Rue des Cordeliers in the Latin quarter of Paris, where he was to reside for the remaining six years of his life. His closest friend, the radical young journalist and lawyer Camille Desmoulins and his wife, the beautiful Lucille Duplessis, came to live on the floor above him. Danton also joined a Masonic lodge whose members included many who were to become leading lights of the revolution, including Sieyès, Bailly and Collot D'Herbois.[2] Others, like the playwright and one-time actor Fabre d'Eglantine[3] and the butcher Legendre,[4] he met in the café Procope. Soon Danton found himself playing a leading role in the influential Society of the Rights of Man and of the Citizen, better known as the Cordeliers Club.

2   The Abbé Emmanuel-Joseph Siéyes was a critic of aristocratic and clerical privileges who saved his skin by keeping a low profile during the Terror. The astronomer Jean-Sylvain Bailly became Mayor of Paris from 1789 to 1791 when his popularity faded and he retired from public life. It was not enough to keep him from the guillotine. Jean-Marie Collot D'Herbois, the actor and playwright, originally argued for a constitutional monarchy, but gradually became more extreme and was responsible for the wholesale massacre of insurgents in Lyons. He ended his life in exile.
3   Philippe François Fabre d'Eglantine, the handsome young dramatist, was famous for naming the days and months of the revolutionary calendar. It did not stop him going to the guillotine with Danton.
4   Louis Legendre was a member of the Jacobin club and a founder of the Cordeliers. Later, a member of the Committee of Public Safety, he tried without success to defend Danton. His greatest achievement, however, was to survive the revolution.

THE REVOLUTIONARY CLUBS

The Cordeliers Club, so named after the former convent building which it first occupied, was a hotbed of radical activity. With its motto, 'Liberty, equality and brotherhood' it led the movement against the monarchy. Later, when people like Danton ceased attending, the Cordeliers were to be taken over by a more extreme faction known as the *enragés*.

Failing to get a seat on the Paris Commune, or municipal government, the successful bourgeois lawyer became one of its assistant *procureurs,* but his career was to take second place to his more radical interests when he joined the newly reconstituted Jacobin club. Formally the Society of the Friends of the Constitution, the Jacobins were located in the Rue St Honoré.[5] Composed at first mainly of professional men, the Jacobins soon became a hotbed of extremism. Danton quickly gained a reputation among them as a skilled political operator. A contemporary described him thus:

> Danton was in the chair; I had often heard of him and now I was seeing him for the first time…I was struck by his height and athletic build, by the irregularity of his pock-marked features, his sharp, harsh and resounding diction, his dramatic gestures and expressive features, his penetrating and confident regard, by the energy and daring of his attitude and movements…He presided with the decisiveness, agility and authority of a man who knows his power.[6]

Well-read and a fair linguist – he is said to have wooed his first wife in Italian – Danton was not averse to shady financial deals. At different times gossip had him in the pay, variously, of the King of France, the Duc d'Orléans, England and Austria. What is certain is that, though heavily in debt in 1789, he was solvent once again only two years later. The spoils of revolution, he once said, go to the victor. Whatever the truth of the matter – and Danton was a master in concealing his traces – it is difficult to resist the conclusion that self-interest fuelled the great man's energies as much as his radicalism.

Hillaire Belloc paints this picture of Danton at the beginning of his brief revolutionary career:

5 Like the Cordeliers, the club was named after a former convent.
6 Quoted in Norman Hampson, *Danton* (London, Duckworth, 1978), p. 32.

He was tall and stout, with the forward bearing of the orator, full of gesture and animation. He carried a round French head upon the thick neck of energy. His face was generous, ugly and determined. With wide eyes and calm brows, he yet had the quick glance that betrays the habit of appealing to an audience. His upper lip was injured, and so was his nose, and he had further been disfigured by the small-pox... His lip had been torn by a bull when he was a child and his nose crushed in a second adventure, they say, with the same animal.... In his dress he had something of the negligence which goes with extreme vivacity and with a constant interest in things outside oneself; but it was invariably of his rank.

The term, 'tribune of the people' might almost have been coined to describe him.

When the King's reforming finance minister Jacques Necker was dismissed from office in July 1789, public discontent boiled over into revolt. The Paris representatives on the Estates General took over the government of the city and began raising a militia which they called the National Guard. On 14 July a hungry mob stormed the old soldiers' home known as Les Invalides and seized a load of muskets and cannon. Their next port of call was the hated royal prison known as the Bastille. Despite attempts by its governor to defuse the situation, the building was stormed, the governor hacked to death and his head paraded around the streets on a pike.[7] Events moved fast after this: revolutionary groups seized power across the land and the recently instituted National Assembly adopted a *Declaration of the Rights of Man and the Citizen*. (Little good it was to do either.) In October the working-class women of Paris, angered at rumours of a counter-revolutionary party having been given for soldiers at Versailles, marched to the palace, disarmed the guards and forced their way into the Queen's apartments, decapitating two of her guards on the way. (She barely had time to escape.) They then forced the King and his family to go with them to the capital, where they were installed in the unused and dusty palace of the Tuileries.[8] Within a few months all church prop-

7   The ancient fortress proved to contain no political prisoners, as had been thought, although it did boast the infamous Marquis de Sade confined on a charge of immorality.
8   Now destroyed. It formerly sealed off the 'open' end of the Louvre Palace.

erty was seized by the state and most religious orders were abolished, along with all titles of nobility.

So far, the King had reluctantly accepted the gradual erosion of his powers, but he reached the sticking point in June 1791 and made an abortive attempt to flee the country along with his wife and children. After they had been caught near the border and returned in captivity to Paris the monarchy was suspended. The following month martial law was declared after some fifty people were killed by the National Guard while demonstrating in the Champ de Mars for the removal of the King. Danton was suspected of having stirred up the disorder and a warrant was issued for his arrest. Whatever his precise role in the demonstration, he judged it prudent to visit his wife's parents in Arcis, returning to Paris only when the pressure was off.[9] After standing unsuccessfully for the Legislative Assembly (in the hope that it would give him immunity from arrest) he secured the position of deputy public prosecutor.[10]

Louis XVI, who still retained a degree of popularity in the country, was eventually restored to the throne in exchange for his agreement to a new constitution, and in March 1792 he asked a loose group of largely middle-class reformers called the Girondins (after the region where they had their power base) to form a government. Hoping to export the revolution, the new government enthusiastically declared war on Austria. This caused Prussia to intervene in support of their southern neighbours and the invading French armies were soon being pushed back. It was not good news for the new government, but events at home were to prove even more dangerous. Food riots in Paris led to an attack on the Tuileries Palace where the crowd forced the King to don the *bonnet rouge*, or cap of liberty.[11] At this stage no decision had been taken on the future of the monarchy, but Louis's fate was sealed when, at the end of July, the Duke of Brunswick, commander of the Austro-Prussian army, unwisely threatened the Parisians with dire consequences if they failed to obey their King.

9   There are unsubstantiated rumours of his having fled to England.
10   Created in 1791, the Legislative Assembly was replaced a year later by the National Convention.
11   It was named after the headgear worn by freed Roman slaves.

On 10 August 1792 the Tuileries was invaded once again by the *sans culottes* (the lowest social class, literally 'without knee breeches'). This time there was no stopping the violence; the palace was overrun and most of the King's Swiss Guard slaughtered despite their attempts to surrender. King Louis XVI, who had been forced to take refuge in the Assembly, was now stripped of his remaining powers and detained in the Temple Prison[12] under humiliating conditions. The commander of the National Guard, General Lafayette, disgusted at what had taken place, surrendered to the Austrians, thus ensuring that he would be one of the few revolutionary leaders to survive the Revolution. The assault on the Tuileries is another event in which Danton's role is obscure. He appears to have gone to Arcis at about this time in order to settle his mother's affairs, but later claimed to have planned the assault on the palace and to have given the order to attack. Whatever the truth of the matter he was popularly hailed as 'the man of August 10th' and elected Minister of Justice, in which capacity he took his place on the high seats of the Assembly known as *The Mountain*. Among his companions were the one-time physician and journalist Jean-Paul Marat, his friend Desmoulins and another rising young Jacobin deputy, Maximilien-Francois-Marie-Isidore de Robespierre. By an extraordinary coincidence Robespierre had also been present as a boy at the King's coronation. Unlike Danton, who had truanted from school, Robespierre had been called upon to give a speech of welcome on behalf of his school.

Robespierre was a talented lawyer of Irish descent from Arras in the Pas de Calais area. An intellectual of some sensibility, he had resigned his appointment as a judge in order to avoid pronouncing sentence of death. After moving to Paris he made a name for himself as a man of principle, first in the Constituent Assembly and then in the Jacobin club. For this reason he was dubbed the 'sea-green Incorruptible' by the nineteenth-century historian Thomas Carlyle. He was in Christopher Hibbert's words, 'a small, thin, dogmatic man of thirty-two with thick, carefully brushed hair and a slightly pock-marked skin of a deathly greenish pallor.'[13] The very model of the revolution,

---

12   An ancient fortress once the headquarters of the Knights Templar.
13   Christopher Hibbert, *The French Revolution* (Harmondsworth, Penguin Books, 1986), p. 203.

Robespierre nevertheless defied its conventions by dressing in knee-breeches and silk stockings and wearing his hair powdered.

'TOUJOURS DE L'AUDACE'

The series of military disasters that France was now suffering gave rise to widespread desertions from the army and rumours of counter-revolution. Danton rose to the occasion in what was to be his finest hour. Although he had at first opposed the foreign wars, he now carried out a series of morale-boosting visits to the army, and to the population at home he made a series of rousing speeches, declaring, *'Il nous faut de l'audace, et encore de l'audace, et toujours de l'audace'* ('What we need is boldness, more boldness and ever boldness'). The force of his oratory did the trick and a re-invigorated army began to push back its enemies. But in attacking the 'traitors within', Danton overreached himself. Against a background of fears that counter-revolutionaries would strike while the army was away defending the homeland, one of the Paris sections[14] demanded, 'immediate prompt justice against the criminals and conspirators detained in the prisons'.[15] They were to get their wish.

For five days beginning 2 September 1792 the mob seized, murdered and (often) mutilated over 1,200 suspects in or on their way to the prisons. Among the first to die were the surviving members of the King's Swiss Guard, but the slaughter soon became indiscriminate. Arbitrary 'trials' were held in which prisoners were hastily singled out for slaughter. In the Salpêtrière Prison, thirty-five prostitutes were killed and in the Bicêtre, one hundred and fifty children. Even innocent passers-by were raped and murdered. One of the victims was Marie Antoinette's gentle friend, the Princesse de Lamballe, who was taken from prison, gang raped and bludgeoned to death; after which her corpse was sexually mutilated and her head displayed on a pike outside the Queen's window. All the while the government stood idly by. Some of its members, Danton among them, actively encouraged the atrocities. Despite having been warned of the dangers by the Inspector of Prisons, he said, 'I don't give a damn about the prisoners.

14 Administrative divisions of the capital dominated by the *sans-culottes*.
15 Hampson, *Danton*, p. 102.

Let them look out for themselves.' The orgy of blood-letting known to history as the September massacres eventually spent itself and the nation turned to the future. A National Convention was set up with the duty of preparing a republican constitution.

Despite a remarkable victory of French arms over the Prussians at Valmy,[16] Danton was forced by the Girondins to resign from the government. Voices now began to be raised for the execution of the King. Danton, who had at first sought to distance himself from this final horror, felt in the end compelled to go along with the rest. Louis was charged with having 'committed a multitude of crimes in order to establish your tyranny by destroying its liberty'.[17] On 21 January 1793 'citizen Capet' went to the guillotine.[18] It was the end of an era.

Flushed with its military successes, France now offered its aid to any peoples desirous of obtaining their liberty. This resulted in war with Britain, Holland and, shortly after, Spain. Returning from one of his many missions to the army in Belgium,[19] Danton was desolated to discover that his beloved Gabrielle had died. His grief was inconsolable – he is said to have had her body exhumed for a final farewell – and Robespierre sent him a moving letter of consolation.[20] A few months later, with two young boys to look after, Georges-Jacques married his fifteen year old babysitter, Louise Gely, in a religious ceremony which defied the revolutionary ethic of de-Christianisation.

---

16   20 September 1792. One of the more extraordinary stories of the time was that the victory had been obtained by bribery. Danton, it was said, had bought the victory by presenting the Duke of Brunswick with diamonds stolen from the Crown jewels.

17   The specifics were surprisingly narrow; he was charged with suspending the assemblies, with attempting to prevent the storming of the Bastille, with escaping from Paris with a false passport, with seeking to overthrow the constitution, with rallying the émigrés, with trying to bribe members of the Constituent and Legislative Assemblies, with allowing the nation to be disgraced abroad, and with ordering the Swiss Guard to fire on the citizens. In other words, instead of being accused of his faults prior to the revolution (profligacy, grinding the face of the poor and so on), Louis XVI was charged only with resisting the revolution.

18   Louis belonged to the Capetian dynasty, though this was not his family name.

19   On 16 February 1793.

20   'I love you more than ever to the death. At this moment I am your second self'. Hampson, *Danton*, p. 99.

Like his first marriage, it turned out to be more than a mere union of convenience.

But failure of the French armies in Belgium led to disorders in Paris. The Convention reacted by setting up, largely at the instigation of Danton, 'an extraordinary criminal tribunal', later to be called the Revolutionary Tribunal, with jurisdiction over the whole of the country.[21] 'Let us be ruthless,' Danton exclaimed, 'so the people won't have to be.' The task proved harder than expected and mobile guillotines had to be sent around the country in order to maintain order. The largest uprising took place in the Catholic region of the Vendée on France's north-west coast.[22] It was quelled in December, but only after great savagery by the revolutionary government. The inhabitants of whole towns and villages were massacred and women and children were buried alive. Perhaps a quarter of a million died in the uprising.[23] A new body was now formed to take over most government functions. It was known as the Committee of Public Safety (*Comité de Salut Public*).[24] Danton was one of its nine members and soon came to dominate its proceedings. But even these measures were not enough to quell disorder. Following a royalist insurrection in Toulon and bread riots in Paris a law, known as the Law of Suspects, was enacted[25] which reversed the normal burden of proof by requiring former aristocrats and others to be imprisoned unless they could prove their commitment to the Republic. An intelligence apparatus was set up to support it with informers in every street. All the elements of Europe's first police state were now firmly in place.

The Gironde leadership gradually lost popular support and found themselves under attack in turn from the more extreme Jacobins. Efforts to reconcile the two factions having failed, Danton and the *Montagnards* resolved that the Gironde must go. In an insurrection on 2 June, the government was overthrown and thirty-one of the Girondin

21   10 March 1793.
22   The revolt, which began in March 1793, was organised by former nobles and aided by Great Britain.
23   Simon Schama, *Citizens* (London, Viking. 1989), p. 791.
24   On 26 March 1793.
25   17 September 1793.

deputies arrested, most of them on the floor of the chamber.[26] At the same time, Danton, who had been seeking a negotiated settlement with the Vendéans and who had opposed the trial of Marie Antoinette, lost his seat on the Committee of Public Safety. Significantly, it was taken by Robespierre. Opinion now began to polarize around these two giants of the revolution whose positions were moving rapidly apart. The first seeds of doubt stirred in Danton when Robespierre expressed the view that liberty must be sacrificed on the altar of the revolution.

'BLISS WAS IT IN THAT DAWN TO BE ALIVE'[27]

Faced with foreign armies approaching its borders, insurrection at home and a deteriorating economy, the extremist Hébertists (named after their leader, Jacques René Hébert) made an unsuccessful attempt at a coup; it gave the Jacobin-dominated administration the excuse it needed. In September 1793 the Convention unleashed throughout France a period of unparalleled violence that came to be known as the Terror. Beginning as an attempt to quell counter-revolutionaries, it soon came to be used against anyone suspected of being opposed to the regime. Robespierre explained the Terror in a speech to the National Convention on 5 February 1794: 'If the basis of popular government in time of peace is virtue, the basis of popular government in time of revolution is both virtue and terror: virtue without which terror is murderous, terror without which virtue is powerless. Terror is nothing else than swift, severe, indomitable justice; it flows, then, from virtue.' And by 'virtue' the Incorruptible meant 'nothing else but love of fatherland and its laws.' Between September 1793 and July 1794 some twenty to forty thousand Frenchmen and women were to go to the guillotine by order of the Revolutionary Tribunal .

Danton had fallen sick earlier in the summer. It is impossible at this remove to say how much of his condition was physical and how

26   They were not to go unavenged. The journalist and popular hero Marat, now president of the Cordeliers, was assassinated in his bath by Charlotte Corday, a young Girondiste from Normandy.
27   William Wordsworth, *The French Revolution as it Appeared to Enthusiasts at its Commencement* (1809).

much a weariness with the world he had helped bring into being. In any event, after obtaining leave of absence from his parliamentary duties, Danton retired to Arcis with his new wife in mid-October 1793. Whether from accident or design, therefore, he was absent from Paris at the beginning of the Terror. On 16 October the once captivating Marie Antoinette, now white haired, gaunt and purblind, followed her husband to the scaffold. Next to go were the leaders of the Gironde who had been arrested and, after a great show trial, condemned; they proudly sang the 'Marseillaise' on the way to the scaffold. When told of the slaughter, Danton prophetically cried out, 'We deserve death as much as the Girondins and we shall suffer the same fate one after the other.'

It is not known why Danton returned to Paris after only six weeks in the country. Some say that it had to do with his having been denounced for speculating in revolutionary currency; others that he had bowed to his friends' entreaties to return to stand up to Robespierre. Perhaps it was simply the love of a good woman. Whatever the case, the Danton who returned was a different man from the Danton of earlier days. Hampson writes, 'From now onwards he made little attempt to disguise his moderate politics behind a façade of verbal violence and there were to be no more of his volcanic eruptions until he found himself in the dock'.[28] The new Danton began to advocate relaxation of the Reign of Terror: 'I propose', he said, 'not to trust whoever might wish to lead the people beyond the bounds of the revolution and to propose ultra-revolutionary measures'. And, 'Perhaps the Terror once served a useful purpose, but it should not hurt innocent people.' He even briefly succeeded in setting up a Committee of Clemency, but his enemies quickly disposed of that dangerous idea.

And so the Terror continued. As Robespierre's unpleasant acolyte, Louis St Just chillingly remarked, 'A man is guilty of a crime against the Republic when he takes pity on prisoners. He is guilty because he has no desire for virtue. He is guilty because he is opposed to the Terror.'[29]

28   Hampson, *Danton*, p. 138.
29   The handsome young Louis Antoine St Just was a devoted supporter of Robespierre. Known as 'the angel of death', St Just, like many of his generation, looked to ancient Greece for his inspiration. Unfortunately for France, he

Even Robespierre now realised that the violence had gone too far and went out of his way to save the lesser Girondins. Like Danton, he had resisted Hébert's policy of de-Christianisation. Desmoulins, a childhood friend of Robespierre, made a powerful plea for moderation in his newsletter, *Le Vieux Cordelier,* but he went too far when he criticized the Committee of Public Safety. Feeling himself to be under attack from both the Hébertists on the left and the Danton moderates (or '*indulgents*', as they were called) on the right, Robespierre resolved to pick them off one by one. On 24 March, after another unsuccessful attempt to wrest power from Robespierre, Hébert and his principal followers were arrested, accused of conspiracy and collusion with foreign powers and swiftly executed. When his old friend Danton attempted a rapprochement, Robespierre replied, 'Liberty cannot be secured unless criminals lose their heads.'

Danton now seems to have lapsed into uncharacteristic irresolution; he would not flee and he would not fight. To fight back, he said, would only mean the shedding of more blood. Warned by Marat's sister of his impending arrest, Danton went to the Convention with a view to challenging his opponents, but declined to act after receiving assurances of his safety from Desmoulins whom he had observed in conversation with Robespierre. It was a serious misjudgement. At a joint session of the Committees of Public Safety and General Security[30] a warrant was issued for the arrest of Danton and a number of his supporters. It was a risky step and two committee members refused to sign. How would the great man react?

Despite warnings from yet another friend, Danton went to bed on 30 March murmuring, 'They dare not.' He was wrong; the following morning he was seized at his home and, along with a number of his colleagues, thrown into the Luxembourg Prison to await his trial before the Revolutionary Tribunal. He was heard to exclaim, 'This time twelvemonth, I was moving the creation of that same Revolutionary Tribunal. I crave pardon for it of God and man.' Denied the chance to appear before the Convention where his oratory could have been effective, Danton knew that there was no hope. He nevertheless af-

---

chose the totalitarian state of Sparta instead of the (relatively) libertarian state of Athens.

30   The body which supervised the police.

fected a forced gaiety, while his fellow prisoner, Desmoulins, the man who had once proudly described himself as *'Procureur-Général de la Lanterne'* (or Attorney General to the Lamp-post – on which the 'aristos' were strung up) fell into the deepest despair.

BEFORE THE REVOLUTIONARY TRIBUNAL

The trial of Danton and fourteen others began on 2 April 1794 before the Revolutionary Tribunal in what was formerly the great hall of the Paris *Parlement*. It was attended by an enormous crowd, with people queuing in the streets. Compared with the Cordelier prisoners, the President of the Tribunal, Armand-Martial-Joseph Herman, and his fellow judges were nonentities. (Ironically, the prosecutor, Antoine Quentin Fouquier-Tinville had used his distant relationship with Camille Desmoulins to help obtain his post.)

The terms of the indictment were decided upon by the Tribunal the night before the trial. Fouquier-Tinville had only been briefed two days before and had little in the way of instructions, save for a wordy report from St Just. The charges alleged that Danton had served the King, that he was an accomplice to the massacre on the Champ de Mars, that he had failed in his duty on 10 August, that he had enriched himself at public expense and that he had conspired to overthrow the Republic. Only one of these counts (unjust enrichment) had any substance in it, but that did not matter; no one had any illusions about the outcome of the 'trial'.

In court, in answer to the usual formal request for his particulars, Danton replied, 'My address will soon be in oblivion; as for my name, you will find it in the Panthéon of history.' Desmoulins answered, 'I am 33, the age of the sans-culotte, Jesus – an age fatal to reformers.' The trial then began with Fouquier-Tinville calling what appears to have been his only witness, the financier Cambon, once a fellow member with Danton of the Committee of Public Safety. Observing that Cambon could not conceal his emotions Danton remarked, 'Come, Cambon, do you think we are conspirators? Look, he is laughing, he believes no such thing.' A challenge by Desmoulins to one of the jurors was refused.

Next day it was the turn of the defence and Danton was the first to speak; the old fire had returned. Carlyle described the scene thus:

> For it is the voice of Danton that reverberates now from these domes; in passionate words, piercing with their wild sincerity, winged with wrath. Your best Witnesses he shivers into ruin at one stroke. He demands that the Committee-men themselves come as Witnesses, as Accusers; he 'will cover them with ignominy.' He raises his huge stature, he shakes his huge black head, fire flashes from the eyes of him, – piercing to all Republican hearts: so that the very Galleries, though we filled them by ticket, murmur sympathy; and are like to burst down, and raise the People, and deliver him!

It was said that Danton's voice could be heard on the other side of the Seine. The oration lasted most of the day. The writer Hilaire Belloc pieced together, no doubt with a degree of imagination, what little is left of the speech:

> You say that I have been paid, but I tell you that men made as I am cannot be paid. And I put against your accusation – of which you cannot furnish a proof nor the hint of a proof, nor the shadow, nor the beginning of a witness – the whole of my revolutionary career. It was I who from the Jacobins kept Mirabeau at Paris. I have served long enough, and my life is a burden to me, but I will defend myself by telling you what I have done.
>
> It was I who made the pikes rise suddenly on the 20th of June and prevented the King's voyage to St Cloud. The day after the massacre of the Champ de Mars a warrant was out for my arrest. Men were sent to kill me at Arcis, but the people came and defended me. I had to fly to London, and I came back as you all know, the moment Garran was elected. Do you not remember me at the Jacobins, and how I asked for the Republic? It was I who knew the court was eager for war. It was I among others who denounced the policy of the war…It was I who prepared the 10th of August.
>
> I went to Arcis. I admit it. I am proud of it. I went there to pass three days, to say goodbye to my mother, and to arrange my affairs, because I was shortly to be in peril. I hardly slept that night. It was I that had Mandat[31] killed, because he had given the order to fire on the people…. You are reproaching me with the friendship of Fabre

31 Commander of the National Guard defending the Tuleries.

d'Eglantine. He is still my friend, and I still say that he is a good citizen as he sits here with me.

You have told me that my defence has been too violent, you have recalled to me the revolutionary names, and you have told me that Marat when he appeared before the tribunal might have served as my model. Well, with regard to these names who were once my friends, I will tell you this: Marat had a character on fire and unstable; Robespierre I have known as a man, above all tenacious; but I – I have served it in my own fashion, and I would embrace my worst enemy for the sake of the country, and I will give her my body if she needs the sacrifice.

It was not simply a defence to all the charges that he was offering, but also an indictment of his enemies. As sympathy in the courtroom began to swing in favour of the defendants a worried Herman passed a note to the prosecutor which read, 'In half an hour I shall stop Danton's defence. You must spin out some of the rest in detail.' In the end Danton was persuaded to stop only by a promise that he could continue the following day. It was not to be honoured.

The defendants had earlier asked for a number of people, including the Mayor of Paris, Robespierre and other Deputies, to be called as witnesses. Realising that this would frustrate the object of a swift trial and condemnation, Fouquier-Tinville said ominously, 'It is high time this part of the trial, which has become a mere struggle, and which is a public scandal, should cease. I am about to write to the Convention to hear what it has to say, and its advice shall be exactly followed.'

That night the tribunal and the prosecutor sent a joint letter to the Convention reporting that, 'There has been a storm in the hall since this day's proceedings began. The accused are calling for witnesses who are among your deputies... They are appealing to the people, saying that they will be refused. In spite of the firmness of the president and of all the tribunal, they continue to protest that they will not be silent until their witnesses are heard, unless by your passing a special decree.' It asked for the Convention's orders. Next day at the Convention, instead of reading out the letter, St Just gave a wholly misleading account of its contents: 'The prisoners are in full revolt,' he said, 'and have interrupted the hearing, saying that they will not allow it to continue until the Convention has taken measures... Innocent men do not revolt.' To gild the lily he added – without any foundation – that the absent Lucille Desmoulins was involved in a plot to kill members of the Committee. If her husband Camille had known of this it would have sent a shiver up his spine.

The Convention immediately passed a decree providing that any prisoner who should attempt to interrupt the course of justice by threats or revolt should be outlawed, but the stratagem was not needed. Next morning, the tribunal convened at 8.30 a.m. instead of the usual 10 a.m. in order to get their business over before the public arrived. No sooner had the decree had been read out than the jurors, prompted vigorously by Herman, asked leave to proceed at once to judgement. Desmoulins tore his written defence into pieces and threw it at the judges. Before the prisoners could say anything they were hurried back to the Conciergerie, the grim prison that still stands on the banks of the Seine, never to return to court.

When the inevitable verdicts and sentences of death were read to them in prison a few hours later Danton had to console a distraught Desmoulins who feared now, not only for himself but for his wife Lucille also. Danton was overheard to comment bitterly to a friend, 'I'm leaving everything in a frightful mess. There's not one of them who knows anything about government… if I left my balls to Robespierre and my legs to Couthon [a paralytic] the Committee of Public Safety might last a little longer.'[32]

The condemned men were taken to the guillotine in two tumbrels, their hands bound. When Fabre d'Eglantine complained that he would never finish his poems, Danton, who was sitting next to him, joked, 'Within a week, you'll be making some great *vers*' (a word that in French also means 'worms'.) As the tumbrel went by Robespierre's house, Danton cried out, 'Infamous Robespierre! The scaffold awaits you! Your house will be razed to the ground'.

It was evening when they arrived in the Place de la Revolution and the scaffold was lit by a blood-red sun. The Cordeliers met death with dignity; all, that is, except Chabot who had taken poison in prison and, bizarrely, had to be executed while unconscious. When Hérault-Séchelles stepped forward to embrace Danton he was pushed away by

32 Hampson, *Danton*, p. 174.

the executioner. 'Our heads will meet there,' responded Danton, indicating the executioner's sack. Now alone on the guillotine covered with the blood of his friends, Danton cried out, 'O my wife, my well-beloved, I shall never see you again!' – but, checked himself, 'Danton, no weakness!' With the executioner's consent, he defiantly sang out some lines that he had composed on the downfall of Robespierre. Addressing the executioner, he said, 'Show my head to the people; it's worth showing.' They were his last words on earth.

Camille was right to be concerned for his wife. A week after her husband's execution Robespierre sent his twenty-three year old wife to the guillotine. (He had been a witness at their wedding.) From thereon, the guillotine was kept continuously busy; so much so that it had to be relocated more than once due to complaints from residents about the smell of stale blood. The Revolution was now feeding hungrily on itself. Fouquier-Tinville, Danton's prosecutor, went to the guillotine on 6 May, followed the next day by his friend, the court president, Herman.

Revolt against the regime was now so widespread that it could be described in many areas[33] as a state of civil war, and a brutal war at that. In Lyons alone, for example, 1,900 men and women were slaughtered, some three hundred of them by cannon fire while chained together. (It was an inefficient form of execution and many had to be finished off by soldiers with sabres, bayonets and muskets.) In Nantes, two thousand prisoners, some of them stripped naked and bound together in pairs, were battened in the holds of barges and sunk in the Loire. A further three thousand died in a prison epidemic. Even worse atrocities were to take place at Bordeaux.[34]

All too late, 'the Incorruptible' saw the need to put a stop to the killing. On 26 July Robespierre made a four-hour speech in the Convention proposing the ending of the Terror and the punishment of those in the Committee of General Security who had exceeded their powers. At first, his resolutions were passed, but they were quickly rescinded and referred to the Committees. Next day, St Just tried to address the

---

33   Ninety per cent of all deaths occurred in twenty-one of France's eighty-six Departments. Schama, *Citizens*, p. 785.
34   Hibbert, *French Revolution*, p. 228.

Convention but his voice was drowned out by cries of 'Down with the tyrant.' Robespierre was arrested but immediately rescued by troops of the Commune and brought with his supporters to the Hotel de Ville (or town hall). The Convention fought back; it declared Robespierre and his associates outlaws and sent in the National Guard to re-arrest them. Robespierre, who at the time was holding a knife in his hand, was shot in the jaw by a young gendarme while about to sign an appeal for Parisians to take up arms in his support.[35] (An alternative reading of events has Robespierre injured in an abortive attempt to kill himself.) He spent an agonising night lying on a board in the chamber of the Committee of Public Safety with his shattered jaw roughly bound up. Next morning he was taken before the Tribunal. The prosecutor demanded death. Without further ceremony, Robespierre was taken to the scaffold where the bandages had to be ripped off in order to fit his head into the guillotine; his last utterance was a scream.[36] Robespierre's place on the scaffold was immediately taken by St Just and nineteen of his colleagues. The Terror was nearly over.

ENEMIES OF THE PEOPLE

The 'trial' of Danton and the other Cordeliers was fixed from the start, and everyone knew it. The jurors were chosen, rather than selected by lot in the normal way – and by the prosecutor rather than by the court. And their number was reduced to seven from the more normal twelve. The accused were denied legal representation and no evidence was called which could possibly have established their guilt. There was no attempt to conduct the hearings with impartiality or even dignity; throughout the proceedings, members of the Committee of Public Safety walked round the courtroom whispering poison in the ears of anyone who would listen. Whenever the accused appeared to be gaining a point the court promptly stepped in to frustrate them. After Danton's death even these draconian arrangements were thought not to have gone far enough. A law was passed[37] which made being an

35 The warrant still exists. It bears only the first letter of his name.
36 Robespierre's companions suffered no better; his brother jumped from a window, breaking his thigh; another shot himself, while a third was badly injured when he tried to escape down the steps on his wheelchair.
37 The law of 22 Prairial (or 10 June) 1794.

'enemy of the people'[38] the only crime and death the only penalty. If proof existed (and it could take any form), 'there shall be no further hearing of witnesses'. Lawyers make great claims for the law, but it is poor protection against totalitarianism when one of the first acts of a tyrant is to bend his country's laws to the perverted notion of revolutionary 'justice'.

An interesting comparison can be made between the French and the American revolutions of the eighteenth century. In 1789, the year of the storming of the Bastille, Robespierre was just thirty-one years of age; Danton, Desmoulins and St Just were aged thirty, twenty-nine and twenty-two respectively. In that same year George Washington was sworn in as first President of the new American Republic. He was, by contrast, fifty-seven years of age. John Adams, his Vice President, was fifty-four and the towering Thomas Jefferson a 'youthful' forty-six. Are young men, particularly bright young men, more inclined than their elders to pursue theories to their logical conclusions regardless of the consequences?

And there is another lesson to be drawn: the Americans sought to secure the liberties of their people by placing limitations on the powers of central government, whereas the French saw a strong central government as the principal guarantor of their citizen's 'rights'. America's reward was its constitution and Bill of Rights; France got the Terror and Napoleon Bonaparte.

Injustices can, of course, occur in any society at any time, but usually through error or individual misbehaviour. Revolutionary France on the other hand inflicted its cruelties deliberately and systematically because they were thought necessary for the greater good. Widely regarded as an ice-cold monster, Robespierre was in fact passionately committed to creating what he saw as the good society, an end which he believed to justify even the most appalling barbarities. The pattern has been repeated many times since, in Soviet Russia, Nazi Germany, China, Cambodia[39] and large parts of Africa. It seems that the worst

---

38   The crime was widely defined to include 'contractors of bad faith' (presumably black marketers), those who disparaged the republican government and the purveyors of 'insidious writings'.
39   Pol Pot was a French-educated intellectual.

forms of repression can sometimes be born, not out of corruption, but from deeply held principles or theories which those in charge have persuaded themselves rank above the claims of simple humanity.

Strangely enough, in revolutionary France the frightening consequences of pursuing such theories to their logical conclusion were to become apparent to the virtuous and principled Robespierre less speedily than they did to the venal and disreputable Danton. Let Carlyle have the last word:

> So passes like a gigantic mass, of valour, ostentation, fury, affection, and wild revolutionary force and manhood, this Danton to his unknown home. He was of Arcis-sur-Aube; born of 'good farmer people' there. He had many sins; but one worst sin he had not, that of Cant. No hollow formalist, deceptive and self deceptive, ghastly to the natural sense was this, but a very Man; with all his dross he was a Man; fiery real from the great fire-bosom of Nature herself. He saved France from Brunswick; he walked his own wild road; whither it led him. He may live for some generations in the memory of Man.

PRINCIPAL SOURCES

CHAPTER ONE – THE TRIUMPH OF CREDULITY

After the trials had ended Governor Phips asked Cotton Mather to write an account of them with a view to publication based on the court records. The result was *The Wonders of the Invisible World* (1693). The author explained, 'I have indeed set my self to Countermine the whole Plot of the Devil against New-England, in every Branch of it, as far as one of my Darkness can comprehend such a Work of Darkness.' Despite its uncritical view of the court, this work, with its unique access to records now vanished, is probably the most reliable account of the few cases it deals with. Nearly as important are Increase Mather's *Cases of Conscience* (1693), John Hale's *Modest Enquiry Into the Nature of Witchcraft* (1697) and the Salem Village Record Book. The Boston Baptist and cloth merchant Robert Calef's *More Wonders of the Invisible World* (1700) was cynically critical of the court and of its apologists like the Mathers. (Calef himself was accused of witchcraft. He dealt with it in characteristically American fashion by filing a £1,000 suit for defamation; no more was heard of his spectral exploits. Even the title of his book mocked Cotton Mather's most famous work.) The revisionist tradition was continued by the local historian and Unitarian preacher Charles W. Upham in his *Salem Witchcraft, Volumes I and II with an Account of Salem Village and a History of Opinions on Witchcraft and Kindred Subject* (1867). Though less in favour today, both Calef and Upham contain much useful material.

Le Beau, Bryan F., *The Story of the Salem Witch Trials: 'We Walked in Clouds and Could Not See Our Way.'* (Upper Saddle River, N.J., Prentice-Hall, 1998)

Boyer, Paul and Stephen Nissenbaum, (co-eds.), *Salem Possessed: The Social Origins of Witchcraft.* (Cambridge, Mass., Harvard University Press, 1974)

Breslaw, Elaine G., *Tituba, Reluctant Witch of Salem: Devilish Indians and Puritan Fantasies.* (New York, New York University Press, 1997)

Burr, George Lincoln, *Narratives of the Witchcraft Cases, 1648-1706* (New York, Barnes & Noble, 1914)

Francis, Richard, *Judge Sewall's Apology* (London, Fourth Estate, 2005)

Hansen, Chadwick, *Witchcraft at Salem* (London, Arrow Books, 1971)

Hoffer, Peter Charles, *The Salem Witchcraft Cases: A Legal History* (Lawrence, University Press of Kansas, 1997)

Lawson, Deodat, *Brief and True Narrative Of some Remarkable Passages Relating to sundry Persons Afflicted by Witchcraft, at Salem Village (1692)* (USA, Kessinger Publishing, 2004)

Rosenthal, Bernard, *Salem Story: Reading the Witch Trials of 1692* (New York, Cambridge University Press, 1995)

Starkey, Marion L., *The Devil in Massachusetts: A Modern Inquiry into the Salem Witch Trials* (New York, Alfred Knopf, 1949)

CHAPTER TWO – LONDON BURNING

Babington, Anthony, *Military Intervention in Britain: From the Gordon Riots to the Gibraltar Incident* (London, Routledge, 1991)

de Castro, J. P., *The Gordon Riots* (London, H. Milford, Oxford University Press, 1926)

Colson, Percy, *The Strange History of Lord George Gordon* (London, R. Hale and co, 1937)

Haydon, Colin, *Anti-Catholicism in eighteenth-century England, c. 1714-80: a political and social study* (Manchester, Manchester University Press, 1993)

Hibbert, Christopher, *King Mob* (Stroud, Sutton Publishing, 2004)

Lovell, Justin, *Notable Historical Trials* (London, The Folio Society 1999)

Rudé, George F.E., *The Gordon Riots; a Study of the Rioters and their Victims* (Transactions of the Royal Historical Society, Fifth Series, vol. 6, London, 1956)

Watson, Robert, *The life of Lord George Gordon with a Philosophical Review of his Political Conduct* (London, Symonds and Eaton, 1795)

CHAPTER THREE – THE MONKEY TRIAL

Coletta, Paolo E., *William Jennings Bryan: Political Puritan* (Lincoln, University of Nebraska Press, 1969)

Darrow, Clarence, *The Story of My Life* (New York, Da Capo Press, 1932)

De Camp, L. Sprague, *The Great Monkey Trial* (New York, Doubleday and Company, 1968)

Ginger, Ray, *Six Days or Forever* (London, Oxford University Press, 1958)

Larsen, Edward E., *Summer for the Gods: The Scopes Trial and America's Continuing Debate over Science and Religion* (Cambridge, Mass., Harvard University Press, 1997)

Levine, Lawrence W., *Defender of the Faith. William Jennings Bryan; The Last Decade 1915-1925* (Oxford, Oxford University Press, 1965)

Scopes, John T. & Presley J., *Center of the Storm; Memoirs of John T. Scopes* (New York, Holt, Rinehart and Winston, 1967)

CHAPTER FOUR – THE BLOODY ASSIZES

Bruce, Charles, *Book of Noble English-women* (London and Edinburgh, W.P. Nimmo, 1878)

Campbell, Lord, *The Lives of the Lord Chancellors* (Philadelphia, Lee and Blanchard, 1848)

Dunning, Robert, *The Monmouth Rebellion: A Complete Guide to the Rebellion and the Bloody Assize* (Wimborne, Dovecote Press, 1984)

Havighurst, Alfred, 'The Judiciary and Politics in the Reign of Charles I' *Law Quarterly Review*, 66, (1950), 229-252

Helm, P. J., *Jeffreys* (London, Robert Hale, 1966)

Heron, G. Allan, 'The Trial of Dame Alice Lisle' *Notes and Queries*, vol 154 (1928), 212

Howell's *State Trials* (London, T.C . Hansard, 1814)

Humphreys, A.L., 'Sources of History for Monmouth's Rebellion and the Bloody Assize' *Proceedings of the Somersetshire Archaeological and Natural History Society*, vol 38 (1892), 312-326

Irving, H. B., *Life of Judge Jeffreys* (London, W. Heinemann, 1898)

Keeton, G.W., *Trial for Treason* (London, Macdonald, 1959)

Luttrell, Narcissus, *Brief Historical Relation of State Affairs,* vol. 1 (Oxford, 1857, reprinted Wilmington, Del., 1974)

Macaulay, T.B., *History of England from the Accession of James II* (United Kingdom, The Folio Press, 1985)

Muddiman, J.G. (ed.), *The Bloody Assizes* (Edinburgh, William Hodge & Co., 1929. An edited reprint of the 1705 edition)

Parry, Sir Edward, *The Bloody Assize* (London, Ernest Benn Ltd, 1929)

Schofield, Seymour, *Jeffreys of the Bloody Assize* (London, Thornton Butterworth, 1937)

Sollom, Emlym, *Tryals for high-treason, and other crimes, with proceedings on bills of attainder,* Part IV (London: Printed for D. Brown, G. Strahan etc..., 1720)

Stephen, Sir J. Fitzjames, *History of the Criminal Law of England.* (London, Macmillan and Co., 1883)

Wharam, Alan, Treason. *Famous English Treason Trials* (Stroud, Sutton Publishing, 2005)

Whitaker, Antony, *The Regicide's Widow* (Stroud, Sutton Publishing, 2006)

CHAPTER FIVE– THE CHATTERLEY AFFAIR

For the English trial I have used the transcript in *The Lady Chatterley's Lover Trial, with an Introduction by H. Montgomery Hyde* (London, Bodley Head, 1990). For the text of the book I have consulted Lawrence, D.H., *Lady Chatterley's Lover* (London, Penguin Books, 2006).

Rembar, Charles, *The End of Obscenity* (London, Andre Deutsch, 1968)

Rolph, C.H. (ed.), *The Trial of Lady Chatterley* (London, Harmondsworth, Penguin, 1961)

Stevas, St. John, *Obscenity and the Law* (London, Secker & Warburg, 1956)

Travis, Alan, *Bound and Gagged* (London, Profile, 2000)

CHAPTER SIX – FEASTING WITH PANTHERS

Douglas, Lord Alfred, *The Autobiography of Lord Alfred Douglas,* (London, Martin Secker, 1929)

Ellmann, Richard, *Oscar Wilde.* (London, Hamish Hamilton, 1987)

Foldy, Michael S., *The Trials of Oscar Wilde: Deviance, Morality, and Late-Victorian Society.* (New Haven, CT ,Yale UP, 1997)

Harris, Frank, *Oscar Wilde.* (Michigan, Michigan State University Press, 1959)

Holland, Merlin, *Irish Peacock and Scarlet Marquess: the Real Trial of Oscar Wilde,* (London and New York, Fourth Estate, 2005)

Hyde, Montgomery, H., *The Trials of Oscar Wilde* (London, W. Hodge and co., 1948)

Hyde, Montgomery, H., *Oscar Wilde: A Biography* (New York, Farrar Straus Giroux, 1975)

McKenna, Neil, *The Secret Life of Oscar Wilde* (London, Arrow Books, 2004)

Millard Christopher S. (compiled anonymously), *Oscar Wilde: Three Times Tried* (London, Ferrestone Press. 1912)

Pearson, Hesketh, *Oscar Wilde, His Life and Wit,* (New York and London, Harper Brothers, 1946)

CHAPTER SEVEN – REVOLT AT HARPERS FERRY

The original trial papers have been destroyed by fire. In their absence I have used:

The Life, Trial and Execution of Captain John Brown, Known as 'Old Brown of Osawatomie', With a Full Account of the Attempted Insurrection at Harpers Ferry, Compiled from Official and Authentic Sources. New York (USA, Entered according to Act of Congress, in the year 1859, by Robert M. de Witt, In the Clerk's Office of the United States District Court for the Southern District of New York)

Du Bois, W.E. Burghardt, *John Brown, a Biography, a New Edition with Primary Documents and Introduction by John David Smith* (New York, Armonk, M. E. Sharpe, 1997)

Hinton, Richard J., *John Brown and His Men* (New York: Funk & Wagnalls, 1894); Reprint New York: The Arno Press, 1968

Malin, James C., *John Brown and the Legend of Fifty Six* (Philadelphia ,The American Philosophical Society, 1942)

Oates, Stephen B., *To Purge This Land with Blood* (New York, Harper Torchbooks, 1970)

Peterson, Merrill D., *John Brown, The Legend Revisited* (Charlottesville, University of Virginia Press, 2002)

Reynolds, David S., *John Brown, Abolitionist* (New York, Alfred K. Knopf, 2005)

Sanborn, F. B. ed., *The Life and Letters of John Brown* (Boston, Roberts Bros, 1885)

Villard, Oswald Garrison, *John Brown 1800-1859; A Biography Fifty Years After* (Gloucester, Mass. Peter Smith, 1965), First published 1910.

Villard has been criticized for adopting too uncritical an approach to reminiscences of elderly participants and for his disposition to be over-sympathetic to Brown. (His middle name, after all, was 'Garrison') See for example chapter XXII of James C. Malin's *John Brown and the Legend of Fifty Six* (Philadelphia, The American Philosophical Society, 1942). Nevertheless, Villard was a trained historian writing only a half century or so after the events who was able, with the help of an assistant, to unearth a mass of useful material which it is possible to use without necessarily accepting all the conclusions he drew from it.

CHAPTER EIGHT – THE END OF A REVOLUTIONARY

Evidence of what took place at Danton's trial is sparse. The press were excluded and the main report appeared in the heavily censored government *Bulletin of the Revolutionary Tribunal*. For a full account of the remaining sources see Hampson, Norman, *Danton* (London, Duckworth, 1978), pp. 165-166.

Andress, David, *The Terror, Civil War in the French Revolution* (London, Little Brown, 2005)

Belloc, Hilaire, *Danton, A Study* (London, Tom Stacey, 1972)

Carlyle, Thomas, *The French Revolution* (New York, Macmillan & Co., 1900)

Dunoyer, A., *The Public Prosecutor of the Terror* (London, Herbert Jenkins Ltd., 1914)

Hampson, Norman, *Danton* (London, Duckworth, 1978)

Hibbert, Christopher, *The French Revolution* (Harmondsworth, Penguin Books, 1986)

Schama, Simon *Citizens: A Chronicle of the French Revolution* (London, Viking, 1989)

Warwick, C.F. *Danton and the French Revolution* (Philadelphia, George W. Jacobs and Co., 1908)

INDEX

Abolitionists, *see* **Brown, John**

America

American Civil Liberties Union (ACLU), *see* Scope, John, trial of

American Revolution, French Revolution compared 288

Harpers Ferry revolt, *see* Brown, John

New England witch-hunt, *see* Salem witch-hunt

Puritan settlers 2, 3, 40

slavery, trial of abolitionist, *see* Brown, John

Barter, John

informant in Lisle case 118, 121, 122 *et seq*

Bleeding Kansas

'border ruffians' 245

deaths thought to have occurred in 254

Free Staters 244-5

'Jayhawkers' 245

Lawrence, sacking of 246-8

effect on John Brown 248

Missouri pro-slavers, and 244-5

compromise agreement (1820) shattered 244

force led by 'Major-General' Reid crossing into Kansas 253

sacking of Lawrence, involvement in 246-7

neighbouring state of Missouri, immigration from 244-5

Osawatomie

'Brown of Osawatomie' 254

'Brown's Station' 245

Pottawatomie massacre 249-52

aftermath 252

approval of by Brown 251

'Dutch Henry', one of main targets 249, 252

motive for 249, 267

'remedy', as 261-2

stain on John Brown's reputation from 266-7

warrant for arrest of John Brown after 252, 257

pro-slavers 245-47, 251-2, 256

slavery, divide over 244-6

two governments 245

Bloody Assizes, *see* **Lisle, Dame Alice, trial of**

'Bosie'

Douglas, Lord Alfred, known as 177, *see also* Wilde, Oscar

Brown, John 219-67

biographical details 239-42

Bleeding Kansas/sacking of Lawrence, *see* Bleeding Kansas

wounding of 225

Stoughton, William 21, 22, 24, 28

Salem witch trials, part in 21, 22, 24, 28

appointment 15

reputation 39

storming off the bench 31

Terror, the 279-82, 286

moderation of reign of, Danton advocating 280

Thoreau, Henry David

John Brown, and

A Plea for Captain John Brown eulogy 260

defence of 261

host of 255

lecture given by, attends 259

Towne family 9-11

Treason

Alice Lisle, *see* Lisle, Dame Alice, trial of

John Brown, *see* Brown, John

Lord George Gordon, *see* Gordon, Lord George

Richard Langhorne vii-viii

United States of America, *see also* America

John Scopes trial, *see* Scope, John, trial of

Lady Chatterley, and, *see Lady Chatterley's Lover*

Virginia

Harpers Ferry revolt, *see* Brown, John

Wilde, Oscar

arrest 193

balance of frailties and talent 218

bankruptcy 204-5

biographical background 171-3

blackmailing of 179-82

bringing about own downfall, reasons for 212

death 211

description of 176-7

Douglas, John Sholto, Marquess of Queensbury

biographical background 182-3

death 211

death of oldest son 183

prosecution for libel by Wilde 186-193

reaction to Alfred's relationship with Wilde 183-4

Wilde's reasons for prosecuting 213-14

Douglas, Lord Alfred ('Bosie') 177-8